AF479050

TEXTBOOK ON SHI'A ISLAM

Syed M. Rizvi, MD

MESSAGE OF PEACE, INC.
(Pyame Aman)
A Division of Muslim Foundation Inc. (Somerset NJ)
P.O. Box 390
Bloomfield, NJ 07003
USA

ISBN 978-158385-162-3

ACKNOWLEDGEMENT

It is with a deep feeling of gratitude that I mention the following individuals for their generous help in preparing this vital book.

Mr. Nazim Zaidi who oversaw the editing, and pulled it all together. Maulana S. Rafiq Naqvi for going through the manuscript. Dr. Hasnain Walji and Dr. Abul Qasim for finalizing the draft. Sister Masooma Beatty of Colorado for preparing the Exercises at the end of each chapter. My nephew, Maulana S. Rizwan Rizvi for designing the table of Zakat. Dr. Mehnaz Baig of California for reviewing the draft. For my sons, Zaki and Zain along with my niece Zehra for going through the manuscript, and Hasan for the final check. Also, a very special thanks to Mr.. Ethesham Kazmi and Hasnain for their tremendous assistance in the transcription.

I will also like to thank the editors and writers of many books commented during this undertaking, in particular the late Maulana M. Jawad Chirri for his book, "Brother of the Prophet of Islam."

I would also like to acknowledge the following authors whose books were used as references.
- Basic Cultural Aspect Seminar I to V, Al-Balagah Foundation, Qum
- Prophet Muhammad, Peermohamed Ebrahim Trust, Karachi
- The Brother of the Prophet (Imam Ali) by late Hujjatul Islam Jawed Chirri, Detroit
- Islam / Practical Teachings by Ghulam Sarwar

- Islamic Teachings by S. Q. Kamoonpuri, PhD, Tanzania

I also want to thank my publisher, Peter and the entire Team at Cold Tree Press for publishing this book and also helping with a dream being fulfilled.

And last but not the least, my wife Kubra for her kind encouragement and patience.

Thank you and God bless you all.

PREFACE

We are currently in a time of turmoil and chaos for the entire world in particular for the Muslims. This is partly due to years of propaganda against Islam, and partly due to the actions of Muslims. As a result, Islam, the religion of peace and tolerance, suffered the most damage. It left a blemish on its name.

Islam was like a huge shade under which exhausted travelers were to find comfort and rest. It was like a fountain of fresh water soothing the soul, where anyone and everyone could quench their thirst.

But unfortunately the reign of leadership went into the wrong hands, and everything good in Islam was perceived as bad.

Shia Islam is the main source coming directly from the last Prophet of Islam. This book is an introduction to this. This is meant to be a textbook for Junior and regular High School students.

I hope that it may be helpful in understanding the real Islam. Thank you.

— Syed M. Rizvi, MD
Bloomfield NJ USA
August 9, 2006
Rajab 13, 1427

TABLE OF CONTENTS

FOREWORD

By Dr. Noel Q. King

We are all saddened by the overwhelming calamities and miseries which have fallen upon our beloved fellow humans, the men and women of Iraq. We know also that that the land of the two great rivers, Tigris and Euphrates, was the cradle of western civilization, and of the origins of Judaism and Christianity and Islam. People have been asking, "Who are the Shiites of Karbala and Najaf that they have so much courage and determination as to face without fear every tribulation, even death itself?" Older Americans remember the fall of the Shah of Iran and the Shi'a who gave Ayatollah Khomeni such effective support and then sustained a terrible war with Saddam. They are wondering what is the relationship of the Shi'a of Iran with those of Iraq. Yet older Americans remember unseating Prime Minister Mousadeq and reinforcing the house of the self-styled Pahlevi monarchy and try to think out the place of Shi'a Islam in it all.

It is against this background that the writings of Dr. Syed M. Rizvi's are so full of lucidity and helpfulness of particular relevance to us in North America, Britain, Europe, Australia, New Zealand, and the worldwide Anglophone reading public in Pakistan, India, South East Asia, East Asia, Indonesia and the islands of the Pacific and especially at present times.

The family of the Rizvi's is well known and respected in South Asia. They were Persian aristocrats from that most ancient holy city of Razes, which stands on the Persian side of Mesopotamia. Long ago in the sixth century Before the Common Era (BCE) it gave shelter to the refugees driven into exile from Jerusalem. In the fourth or fifth century the Patriarch Tobit went from Jerusalem to Razes to bring back a suitably pious bride. Indeed the story of Toby and his struggle with a great fish and against demons yields us the name of Toby who was one of Shakespeare's most amiable characters. The Mughal Emperor of India brought back members of the Razavi (Rizvi) family to help him uphold the peace and prosperity of Hindustan. The Persian administrative, military and scientific (especially the medical and horticultural) migrants married into the Indian royal families. The daughter of one was Nur Jehan, who is among the greatest Queens of all time. Her close relative, Mumtaz was the Lady of the Taj Mahal who was mother of an Emperor. A Rizvi was appointed by the Mughals to be a lord of the north-east marches, that is the zone in the Terai above Gorakhpur. He brought under cultivation vast jungle areas where the rivers debouched from the Himalayas. The family settled people on the nearby laid out fields. They experimented with various crops and trees and made those lands into a food bowl. Some of them carefully studied yunani medicine and many became well-regarded scholars of religion. The family was known also for its patronage of art, poetry and architecture. While the family wholeheartedly and carefully practiced the Shi'a faith it was known for its fair and evenhanded treatment of Muslims of other schools and of Hindus including the kanphata yogis. In our own times the family is known for its friendship with Christians and Jews as well as Marxists. It helps them to be true to their own faith and beliefs while respecting the faith of others.

Dr. Syed M. Rizvi, when I first met him one raw New Jersey winter's dawn some twenty year ago, immediately brought to mind his noble ancestors. Allow for an old man's imaginative alignment of New Jersey with the North-East Marches. But as I got to know him I saw in him a veritable embodiment not only of Hindustan but of the ecument, the inhabited earth, and the jungle too. Readers will learn many things not only of this world and the environment and the world to come as well as the divine purposes but of themselves, not only in material matters but regarding our own spirituality and the divine call to us humans to join in the task of love and service. I commend his writing to discerning readers with confidence and enthusiasm.

Short Biography of Dr. Noel Q. King

Born 1922 Taxlila N. W. Punjab
Served with Punjabi Troops in India, Burma and Europe.
1948 BA Oxford in History
1949 MA Oxford in Theology
1954 PhD Nottingham (UK) in East Roman History
and Religion
1955 Professor of Theology and Comparative Religion,
University of Ghana / Gold Coast
1962 Mukerese University, Uganda
1968 University of CA, Santa Cruz – Professor of History
and Comparative Religion
1998 Emeritus Professor of the same, Venial Prof at Papua
(New Guinea, Sydney, Patiela, Amristar, research in Institute
of Central Asia, Islamabad.
Author of works on late East Roman History and annotation
of translators od Swahili epics and Arabic Travel naagitines.

INTRODUCTION

Islam is not just a religion but also a way of life. Most of the world's religions are the same in the sense that they instruct their devotees to be good in this world. However, Islam encompasses not only this worldly life, but also death and the life thereafter, all in a more comprehensive, complete and logical manner than any other religion.

Islam covers all aspects of life, from birth to death and everything in between. Education, manners, and marriage are all covered under the umbrella; children, parents, neighbors, teachers, and society overall. Islam also has laws governing plants, animals, and other aspects of this world.

Everyone is a sheep and a shepherd. All of us have our duties and obligations. The Qur'an says, "And that man shall have nothing but what he strives for." (53:39) What we sow, we will reap, what we work, we will benefit. Islam is an ideal religion and total submission to Allah is needed. Find out the laws of Islam, the meaning of these commandments of Allah, and follow them unconditionally and you are guaranteed success in life and death. As individuals, we have to submit to the command of Allah completely in order to meet our full potential as human beings.

Islam places great emphasis on individuals because the individuals are responsible for forming societies. Islam insists that every individual be good—hence the system of rights and obligations—so these individuals can create highly productive and morally excellent societies.

The word Islam comes from "silm" meaning peace. Islam is a religion of peace. There is no place for injustice or terrorism in Islam. The last Prophet has said that a Muslim is one from whose hands and tongue others get no harm. In the eyes of Allah the rich person is not the one who has the riches or all the worldly things, but the one who has goodness in his heart and actions. The Qur'an says: "The nearest to God among you are those who fear God the most."

The best way to achieve this end is education. Islam emphasizes education, understanding, and wisdom. These are the criteria which Muslims should meet and achieve excellence.

The world is created in a harmony based on the law of nature or *Deen e Fitrat*. Look at the world and you will find smoothly running systems, where everything follows the command of the Creator. All the creations of Allah, the sun, the moon, the galaxies, the animals, and the birds, even the angels follow His command and obey Him as ordained. They have no choice. Even human nature has been the same. Everyone likes good things and dislikes the bad. No one is created inherently bad. It is the society and system of the world and the choices they make that turns them into tyrants or noble. But, there is another side of human beings. Human beings have been given a special status; they have been created independent to a greater extent than any other creatures. The Qur'an says there is no compulsion in religion. Allah has laid down His command and given us the freedom to believe and act on it, or reject it. Having warned us that there is an inevitable Day of Judgment, the desire goal is to go to heaven and only good deeds with good intentions can carry you there.

In the Qur'an, Allah has mentioned in numerous places that He has not created us in vain. There is a purpose of creation. In this world, we do not move from one place to another without a purpose. How then could it be possible that this entire world is created without a purpose? The Qur'an has summarized this in one Ayat: "I have not created the jinn and the mankind for any other purpose but to worship (Me)." (51:56)

Worship here means understanding His command and submitting to it totally. Obviously, it does not mean to sit in the mosque and just worship Him all day and night. It means always to remember Him and keep His command foremost in your thinking. Do what is right, *maroof*, and avoid that which is not right, *munkar*. In other words, we are created to do right and believe right and remember God with honor.

Islam does not believe in the "isms," i.e., Capitalism, Communism or even in Muhammadanism. Some past non-Muslim scholars made use of "Muhammadanism" to describe Islam, as they failed to understand Islam. The followers of Islam are called Muslims, a name given by Prophet Ibrahim, as mentioned in the Qur'an: "This is the faith of your father Ibrahim. He named you Muslim." (22:78) A Muslim is one who submits himself to Allah and the peaceful path of Islam.

The two Islamic terms of *Deen* and *Shariat* should be differentiated. *Deen* is religion, while *Shariat* is divine law. *Deen* means the belief in the oneness of Allah, prophethood, and in the Day of Judgment. These beliefs have been the same all along. The *Shariat*, on the other hand, changes according to the current needs of a particular time but is based upon the *Deen*. All prophets from Prophet Adam to Prophet Nuh, Prophet Musa to Prophet Isa, up to Prophet Muhammad brought one *Deen*—Islam. They were all Muslims. The *Shariat* was changed from time to time, according to the needs of the time. After giving a complete code of teaching in the form of books and teachers, Allah declares: "Surely the true religion with Allah is Islam."

This book contains important information on Islam, Shi'a and Sunni differences, and other related issues. You should look at this as an entry into further learning and study, because a person spends his whole life learning and improving yet never reaches a stage in which he can honestly say he has finished. The exercises are not meant to be assigned all at once, because most of them require you to think deeply, communicate clearly and completely, and perform some additional research. But, none of them should be left out, either, as they provide crucial experience to the student for developing his own skills and understanding. The exercises might ask you to write a story or poem, make a plan for a certain aspect of your life, prepare a paper or speech, find verses in the Qur'an, or to answer a question for which the answer is not provided in the text but which you have to think about in order to find the answer. Some of the questions give you choices to pursue your individual interests. Many of the questions do not have a single right answer or right way to solve the problem. The goal of the exercises is to have you ponder, think critically, and learn how to find things out on your own by using resources. These skills are important life skills no matter what you do with your life and also because Allah advises us to ponder our life.

Textbook on Shi'a Islam

Chapter One

BELIEFS IN ISLAM

Islam emphasizes correct beliefs and righteousness of actions together with humbleness of spirit. According to the Qur'an (2:177), it is not only the righteousness that you turn your face east or west (in prayer), but righteousness is to believe in (1) Allah; (2) the Day of Judgment; (3) Angels; (4) the Books sent by Allah; (5) the Prophets sent by Allah; (6) Alms, Charity and giving of your wealth in love of Allah; (7) Establishing prayers; (8) Giving *zakat*; (9) Keeping one's words; and (10) Showing patience in time of distress. These are some of the signs of true believers. People are not righteous because they make a show of being better than other people, but true righteousness depends upon the purity of their hearts.

Islam emphasizes (1) Beliefs (*Aqeeda*); and (2) Actions (*Aamals*). Belief without action is like a fruitless tree and action without belief is like a bitter fruit. There are three basic beliefs: (i) Tauheed meaning oneness of Allah; (ii) Nabbuwat meaning prophethood; and (iii) Qiyamat meaning the Day of Judgment. Tauheed also includes divine justice, without which it is incomplete. In the same way, the Nabbuwat includes Imammat for continuation of the work of Allah. Hence the correct beliefs are: (i) Tauheed (oneness of Allah), (ii) Adl (Divine justice), (iii) Nabbuwat (Prophethood), (iv) Imammat (vicegerents of prophethood), and (v) Qiyamat.

TAUHEED

Belief in Allah, or Tauheed, is the basic code of Islamic belief. This is the only door to enter the castle of Islam. This Belief means that Allah is our Creator, and the Creator of this world. He is one, everlasting. He was not created by anyone else, and will never perish.

In the Qur'an it is summarized this way, "Say: He, Allah, is one, Allah is He on Whom all depends (He is eternal and absolute). He begets not, nor is He begotten. And none is like Him." (112:1-4)

Basically, believing in one creator is human instinct. It is universally observed in almost all religions. In Islam, this belief has been crystallized and further clarified.

Tauheed is the most basic belief in Islam, and there is no compromise allowed in this matter. There is no mix-up in this belief. In Islam, He is absolute, He has no partner, He is wise, He is powerful, Almighty, and He is everywhere. The Qur'an has mentioned this belief several times. It may seem difficult superficially, but for one who can think and read the signs of His presence; it is not difficult to find Him.

One day the Prophet was passing through a street with his companions when he noticed an old lady making thread from a hand machine. He went to her, and asked her whether she believed in Allah. She answered, "Yes, of course I do." The Prophet asked her to prove her point. She stopped the machine. She turned towards the Prophet, and told him that if this small machine could not work without someone running it, then how could this world be formed without a creator, and how its system could run without someone operating it.

Someone asked Imam Ali if he had seen Allah. The Imam replied, "I will neither believe nor worship Him unless I have seen him. But I have not seen him with my naked eye. I have seen him with the eyes of my heart and brain. Look at the universe and everything is singing the song of its Creator."

The belief in Allah has two parts in *La ila ha illah allah*. One part is *la ila ha* meaning "there is no God." The second part *illah allah* means "but Allah." One who believes in Allah should first deny any other false gods, then and only then can he believe in one Allah. We must be very careful to avoid polytheistic beliefs and actions such as believing in Allah as having children or family or having divisions within him that act in different ways or perform different functions. God cannot be divided into different parts or jobs. It is impossible to limit Him. He can only be recognized as an absolute oneness.

The Qur'an has categorized His attributes as positive and negative attributes. The positive attributes are called *Sifate-Sububityyah*. Following are the eight positive attributes:

1. *Qadim*: He is Eternal and has no beginning and no end.
2. *Qadir*: He is Omnipotent, has power over everything.
3. *Alim*: He is Omniscient. He knows everything.
4. *Hai*: He is alive and will be forever.
5. *Mureed*: He does everything according to His intention and will.
6. *Mudrik*: He is aware of everything. He sees all and hears all.
7. *Muttakkallim*: He can infuse and create speech in anything.
8. *Sadiq*: He is true in His Words and Acts, and true in
   His Promises to mankind.

The negative attributes are called *Sifate-Salbiyyah*, which He does not possess. These are also eight:

1. *Shareek*: He has no colleagues and no partner.
2. *Murrakab*: He is not made or composed of different things.
3. *Makan*: He does not need and does not have a place to live. He is everywhere.
4. *Mahalle-Hawadis*: He is not subject to change. No change of state or place occurs in Him.
5. *Mar-ee*: He was never and never will be visible.
6. *Ehteyaj*: He is not dependent on anyone.
7. *Hulool*: He does not enter into anything and nothing enters into Him.
8. *Sifate-zaedh*: His attributes are not separate from His essence.

Two important points have to be remembered with regard to the positive attributes. The first important point is that the positive attributes are not something assigned to Him. These are inseparable from him. For example, a child goes to school and gradually gets educated. For him, education is separate. He is separate and his knowledge is separate. For Allah, these attributes cannot be separated from Him. The second vital point is to recognize Allah by one's own thinking and feeling and not because one has read it or someone has told him. Everyone has to perceive Him. He should be recognized by His creation. Don't be afraid to think about Allah and His nature, but check your thoughts carefully that they do not misrepresent Allah.

The belief in one God imparts unity among Muslims, as they are all believers in one God. There are multitudes of other advantages in this belief. Some of these are as follows:

1. By virtue of us being created by one Creator, we all become brothers in a way.

2. The sense of brotherhood creates similar feelings towards other people who are not the believers in Islam. Imam Ali wrote to one of his governors, Malik-e-Ashtar, "Remember there are two types of people under you. One who are believers like you. They are your brothers in Islam. The others who do not believe in Islam, they are your brothers in humanity."

3. By believing in His command to be good, everyone should excel as human beings.

4. By believing that He is watching us, everyone should try to be good, even in the darkness of the night and loneliness of his home. Allah is watching us all the time.

5. We will be presented to him on the Day of Judgment. This should stop us from doing bad deeds.

6. A good believer surrenders himself totally to Allah. Allah returns the favor by making the entire universe subservient to

him. The Qur'an says, "Do you not see that Allah has made (resources) subservient to you whatsoever is in the earth…" (22:65) This gives a clue to intelligent people to use all resources wisely and not to misuse these. We should not waste anything, be it personal energies or otherwise. The Qur'an says, "Eat and drink but do not waste." It also inculcates among the believers a sense of self-respect. As a human being he is the master of this universe, and everything is created for him, but the universe does not revolve around him as if nothing else has any value or importance. He should not degrade himself by worshipping anything lower than Allah, like idol worshipping. He is only to worship Allah.

7. A believer knows that Allah has created him and there is a Day of Judgment ahead of him. Thus, he will never be belligerent, arrogant or nasty to anyone.

8. Believing in Allah makes the believers dutiful and upright in every step of life. Belief keeps on reminding the believer of his rights and responsibilities.

9. Like a child feeling secure under the protection of its parents, the believer feels secure thinking that Allah is the protector, and this makes him confident, brave, and courageous. If he is following the right path, he is not to fear anyone or anything in creation.

10. A believer believes, and rightly so, that he is part of this universe. He is not a narrow-minded person living in a hole. He is broad-minded. He is friendly to the world and sees the world from that perspective.

11. The stronger he believes in God, the more determined he would be in his resolve. He will be more perseverant and more patient. He will not be perturbed by the temporary spasms. He will look at Allah, and pray to Him for guiding him in times of need.

12. The believer surrenders himself totally to Allah. He will always

watch for His command. The concept of action is different for him. He will always try to do the right thing (*Maruf*), and stay away from bad things (*Munkar*). The youth need to realize that it is easier to stay away from bad things altogether than to taste them for a time and then try to put them away when older; some may never receive that chance of old age to put the bad habits away, and most others will find it difficult to get rid of bad habits and will regret having allowed themselves to begin them while young. The youth also must realize that we are responsible for our thoughts and actions and we cannot be less-than-perfect.

13. The believer will use anything of this world wisely and not waste it. He will not need a state officer or ordinance to ask him not to waste water, for example. He knows if he wastes even water, he will be answerable to Allah one day.

14. A believer knows that, he is only a temporary owner of his possessions; the actual owner is Allah. He is very conscious in all his dealings, and knows that even his own children belong to Allah. He is only the custodian or guardian of those things temporarily entrusted to him by Allah.

DIVINE JUSTICE (ADL)

Allah is all-powerful. This attribute of Allah sometimes gives a wrong connotation to some people that He can do anything, even can pardon a wrongdoer, a killer. We should remember that He is all-powerful, but He is also wise, just, and perfect. These attributes defy any wrongdoing from Him. He cannot send an unrepentant killer and his victim both to heaven; it does not make sense. He will always do justice. In the Qur'an, Allah has mentioned His justice several times. For example "Surely Allah does not do injustice to the weight of an atom…" (4:40) "And We will set up a just balance on the day of resurrection, so no soul shall be dealt with unjustly in the least;" (21:47) "Allah commands justice, kindness and charity and giving to kindred and forbids unnecessary oppression." (16:90)

Imam Ali has defined justice as placing a thing in its proper place. It should be remembered that there are two types of rights and responsibilities: rights and responsibilities of humans to other human beings, and right and responsibilities of human beings to Allah. It is possible for Allah to forgive when someone does not fulfill some of His rights and some of the responsibilities towards Him. If someone does not fast, Allah out of His mercy and wisdom may or may not forgive him. On the other hand, Allah cannot forgive rights of other human beings until it is forgiven by the human being whose rights have been violated. If someone owes another person some money and doesn't pay it back, Allah can't forgive it unless the loaner forgives it.

PROPHETHOOD

Allah asks us to follow His commands and to follow the right path. We are ready to do so but how do we know what His commands are and what the 'right path' is? We need someone to teach and show us the right path. This is the reason He sent prophets — to give us clear commands from Allah and guidance to the right path. A prophet cannot be an ordinary person. He should be a pious and holy person, high enough to be near to Allah in spirit directly or with the help of angels. On the other hand, he should also be a down to earth person in order to give His orders to us directly to be followed. The Qur'an says:

1. "(All) people are a single nation; so Allah raised prophets as bearers of good news and as warners, and He revealed with them the Book with truth, that it might judge between people in that in which they differed;" (2:213)

2. "Nor do We chastise until We raise an apostle (prophet)."(17:15)

3. "Even as We sent a messenger from among you to convey Our messages to you and cleanse you, and teach you the Book and the wisdom, and what you did not know;" (2:151)

The missions of prophets are:

1. To guide mankind towards the right path.
2. To inform the people about the unseen and hidden realities which they can never know or perceive without help.
3. To purify the soul and develop good morals.
4. To certify the actions of people on the Day of Judgment.

The following are the characteristics of prophets:

1. Allah appoints prophets. The Qur'an says, "Allah best knows where He places His message." (6:124)
2. All of the prophets were perfect infallible (sinless) human beings. The Qur'an says about Prophet Muhammad: "Nor does he speak out of desire." (53:3) If prophets make mistakes how can we follow them? If prophets were not sinless in all their deeds and words at all times we would become confused about which of their words and actions to follow and which not to.
3. All prophets were endowed with distinct signs (miracles).
4. All prophets taught the basic beliefs of Islam – particularly Tauheed.
5. All prophets successfully completed their missions of delivering a message, even though some people choose to reject the message.

Prophets are either called Nabi or Rasool depending on their mission. Nabi means messenger. The Nabi delivers the message to people. Rasool gives a message and also brings a Shariat (Divine law) with him.

There were a total of 124,000 Nabis, (the messengers), but only 313 were Rasools. Among them the five most important grand prophets are: Prophet Nuh (Noah), Prophet Ibrahim (Abraham), Prophet Musa (Moses), Prophet Isa (Jesus), and Prophet Muhammad. Prophet Muhammad was a Nabi by birth, but he declared his status as Rasool at the age of forty. Rasool is higher in rank than the Nabi.

The Qur'an has mentioned 25 prophets by name. They are: Adam, Idrees, Nuh, Hud, Salih, Ibrahim, Ismail, Ishaq, Lut, Yaqub, Yusuf, Shoaib, Ayyub, Musa, Harun, Dhulkifl, Dawud, Sulaiman, Ilias, Alysa, Yunus, Zakariyya, Yahya, Isa, and Muhammad.

IMAMMAT

Imammat is basically the continuation of divine leadership that started from prophethood. Imammat is different from prophethood and hence has a different designation. When the message of Allah and Shariat of Islam was completed, there was no longer a need for the Prophet. The Qur'an says, "This day have I perfected for you your religion, and completed My favor on you and chosen for you Islam as a religion." (5:3) This verse was revealed at Ghadeer Khum the day the Prophet publicly announced Imam Ali as his successor. The analogy is that of a building which is completed. The builders are not needed any more. The maintenance crew and the custodian of the building will take over. After the religion is completed, the prophet is no longer needed. The world, however, still needs a guide. Guidance of humanity needs to be continued. As the Qur'an says, "Nor do we chastise until we raise an apostle (prophet)." (17:15)

The first person on earth was a Prophet. Like a good administration before starting a school, Allah first appointed a principal. By the same token, as long as the school continues to exist, a principal will be needed to run it smoothly. Presently, there are more than six billion people who need to be guided. The Qur'an is quick to declare a rule, "Whatever communication We abrogate or cause to be forgotten, We bring one better than it or like it." (2:106)

Of course, none can be better than Prophet Muhammad but someone like him, according to this verse, should be brought as guide. The Qur'an also testifies more than once: "And you shall not find any change in the course (law) of Allah." (33:62), and "For you shall not find any alteration in the course of Allah; and you shall not find any change in the course of Allah." (35:43) The chain of Prophets was ended and replaced by the chain of Imams, the divine representative of Allah, to guide humanity in the completed message and the right way as delivered by the prophets. There is also an authentic hadith of the Prophet accepted by all Muslims: "Anyone (Muslim) who dies without the recognition of the Imam of his time dies the death of jahiliat (unbeliever)."

Imammat has been a great controversial point in Islam especially between Sunnis and Shi'as. Sunni brothers hastily say that Shi'as believe in Imam Ali as the rightful guide because of his close relationship with the Prophet. He was the cousin and son-in-law of the Prophet. The fact is that Shi'as believe in the divine continuation of guides from Allah. Whoever fits this definition they accept him to be the Imam. Since no one else but Imam Ali satisfactorily fits into the definition of Imam and the Prophet announced him as such, according to the command of Allah, they call him their Imam.

Let us ponder with balanced and open minds the Imammat. As stated earlier, Allah created a guide in the form of Prophet Adam before creating any human being. How is it possible that Allah suddenly disconnected the line of divine guidance after the demise of Prophet Muhammad in spite of His promises? Who else can keep this promise better than Allah?

There could only be three explanations:

1. After the Prophet there was no one who could take the position of Imammat and hence it was discontinued. But Allah is all-powerful and could very well create such a person as noted above in the Ayah 2:106.
2. Allah was happy with human beings up to the time of the Prophet and after that He got angry with them and stopped sending guides. But He himself has said that He is kind to his people and that He does not change his rules.
3. Human beings have reached the pinnacle. The Muslims have become so good, so reliable, and so perfect that they do not need a guide anymore. Looking at the state of affairs through which Muslims have passed the last fourteen centuries, nothing could be farther from truth than this explanation.

If the above three explanations are not true, and of course they are not true, then it is obligatory on Allah by the rule He made Himself that divine guidance should continue. The Qur'an still guides and gives the proof by saying, "And remember the Day when We will call all people with their Imams." (17:71).

Thus, it does not meet the criteria of wisdom and fairness that the Prophet left this world without designating someone as his successor. Remember the hardship Prophet Muhammad had taken to establish and spread the word of Allah. Also that he did not leave any avenues of life unexplained or incomplete. How could he leave this important issue unresolved? He did not die in a hurry. He was told that his days to meet Allah were coming. He had plenty of time to carry out his duties. How then could he leave this important matter to the *Ummah*?

It is also a matter of concern that elders and respected members of the *Ummah* left the dead body of the Prophet unburied and instead hurried to assemble at Saqifa to choose his successor so the *Ummah* would not disintegrate. With all due respect, does anyone think that the companions of Prophet Muhammad were more concerned about the disintegration of the *Ummah* than the Prophet? What about Allah? Did He change his *Sunnah*? Was He not concerned anymore about the *Ummah*?

It is also intriguing to note that Caliph Abu Bakr, though he was very sick on his deathbed going in and out of consciousness, appointed Umar as his successor so that the *Ummah* remained united.

Caliph Umar after being injured and suffering on his deathbed did not forget the issue of his successor. He appointed a six-member committee to elect a caliph. Even after using all sincerity at our disposal, it is hard to believe that these people were smarter and more caring about Islam to announce successors for the Ummah than the Prophet, and even Allah.

The Qur'an clearly orders us: "O you who believe! Obey Allah and obey the Apostle, and those in authority among you." (4:59) This verse makes it incumbent upon Muslims to follow the same sequence as described in this verse. It is up to Allah to send Prophets. Naming his divine successors should be declared by the Prophet and followed by the *Ummah*. And who should be appointed? The best among the *Ummah* after the Prophet should be appointed as a successor. It is the unanimous decision amongst Muslims during the last fourteen centuries that Imam Ali was the best after the Prophet. Thus, Imam Ali should have been selected. There are many traditions that make it clear that "those in authority among you" refers to Imam Ali in particular and the rightly guided Imam in general.

Indeed the Prophet had appointed Imam Ali as his successor and it was announced time and again by the Prophet. According to historical records, not only was Imam Ali declared as the Prophet's successor, but it was also reiterated several times.

1. On the first day of open declaration of Islam and his Prophethood at the feast of Zul-Ashira, the Prophet declared that Ali

would be his successor and his Vizier in his mission. There is no need of any reference as every writer and historian East and West agree that if Imam Ali had not stood up on the day of Zul-Ashira, the Prophet would have been embarrassed and crippled, and Islam would have vanished on that day. Ali was the first to accept Islam openly and believe in the Prophet. The Prophet's declaration of making Ali his vicegerent was unequivocal.

2. When the Prophet sent Abu Bakr to read the *Surat Tauba (Barat)* to the Meccans, Angel Gabriel came and asked the Prophet to call back Abu Bakr as no outsider could be deputed for this job. It should either be read by the Prophet himself or someone from him should be asked to recite the *Surah*. Imam Ali was then sent and Abu Bakr was called back.

3. On his mission to Tubuk the Prophet left Imam Ali in Medina as his successor. When Imam Ali showed some concern, the Prophet declared that he (Imam Ali) was to the Prophet the same as Prophet Haroon was to Prophet Musa except that there would no more Prophets after him. This meant he was the prophet's successor even after Muhammad's death and thus would outlive him to perform this duty.

4. During his return journey after performing his last Hajj, the Prophet declared, at a place known as Ghadeer-e-khum, Imam Ali as his successor. Ghadeer-e-khum is a place between Mecca and Medina and an important converging point for people to take off in different directions. The Prophet asked the entire caravan of about 120,000 of his companions to stop at this place. The date was 18 *Zilhaj*, 10 *Hijri* and it was mid-day. The Prophet led the *Zohar* prayer, and then he got on the pulpit and declared in no uncertain terms that Imam Ali was the guardian and guide of his *Ummah*, in the same way as he (the Prophet) was their guardian and guide. He used the same word as he chose for himself that is, "For whosoever I

am *Maula*, Imam Ali will be the *Maula*" meaning here guide and supervisor for all their affairs. Everyone was requested to congratulate him, and to call him *Amirul-momineen* meaning the leader of the *momineen* (believers). The official poet of the Prophet, Hassan bin Sabit wrote an extempore poem and read it to the Prophet. Caliph Umar's famous words on this occasion were inscribed in the books of history saying: "Congratulations from me Oh Son of Abu Talib for becoming our *Maula* and *Maula* of all *momimeen*."

QIYAMAH (THE DAY OF JUDGMENT)

Common sense dictates that if commands are given to people then there should be some mechanism to judge whether or not they are carried out, and if carried out, then whether it is done correctly or incorrectly. By the same token, one who carries them out correctly should be awarded and those who don't should be punished. If there are rewards or punishments regarding the commands, they would not be carried out often.

The day when everything and everyone will be judged, good deeds will be rewarded, and bad deeds punished is called, in Islamic terms the Day of Judgment, or Qiyamah. In the Qur'an, there are many verses regarding this day and this is one of the basic beliefs of all Muslims as well as many other people.

BOOKS OF ALLAH

Allah has revealed many books to various prophets. According to the Qur'an, the Muslims should believe in all these books and we all do. Denial of any one will mean denial of all. The four books mentioned the Qur'an are:

1. Torait (Torah revealed to Prophet Musa);

2. Zaboor (Psalms revealed to Prophet Daud);
3. Injeel (Gospel revealed to Prophet Isa); and
4. Quran (the last Divine book revealed to Prophet Muhammad).

QUR'AN

It is the basic constitution of Islam. It was revealed to Prophet Muhammad over the period of 23 years. Today, the Quran is exactly the same as revealed originally to the Prophet without even a slight change. Whatever is between the two covers is all the message of Allah without omission or addition. It starts from *"Ba"* of *Bismillah* of *Surrah al-Fatiha* and ends with "Seen" of *Surrah Wan Naas*. Not only that, it is also believed that the Prophet compiled it as the Qur'an is read today. It is wrong to say that any Caliph compiled it. Caliph Uthman obtained copies of the Qur'an and sent it to all other states. If any Qur'an was not according to the original, as noted by him, he burned them.

The interpretation of the Qur'an is a different story. Different interpretations of the Qur'an are probably responsible for the divisions amongst Muslims. Shi'as follow the interpretations given by the Ahlul Bayt because the Prophet taught them starting with Imam Ali.

Imam Ali did compile a Qur'an, but it was the same as the original Qur'an, with no change in its content. It did have some details about the reasons for revealing of some of the Ayahs or Surahs and their background and explanations. He accepted and recited the present Qur'an as it is.

ANGELS

Angels are special creatures of Allah. These are the creatures of light, contrary to the creatures we know as human beings, which are made up of clay (like the various chemical elements in the soil). The

Jinns on the other hand are created by fire. So, we understand that the chemical elements that make us are not the same as what makes angels and *jinns*. The most infamous among *Jinns* is *Iblees*. *Iblees* was a special *jinn* because he was praying and worshiping Allah a lot. He was never an angel, but he was often associated with them due to his special status. Later on, he openly disobeyed Allah and was thrown out of the Heaven. His pride prevented him from obeying Allah in regard to His new creation, man. *Iblees* considered himself better than man because he considered being made of fire superior to being made of clay.

The angels are infallible (sinless) creatures of Allah. They cannot do anything wrong. They do not have free will. They are created to carry out work as commissioned by Allah without fail. They are millions in number, and Allah assigns some of them to record our deeds, to pray for us, and so on. The most prominent among them are:

1. *Jibrael* (Gabriel): He brought the message of Allah to his prophets and other messengers.
2. *Mekaeel* (Michael): He distributes sustenance to the world as ordained by Allah.
3. *Israeel* (Israel): This is the Angel of death.
4. *Israfeel* (Israfeel): This angel will blow the trumpet before Qiyamah.

Angels are assigned to various jobs, like the two angels sitting on each shoulder of every human being recording all their actions. The two angels are known as *Kiraam-ul-Katebeen*. It is also believed that angels come to the grave after one's death and ask you questions about your beliefs. These angels are called *Munkir* and *Nakeer.*

EXERCISES

1. Write a short story or poem that shows the difference between

two main characters, one who is a righteous person and another who thinks him/herself to be righteous but really isn't. Make sure your story or poem uses the concepts of true righteousness mentioned in this chapter as well as what you already know about what makes a good person.

2. Provide some examples of evidence in the universe for the existence of Allah that are meaningful to you and explain how they are special examples for you.

3. It is said that a heart cannot have two masters.

    a. What does this mean in terms of tauheed?

    b. What things might occupy your heart besides Allah that you personally need to be careful about?

    c. Come up with three experiments to help your heart have only Allah as its master. Try one of them as agreed upon by you and your teacher for one full week and then prepare a 3-5 minute speech about the effects of your experiment.

4.

    a. What characteristic of Allah exists which makes you know you will not be treated unjustly by Him?

    b. Injustice does happen in this world, how can you reconcile that with the justice of God? What is the source of that injustice? What difference would it make if people were like robots that had no choice but to do right and couldn't choose to do wrong?

    c. Why do you think we have the choice to do wrong even though it may cause harm to ourselves and others?

5. Choose one of the prophets mentioned in the Qur'an. Find all the verses about that particular prophet in the Qur'an, and also find all the verses about the prophet from another religious text such as the Bible. If you cannot find information on that prophet in a second source, choose a different prophet. Make a chart to compare the information about

the prophet in the both sources – what do sources agree on? What information is in Qur'an but not in the other religious text, and vice versa?

6. The word "Maula" sometimes can mean friend in Arabic. Re-read the events of Ghadeer Khum. How do you know, using logic and common sense based on the events of that day, that the Prophet did not mean friend when he said "Maula" that day?

7. Most people who think carefully are concerned about the Day of Judgment and what will happen to them on that day. Allah promises us that each person will be judged justly only according to whatever good and bad he has committed. To prepare yourself, it is wise to adopt good deeds and leave aside bad habits. Pick a good deed to adopt regularly (daily, weekly, etc.) and put it into practice. Write about what you have chosen and how you are carrying it out.

8. We believe in the Torah, Psalms, Gospel and the Scrolls of Abraham in addition to the Qur'an. Christians and Jews today have books which they call Torah, Psalms and Gospel. But, there are many versions of them with different words, translations, and sometimes even entirely different chapters, and they do not possess the original text of Torah, Psalms, or Gospel with which to compare the various versions. This leads them to some differences in their divisions in beliefs and practices. As Muslims, we do not think any of these to be exactly the same as was originally revealed by God, so we understand that they contain elements of man's interference, either by decision or by accident. Think about this situation, and then answer the following questions:

   a. What verses in the Qur'an and what other evidence do we have that lets us know the Qur'an is different from these books, and that it is still the original, unchanged Word of God?

b. Why is it important to learn Qur'anic Arabic with understanding instead of relying solely on a translation of the Qur'an?

c. What role does a commentary (tafsir) of Qur'an such as the one that Imam Ali had play in developing our understanding of God's Word?

9. Iblees was once a much-honored worshipper of Allah. Then pride made him one of the lowest of creations. This is a warning to us that just because we are good one day, we are not safe from the danger of becoming bad the next day. Even the highest ranking person can fall. But also, the lowest person can be the highest — think of *Sura Yusuf*, and the story of Prophet *Yusuf* as a possible example. He went from being a captive to being one of the highest people in the land, and became a spiritual leader.

    a. What are some warning signs to look out for that pride or another character flaw that could be lowering your spiritual rank?

    b. What can you do to turn yourself around if you've made mistakes and want to raise yourself back up?

10. Choose one of the following topics to learn more about it and write at least one page about what you have earned:

    d. What questions do *Munkir* and *Nakeer* ask?

    e. What happens with the records of your deeds written by the angels on your shoulders, *Kiraam-ul-Katebeen*?

    f. How did *Jibraeel* deliver Qur'an to the Prophet?

    g. What exactly does the Angel of Death, *Israeel,* do?

    h. What can you find out about *Ruh ul Qud* — the Holy Spirit?

    i. Are there other angels that you can find? And what do they do?

Chapter Two

ACTIONS IN ISLAM

Good beliefs beget good actions. Our beliefs have to be converted into action to prove our goodness, just as small seeds give rise to big fruitful trees. In Islam, good actions are as important as good and sound beliefs. These actions called *Furu-din* (meaning branches) are divided into the following ten groups:

1. *Namaz* (Salat).
2. *Roza* (Saum).
3. *Hajj* (Pilgrimage to Mecca).
4. *Zakkat* (Alms).
5. *Khums* (Special obligatory charity).
6. *Jihad* (Struggle in defense of truth).
7. *Tawallah* (Love of good things).
8. *Tabarah* (Disassociation from bad things).
9. *Amar-bil-Maroof* (Ordering good things).
10. *Nahil-Anal-Munkir* (Keeping away from bad things).

SALAT

Prayer is an act of utmost devotion of a man towards his Creator—Allah, wherein he submits himself totally to Him. It is an act of total surrender. This is what Islam is all about—submitting to Divine Laws. Hence, The Prophet of Islam stressed offering of prayers more than anything else. The Prophet said, "If Salaat (prayer) is accepted, other deeds may be accepted." He also said, "Someone who doesn't care about it, and thinks it is trivial, i.e., unimportant, he would be punished on the Day of Judgment." It is, therefore, very important to say the prayers—the obligatory one, at least—and say them properly in a serious manner, feeling the presence of Allah. In fact, prayer is a "dialogue," for the most part with Allah.

As a number of treatises are available on how to say Salat and its essential requisites, we will be omitting our discussion on this topic. Readers can easily find various publications on this subject. (Salaat — Pyame Aman Publications.)

SAUM

Saum means to fast and abstain from those things that break the fast, from true dawn (*Subhey Sadiq*) to after sunset (*Maghreb* time) in obedience to the commandment of Allah. The *wajib* (obligatory) fasts fall into six categories: (1) Saums during the month of the Ramadan; (2) Saum of *kaffara*, which become obligatory or *wajib* due to various reasons including expiation for certain misdeeds; (3) Saums which are lawfully skipped and become *Qaza*, meaning they will be made up later; (4) Saums for ten days of *badal-ud-adi* during *Hajjj*; (5) Third day of itikaf; and (6) some saums which become obligatory or wajib on account of nazr, or making a vow.

Conditions of Saum: Following are the conditions of validity of the Saum:

1. Adulthood. (*Baligh*)
2. Sanity.
3. Good health (Not being exposed to danger of illness by keeping fast.)
4. Remaining free from any *Najasat*.
5. Not traveling

Things or actions that break the fast are:

1. Eating or drinking.
2. Sexual relations.
3. Indulging in any action that causes semen to come out.
4. Speaking or writing or conveying derogatory remarks about Allah, the Prophet, Imams and/or Bibi Fatima.
5. Allowing thick dusty smoke or steam to reach the throat purposely.
6. Submerging the head in water.
7. Remaining in conditions of *janabat* or *haiz* until dawn.
8. Liquid Enema.
9. Vomiting.

The following persons are exempted from saum:

1. Men and women who are too old and cannot keep the fast.
2. A person who has a disease in which she/he remains thirsty or in which regular eating or ingestion of medicine is necessary.
3. A pregnant woman, or a woman in *haiz,*
4. A breast-feeding mother.

In some conditions, people who are exempted from fast are permanently exempted, while others are temporarily exempted. Some will need to make up their fasts later when their condition improves.

HAJJ

Hajj means undertaking pilgrimage to the holy mosque of Ka'abha in Mecca on the 8th to 13th of the Islamic month of *Zilhajj.* It is incumbent upon every Muslim who has the necessary means to perform Hajj, or to visit Mecca, at least once in his lifetime. The conditions for performing Hajj for an individual are:

1. He or she must be *baligh*.
2. He or she must have means to meet the expense of the journey as well as the needs of his or her dependents in his or her absence.
3. He or she must be in good health to undertake the journey.
4. There is no immediate risk of life in undertaking the journey.

The essential formality of Hajj is the *Ehram* i.e., the male should remove his stitched clothes and wrap himself in two pieces of unstitched clean cloth, one covering his body from his shoulder to his loin and another from his waist to feet. A female should wrap these two pieces over and above her usual cloth or can wear stitched clothes designated as her pilgrimage garment. The *Ehram* clothes should have been lawfully acquired and it should be not be silken or transparent. Most women are able to adopt regular sewn white or other color clothing as their *Ehram*.

The moment the individual puts on the *Ehram*, he becomes *Mohram* and some things become *haram* (forbidden) for him and he should put aside all worldly thoughts and desires beyond what is minimally necessary. After putting on *Ehram* the pilgrims in response to the call of Allah issued through Prophet Ibrahim recite:

Labbaik, Allahomma Labbaik! La Sharika Laka Labbaik, Innal-Hamda Laka Wan-Nemata Laka, Wal Mulka La Sharika Laka Labbaik. (Yes here I am, Allah, here I am. There is no partner for you, yes here I am. Verily the praise and the bounties are yours and the domain is yours. Yes I am here, O' Allah.)

It is worth noting that the call of Allah to mankind issued through Ibrahim thousands of years ago has been made to ring and resound into the ears of men through Islam, and today the holy house of the Allah, the Ka'abah, is visited regularly and punctually every year on the fixed date in the month of Zillhajj of the Islamic calendar.

After putting an *Ehram,* the Hajji, or pilgrim, is required to perform the following actions:

1. *Tawaf*-or circumambulation i.e., going seven times around the Ka'abah.
2. After the *Tawaf* is completed, a prayer (namaz) of two *rikat,* same as that of the morning prayers, must be performed.
3. After the prayer ,the pilgrim has to cut his nails.

These formalities are performed immediately as pilgrims arrive in the city of Mecca for the pilgrimage, this is called *Umrah* and the cutting of the nail and/or hair is called *Taqseer.* This could be performed from the first of the lunar month of Shawwal to the 8th of ZilHajj.

On the 8th ZilHajj the pilgrims put on the *Ehram* again. On the 9th ZilHajj the pilgrims go to the plain of Arafat and stay there until sunset. After sunset the pilgrims proceed to Mashar and stay there at night. On the morning of 10th ZilHajj the pilgrims go to the plains of Mina, and offer sacrifice and perform the *Taqseer* (shaving his head clean this time instead of cutting his nails; ladies only cut a small portion of hair). After completing the *Taqseer,* the pilgrims should put off the *Ehram* but must remain in Mina for two or three nights. During the day, they are required to stone three symbols of *Shaitan* in Mina and then the pilgrims go to Mecca to perform *Tawaf* and offer two *rikats* prayer. After completing the *Tawaf,* the pilgrims perform the *Sai* between the hills of Safa and Marwa. This is a process of walking between them seven times as Hajra did looking for water for her son Ishmael. After completing *Sai,* the pilgrims conclude the pilgrimage by repeating the *Tawaf* called *Tawaf-e-Nisa* and offering the Namaz *Tawaf-e-Nisa* which are compulsory in Islam. If a person is married and forgets to perform this *tawaf,* he is not lawfully allowed to have relations with his spouse again until it is completed. During the pilgrimage, marriage relations are not permitted and it is this last *tawaf* and *namaz* that officially makes it lawful again. This completes the pilgrimage.

After the Hajj (or before), the pilgrims proceed to Medina to visit the shrine of the Prophet and the graves of the four Imams in the Cemetery of Jannat-ul-Baqi. The four Imams who are buried in Jannat-ul-Baqi are: second Imam Hasan ibn Ali, fourth Imam Ali ibn Husyan, Az-Zainul-Abidin, fifth Imam Mohammad ibn Ali, Al-Baqar, and sixth Imam Jafer ibn Muhammad, Al-Sadiq. This is a highly recommended act.

ZAKAT

Zakat, or the prescribed poor-rate, is one of the basic pillars of Islam. Islam in its system of Zakat and Khums has rendered a death-blow to the accumulation of wealth with any particular individual, making it automatically and most healthily shared among the members of the human family. The rank of the injuction about the payment of Zakat, or the poor rate, among beliefs of Islam is immediately after the prescribed prayers. The Qur'an says: "And keep up prayer and pay the poor-rate and bow down with those who bow down."(2:43).

Zakat is basically paid on nine items, namely wheat, barley and dates, which are agricultural produce, gold, silver, camels, cows, sheep and goats. See the table at the end of the chapter for more details about payment of zakat (Table 1).

Zakat can be used for the following purposes:

1. For poor people who do not have enough expense for one year.
2. For needy people.
3. For the tax collectors who collect the Zakat.

4. For those fighting legitimate war with non-Muslims or in favor of Islam.
5. For setting free the captives.
6. For paying off debts of the people who cannot do it by themselves.
7. For undertaking public works of any type.
8. For payment to travelers who are in need of money.

KHUMS

Khums is also a fixed-rate annual tax on one's annual net savings. The rate of Khums is one-fifth or 20% of the net savings, which stands to the credit of an individual after meeting all necessary expenses at the end of the year. Payment of Khums is in addition to Zakat. Khums is also wajib. According to the Qur'an, "And know you that whatever thing you gain, a fifth of it is for Allah and for the Apostle and for the (Apostle's) near of kin and the orphans and the needy and the wayfarer. If you believe in Allah, and in that which We revealed to Our servant on the day of distinction, the day on which the two parties met; and Allah has power over all things." (8:41)

Another Verse in the Qur'an on Khums says: "Whatever Allah has restored to His Apostle from the people of the town, it is for Allah and for the Apostle, and for the near of kin and the orphans and the needy and the wayfarer, so that it may not be a thing taken by turns among the rich of you, and whatever the Apostle gives you, accept it and from whatever he forbids you, keep back, and be careful of (your duty to) Allah; surely Allah is severe in retributing (evil)." (59:7)

The preceding verse clearly shows the importance of Khums and its order. A Muslim being the one who has submitted himself to Allah has to implicitly obey the command of the Prophet, which is nothing but the command of Allah and should not interfere with it by using it of his own discretion. The Shi'a Muslims who are the followers of the Islam-original, as prescribed by the Qur'an and preached and practiced by the Prophet and his family (Ahlul-Bayt), follow the law of disbursing the Khums as the Prophet himself enforced it during his lifetime. Khums comprises of two equal parts. The first part is marked for Allah, the Prophet and the Imams of the age. It is given either to the Imam or to his representative and is mostly used for educational purposes. The other equal part of the Khums goes to the needy *Sadaat*. The first year someone is preparing to calculate Khums, he or she simply makes an accounting of his savings, and then paying Khums at 1/5 of it. The next year, he reassesses his earning and property. If, in this second year, he has more assets than the previous year, he pays Khums on one-fifth of the difference between his assets of the two years.

JIHAD

Jihad is the struggle or endeavor in the way of Allah. Jihad literally means 'to strive' and striving can be of various kinds and can mean different things. It includes fighting when it becomes the only alternative to defend the faith and the faithful. Jihad can be of many types, some of which are given below:

1. *Jihad Bin-Nafs* is fighting with one's own rebellious self, which is the greatest Jihad, called Jihad-e-Akbar.
2. *Jihad Bil-Maal* is an endeavor with one's wealth, which means spending or sacrificing one's own wealth in the way of the Allah.
3. *Jihad-Bil-Ilm* is striving to spread knowledge for the benefit of those who need it without any strings of any worldly gains or fame in return for the services.
4. *Jihad-Bis-Saif* is striving with sword only in defense when it becomes unavoidable to defend the truth, Islam, or the truthful, the Muslims. This kind of Jihad is allowed only

at the command of the Prophet or Imam i.e., his apostolic successors and in the absence of the Imam, the Muslims can fight only to defend their faith or their lives, and this kind of defense is called *Difa* or self defense. (See verses in Qur'an: (1) 2:216 and (2) 2:244.)

Jihad should be exclusively in the way of Allah and must not be undertaken for any territorial ambition. The wars that were fought by Muslim kings had no sanction of the Qur'an, the Prophet, or any of the Imams. Those were fought to satisfy the monarchical and territorial ambitions, which are not allowed in Islam.

Suicide bombers, unnecessary violence, terrorism and the innocent killing do not have any place in Islam whatsoever.

AMR-BIL-MAROOF

Amr-Bil-Maroof means the enjoining of good. Under this injunction of the faith it is compulsory for every Muslim to be good, to do good, and to urge others in Islam to do the same. The Qur'an says: "Why do you speak of a thing which you do not do by yourself?" At another place the Qur'an clearly indicates this ordinance: "You are the best of the nations raised up for (the benefit of) men; you enjoin what is right and forbid the wrong and believe in Allah; and if the followers of the Book had believed it would have been better for them; of them (some) are believers and most of them are transgressors." (3:110)

It must be remembered that the *"Khair-ul-Ummat"* mentioned in this verse, means the best of the *ummah* refers only to the Prophet and his Ahlul-Bayt. There is another verse reiterating the same ordinance. It says: "And from among you there should be a party who enjoin good and enjoin what is right and forbid the wrong, and these shall be successful." (3:104) It must be emphasized here that the people who invite to goodness must themselves be good.

Those who preach abstinence from evil should themselves be free from it. The Qur'an also lays down the method for every Muslim to do the *Aml-Bil-Maroof* and it says: "Call to the way of your Lord with wisdom and good advice, and argue with them in the best manner." (16:125).

NAHY-ANIL-MUNKAR

Nahy-Anil-Munkar means prevention of evil or avoiding the forbidden. This injunction of abstaining from the evil and preaching others to do the same goes along the previous one (*Amr-Bil-Maroof*) which is connected with being good and preaching to others to be good. The same principles or rules, which apply to *Amr-Bil-Maroof* is applicable here i.e., Muslims have to keep themselves away from every evil and wickedness before preaching to others the abstinence from it. It is obligatory on every Muslim to abstain from every evil in word and action and to avoid evil society. "He will certainly help those who, if given power in the land, will worship Allah through prayers, pay the religious tax, enjoin others to do good, and prevent them from committing evil. The consequences of all things are in the hands of Allah." (22:41)

In short, the spirit of every teaching of the Qur'an is to abide by truth and goodness and to shun evil and to enjoin upon others to do the same. Sometimes we become so focused in the details of the *wajib* actions in Islam that we underestimate the importance of good character. We are all representatives of our faith, our families, and ourselves before the rest of mankind. If a man prays and performs perfectly all the *wajib* actions and yet has bad character and treats others poorly, acts foolishly or selfishly, or engages in misdeeds, then he is missing the heart of the teachings in Islam and is missing the purpose of following Islam, which is to reform oneself to be the best person that you can be according to the Word of Allah.

TAWALLAH

Tawallah means attachment, or love, and also means the love of the good. Whatever are the hereditary characteristics of a person; environment always plays its own role in molding man's character, conduct, and ideology and practice. A human child brought up in a good and healthy environment has a better chance to be good and kind; likewise those children brought up in an evil and wicked society may turn evil and wicked. It is with these natural phenomena in mind that Allah ordered the Prophet to command his followers, the Muslims, to love his nearest kin as a recompense for the labor of his prophethood so that the Muslims, bound in duty, might love the relatives (the Ahlul-Bayt) of the Prophet and by being attached to them, they would remain on the right path, and be good. "Say (O' Muhammad), I do not ask of you any reward, but the love of my close relatives." (42:23)

Under the command of Allah it is incumbent upon every Muslim to love the Ahlul-Bayt, otherwise he has not paid for the favor of the guidance of Allah received through the Prophet. It is incumbent upon all Muslims to love Allah, to love his Prophet, and to love Ahlul-Bayt. The Holy Prophet has repeatedly pointed out who his Ahlul-Bayt are. Repeatedly, the Prophet said his Vicegerent Ali Ibn Abi Talib, his daughter Fatima Zehra, and his two grandsons Hasan and Husayn are his Ahlul-Bayt. He prayed to Allah saying: "O Lord these are my Ahlul-Bayt." He said this several times and it is written in many books. It is the unanimous report of all historians that on the memorable occasion of proving the truthfulness of Islam against the contesting Christian of Najaran, the Prophet appeared in the field with Husayn, who was only a baby, in his lap, Hasan held by his other hand followed by his daughter Fatima and behind her, her husband Ali ibn Abi Talib, the Vicegerent of the Prophet. Standing in the open field and the Christian looking at him turning his head towards heaven he declared: "Lord these are my Ahlul-Bayt."

Why has the love of Ahlul-Bayt been made incumbent? The Ahlul-Bayt were the people purified by Allah Himself and those purified by Allah were naturally infallible ones (Masoom) who never committed even a minor sin or fault in their lives. They overcame every temptation and served as examples of ideal human being. Allah Himself declared to mankind that He had Himself purified them to the limit of purity. The Qur'an says: "Allah only desires to keep away the uncleanness from you, O people of the House! And to purify you a (thorough) purifying." (33-33) The Ahlul-Bayt were the godly ones of the family of the Prophet whom the Muslim world, as a whole, unanimously acknowledges as the pure personalities and hold them as the infallible ones purified by God Himself. In their love of the divinely purified ones, the devotees will naturally be inclined to goodness and self-purification.

TABARRA

Tabarra means keeping aloof from the enemies of Allah, the Prophet and his Ahlul-Bayt. Disliking evil and wickedness is quite natural. Righteous parents advise their children to stay away from wicked people. It is because everyone knows the destructive effect of a bad company. *Tabarra* means to dislike evil and keep aloof from evil ones. *Tabarra* never means abusing or using of any vulgar or offensive terms against anyone, but is only the expression of ones' disliking of evil characters and wicked conduct by invoking Allah's curse on the tyrant among them. Cursing the wicked ones is a godly act, for Allah Himself curses them and declares that the angels and men should also do it, which means that the men, the true believers of Allah, should do the same. About those who offend Allah and the Prophet the Qur'an declares: "Surely (as for) those who speak evil things of Allah and His Apostle, Allah has cursed them in this world and the hereafter, and He has prepared for them a chastisement bringing disgrace." (33:57)

Real *Tabarra* does not mean only verbal declaration of the disliking or hatred against the wicked and invoking Allah 's curse on them but it also demands a person to keep aloof from the evil which entitled the wicked one to the hatred of men and curse of Allah. The Qur'an says: "Surely those who disbelieve and die while they are disbelievers, will be subjected to condemnation of Allah, the angels, and all people." (2:161)

EXERCISES

1. Name the 10 branches of faith in Islam.
2.

   a. Why do girls and boys begin obligatory fasts at different ages?

   b. Try to think of what can be gained by fasting. How might it help you to be compassionate? How might it help you to get rid of a bad habit?

   c. Give an example of someone who should not fast.

3.

   a. When Malcolm X performed Hajj, he realized that Muslims were of every race, color, cultural and linguistic background and that racist ideas and lifestyles were wrong. What do you think he saw and experienced that changed his thinking?

   b. If possible, interview someone who performed Hajj or read about someone's Hajj experience and find out how it changed the person.

4.

   a. If everyone in the world properly obeyed the commandments of charity, how would society be different? How might life be different for a widowed mother, for example?

b. Imagine that you decide to calculate khums and in the first year your assets are $1000, in the second they are $900 and in the third year they are $1000 again. In which year would you pay khums, and how much would you pay?

5. Why is Jihad against one's self called the Greatest Jihad? Are other forms of jihad possible to be done properly if the Greatest Jihad is neglected?

6. Who can order jihad that involves fighting against oppressors?

7. What are the relationships between the acts of enjoining good and forbidding evil and the spirit of loving Allah, the Prophet and Ahlul-Bayt and hating their enemies? Is it possible to do one without the other(s)? Why or why not?

Chapter Three

SPECTRUM OF HUMAN EXISTENCE

The human essence from womb to tomb and thereafter, has been shown in Figure 1 to explain the various events that happen one after another. The Qur'an invites us to think about how this short-spanned physical world is going to shape the endless and eternal life. From this self-explanatory map, a person of rational thinking can easily arrive at the following conclusions:

1. Allah first created the soul and kept it in a specific place.
2. The soul was introduced in an organic body after the process of fertilization.
3. The body with a soul stayed in the mother's womb for around nine months from where it arrived in this physical world at the time of birth.
4. The life in the physical world is an infinitesimal portion of the actual life. Death is not the end of life but the beginning of the second phase of eternal life. Death separates the body from the soul.
5. After experiencing death, the departed soul of every man and woman continues to live in a place, which is conditional with his or her performance in the world. The intermediate place, which is a bridge between the first physical world and the second metaphysical world, is known as Barzakh.
6. The stay in Barzakh may be very long but definitely not permanent. The soul will remain at this place from the time of death until the end of the world, or the beginning

of the new world i.e., the day of Qiyamah, (the resurrection day).

7. The world will end at a definite time, which only Allah knows. After the execution of the Qiyamah, Allah will then resurrect the entire human race for the final judgment. This will be the most important day for every soul.

Thus, every man and woman who is born in this world will acquire a final and eternal life, which he or she will spend either in a place known as Jannat (heaven) or in Jahanam (hell).

PHASES OF LIFE

As Figure 1 shows, human beings have the following stages and phases of life:

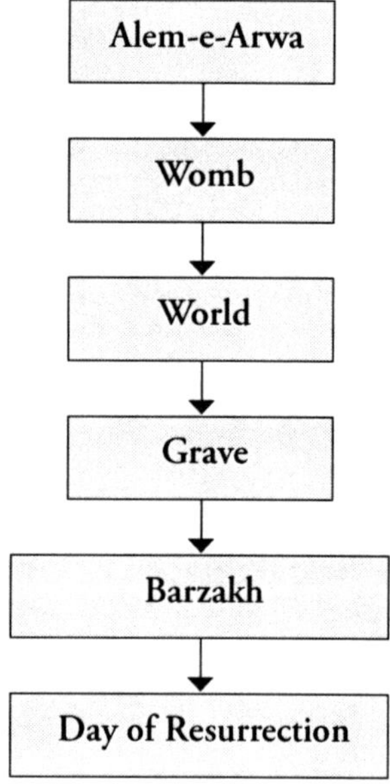

Figure I: Spectrum of Human Existence from Womb to Tomb

PHASES OF LIFE

1. Life before birth.
2. Life after birth.
3. Life after death.
4. Life after resurrection.

LIFE BEFORE BIRTH

Human beings have come in this world from the body of their mother as a newborn baby, but their appearance in this world as a new living species is not the first stage of their existence. Allah created human beings much before their birth. Before birth all human beings existed somewhere as an individual soul. This is what the Qur'an, and Hadith tell us about the origin of a human being's existence. The Qur'an says: "When your Lord asked all the offspring of Adam (before birth) am I not your Lord? All of them testified and bore witness to their testimony that on the Day of Judgment they would not say, 'We were not aware of this fact.'" (7:172) This verse of the Qur'an reminds us that this testimony was made between Allah and us before our birth, in which we acknowledged that none other than Him is our God. It also confirms that we had an existence in conscious life before birth.

What is the soul?

Every living creature has two important components. One is the organic body and the second is the soul. Some scientists do not believe in the existence of souls. As far as organic body is concerned, scientists have discovered a large number of secrets about it. They have studied much about the body and its composition with the help of powerful microscopes, but scientists still do not know everything about the body and, therefore, cannot answer many basic questions such as:

1. How exactly do the different organs of the body work?
2. Why a dead body cannot move, when the same body was doing incredible things just before the death? What exactly is death?
3. What leaves the body at death making it totally inert and motionless immediately after death?
4. Why don't the same atoms and molecules, which are present in the body, show life in other substances?

Scientists will never be able to fully understand all such questions. As far as the soul is concerned, we have no knowledge of it. The soul is totally invisible and beyond the reach of any powerful microscope. The Qur'an has enlightened us about the soul by giving this information: "And they ask you about the soul. Say: the soul is one of the commands of my Lord, and you are given but a little knowledge." (17:85)

This verse of the Qur'an educates us how to deal with the mysteries of the soul. From this verse, the following important points can be inferred:

1. There are many natural facts and phenomena, which scientists will never be able to comprehend and the soul is one of them.
2. The soul is a divine command.
3. The prophet did not speak much about the soul because the soul is unimaginable, and man could never conceive it. Thus, the whole picture of the soul is beyond human perception.
4. As little is known about nature of the soul, it cannot be said with certainty about such things as: (i) Where the soul lives in the body, and (ii) whether the soul lives in the brain or is spread everywhere in the body.

All scientists believe without any difference of opinion that each and every organ of the body strictly follows the instructions of the brain. In bygone eras, scientists thought the soul was in the heart, and instructions for the body came from there, but now they have learned it is the brain that does these things. The brain gives instructions to special organs to perform a job, and only then do the organs complete the job, but the soul is the master control center of the brain. This is also clear from one of the hadith of the Prophet in which he states: "Actions will be judged according to intentions." The intentions are always formed by the soul, and actions are simply its manifestation. The brain is only an instrument that brings intentions into actions. The other parts of the body are the means by which functions are carried out. The Qur'an says: "On that day we shall set a seal upon their mouths, and their hands shall speak to Us and their feet shall bear witness of what they earned." (36:65) This means that all our organs, which were used by the soul to seek pleasure, will testify against our soul.

LIFE AFTER BIRTH

The second phase of human beings' existence is perhaps the most crucial and difficult period. The span of life is relatively very short; 60 to 70 years on average, but it has a direct effect on the nature of our endless life. How does the present life shape the nature of eternal life? This is the most important question which all of us should strive to know. The Qur'an has repeatedly mentioned that the nature of our endless life depends upon how we live in this temporal world. For this, we all will be judged on two things: (i) Beliefs and perceptions, which are termed as *Eemaan;* and (ii) actions and deeds, which are termed as *Amaal.* So this life is like a test or competition of beliefs and deeds that has eternal consequences.

All human beings will be judged for these two things, and will go either to heaven or to hell accordingly. The first basic qualification required of a person to enter heaven is the perfect religion. The

Qur'an explicitly warns all of mankind that Islam will be the religion acceptable on the Day of Judgment. It says: "Surely the (true) religion with Allah is Islam." (3:19) The second important requirement is *Amaal*, or actions and deeds. Islam provides a full scheme of work called *Shariah*, or Islamic law, which identifies explicitly all good and bad actions including the obligatory and forbidden acts. All those Muslims who do not follow the rules of *Shariah* could be in trouble.

Successful life

As the second phase of our life, i.e., life in this physical world is the most important and difficult period of our entire life, it is therefore essential to know how to make it more successful and productive. There is a large amount of Islamic literature that includes more than 6,000 divine verses, more than 15,000 ahadith of the Prophet, more than 300 sermons and supplications of Imams, and a huge stock of books by ulemas, telling us the details about living a successful life, and how to obtain success. One hundred and twenty-four thousand prophets were sent for this purpose.

Based on this literature, here are some key points for living a successful life:

1. The first, and foremost, thing in the agenda of life is the true intention of totally submitting to Allah, which implies we should have this feeling in the core of our beings. We should please Allah by all possible means. We should do anything and everything to seek His pleasure and His nearness.

2. We should know that every pleasure and success in this world is temporary. Real success is success on the Day of Judgment. The Qur'an repeatedly warns everyone that the stay here is very short.

3. Acquire useful knowledge to strengthen *Eemaan*. The Qur'an

has stressed the importance of exploring the universe and studying nature.

4. One must know the laws of Islam in order to fulfill the obligatory duties, and to abstain from prohibited acts. The *Sunnah* of the Prophet, as interpreted by his Ahlul-Bayt, covers each and every aspect of an ideal life. Thus, it is essential to follow his *Sunnah* and the teachings of the Imams in every aspect of life.

5. Remember the saying of Imam Ali that Islam in a nutshell means fearing the Creator and loving the Creation.

LIFE AFTER DEATH

Allah has created life and death. "Blessed be He in Whose hands is all sovereignty. He has power over all things. He created life and death that He might put you to test and find out which of you acquitted himself the best. He is the Mighty, the Forgiving one." (16:31) and (68:1) In such a short verse the Qur'an has given a complete and perfect definition of life and death. It gives a full account of the origin and the prospect of life and death. Following are the highlights of the important features of life and death from this short verse of the Qur'an:

1. Life is not an accidental product of some spontaneous biochemical reactions; rather it is a great creation of the Almighty Allah.

2. Death is not the disorder of biochemical functions of organic systems of the body; rather it is another kind of creation of the Almighty Allah.

3. Both life and death have well-defined purposes for human beings.

4. Death is not the end of life but the beginning of another kind of life.

WHAT HAPPENS AFTER DEATH

Death is the termination of organic functions. It can be said that death is caused by the separation of soul and body. So, death is the end of the organic life but not the absolute end of life. This means that there is a kind of life after death, and that death is simply a major change in the present condition of life. The entire edifice of Islam is based on the fact that death is not the end, but a sharp turning point from where another kind of life begins.

After death, the dead body is buried and according to the Islamic *shariah* there are proper ways to bury a believer that we should observe. Upon death, the soul goes to Barzakh (purgatory), the resting place of souls. *Barzakh* is an Arabic word, which means "a barrier," or a thing that separates two things. The Qur'an uses this word to tell us that there in another world between this physical world and the eternal world, where we will live after death until the Day of Resurrection.

The Qur'an says: "And behind them is the *Barzakh*, until the Day of Judgment." (23:100).

To go to *Barzakh*, the first step is burial. This is a place where the soul of the dead person meets two angels who ask him certain fundamental questions.

The questions are:

1. Who is your *Ra'b* (creator)?
2. Who is your Prophet?
3. What is your Religion?
4. What is your Book?
5. Who is your Imam?

These questions apparently seem to be very easy and straight-forward, and even a small boy who has learned the answers can reply them easily. In fact, only the true and practicing Muslims will be able to answer these questions correctly, and the rest of the people will be stunned and perplexed. These questions and their answers are to show the dead person what his status will be in the *Barzakh*, and thereafter. The souls are classified into good and bad souls. *Waadi-e-Salam* is the place for the good souls and *Waadi-e-Barhoot* is the place for the bad souls, based upon a person deeds in life they may or may not be at peace.

FOURTH PHASE

The fourth phase of human existence is Resurrection. Resurrection is the second stage of life-after-death. This is the beginning of the life that has no end — it is the eternal life. This is the end, and also the beginning of which there is no end. On the day everybody is resurrected and made living again, the Day of Judgment will begin. The Day of Judgment is a fundamental belief of the Islamic faith. There is a basic rational behind resurrection. This is a phase when every person who has lived anywhere and any time, will be brought to the divine court for final judgment. Allah will be the judge and will decide the ultimate fate of every person. All Muslims are repeatedly reminded of this in Sura Fateha, which all Muslims recite daily at least ten times in prayer. He — being Allah — is the master of the Day of Judgment.

EXERCISES:

1. What does Islam say about your soul before you were born and after you die?
2. Write a short story or poem about a soul telling its tale of existence from before being born all the way to heaven or hell. Make sure all the steps in Figure 1 are included. Is the soul in your story going to be successful or unsuccessful in getting to heaven? How will that affect what happens along the way?

3. What do you think about the location of your soul? Is it at a specific place within your body, or your whole body, or the whole universe? What makes you think that way? Is there any way we can really know where the soul is? How do you think it is attached to your body or how it resides in it? The Qur'an says when you die the soul comes up and out through your throat, in *Sura Yaseen*. Think about what that might tell you about the soul.

4. Are you your soul, your body, or both? Explain your thinking.

5. What are the questions you will be asked in the grave? What are the answers? What can you do to prepare for the questions so that you can answer them most easily?

6. What is the difference between knowing the answers to those questions asked in *barzakh* and really living the answers? What would it look like if you knew the answers but did not live by them? What would it look like if you knew AND lived the answers?

7. Does submitting to Allah in Islam mean that you no longer have free will, that you no longer have choices that you no longer think for yourself? How would you answer this question convincingly in a debate with someone about it?

8. What are the two things we will be judged for on Judgment Day?

9. If a soul is not made of matter, could a scientist of today study it in any way? How do we know anything that we know about the soul? Did we learn it from science? What kind of things can we learn from science and what kind of things do we have to learn in other ways?

10. If no one told you that you had a soul, would you still know? Can you feel it somehow? Enter a darkened, quiet room and either lie on your back or sit cross-legged against a wall. Listen to and feel your breathing and be still and relaxed for a minimum of five minutes. Do you sense anything

that you think is soul? Is it the same thing as your mind and thoughts or more or less?

11. Read the story of Prophet Ibrahim in the Qur'an, particularly the part in which he finds out or shows that the Sun and other things are not God, but he finds that God is Allah. Now imagine a small group of people who are isolated from the rest of the world on a tiny island that no one knows about. So, they don't have the Qur'an and they don't know the name Muhammad. Might they still be Muslims, people who believe in the One God and submit to Him? Does your answer imply that Allah judges people according to their circumstances? Explain. If you said yes, could someone deceive themselves into using that as an excuse for wrong behavior? Could they be sure Allah will accept that excuse?

12. If you have a friend or family member who has died, are they already in heaven or hell? Where are their souls right now?

Chapter Four

HISTORY OF THE PROPHET HOOD

Before the human world was created by Allah, He created another type of creation. They were called Jins who were made up of fire. The Jins remained noble for quite sometime obeying Allah. Later, they turned away from Allah's commands, and became disobedient and mischievous. They carried evil deeds on the earth, killing each other and spoiling the earth. They turned tyrant and life became impossible. Allah sent warnings to them which did not deter them from their evil deeds. With Allah's order all of them were destroyed except one whose name was Iblees. Iblees remained good and continued to worship Allah. He was taken to heaven, where he stayed as an obedient servant of Allah.

When Allah created Prophet Adam, He ordered all the angels to bow down before him. All angles did, except the jinn, Iblees. Allah asked Iblees the reason for not bowing before Prophet Adam. In reply, Iblees proudly said that he was created by fire and Adam was created by clay, and therefore, he thought himself to be superior to Adam.

Allah explained to Iblees that this prostration to Adam was His order and since he disobeyed Allah, he would be thrown out of heaven. Instead of apologizing, Iblees asked Allah to give him long life up to the day of Resurrection. Allah granted him a long life up to a certain time. From then onward Ibless was called Shaitan-ur-Rajeem. He challenged Allah that he would desist human beings from following the righteous path and encourage them to disobey Him except for true believers. Allah ordered that all those who would turn away from the right path by the Shaitan would be sent to hell.

THE PROPHETS

With the first Prophet Adam Allah continued to send prophets to this world and as many as 124,000 were sent to this world to guide the humanity. The last prophet is Prophet Muhammad.

The first and the foremost point in Islamic beliefs, is the fact that all the prophets and their vicegerent were infallible. They restrained themselves from doing any wrong or any minor or major sin by Allah's mercy and it did make sense. Allah has ordered us to follow these prophets and their vicegerents unconditionally. If they do any sin it would be useless to follow them.

The second important point in Islamic belief is that all these prophets and their vicegerents were appointed by Allah.

PROPHET ADAM

The first prophet, Adam was made of clay by Allah Himself. Allah later entered soul in him and he became alive. When his soul came to his nose he sneezed and said *Allhum-do-Lillah*. Allah responded by saying *Akramakumallah*. From that time it became a tradition to say these words on sneezing. Allah had already informed the angels of His creation and had asked them to bow down to him. As stated earlier all of them did, except for Iblees the Jinn, who was consequently thrown out of heaven. Prophet Adam was kept in heaven. Later on, Hawa was created and Adam and Hawa were married. They were allowed to live in heaven and eat whatever they wished, but were prohibited from going near a particular tree. One day Shaitan brought a fruit from the same tree and they ate it. It was a misunderstanding as Adam thought that only going near the tree was prohibited, and eating the fruit was not. Anyhow, as soon as Adam ate the fruit, both Adam and Hawa realized the error of their judgment and repented it. Adam was sent to this world along with Hawa. He continued to repent in this world. God gave

Adam the knowledge of some names, and with the help of these names he was pardoned.

Adam was blessed with two sons: Habeel (Able) and Kabeel (Cane). The former was a noble person, but latter was not. One day, both of them made some sacrifices in the name of Allah. Habeel's sacrifice was accepted but Kabeel's was rejected. This enraged Kabeel, who then killed Habeel in revenge. Kabeel was worried as to what to do with Habeel's dead body. At that time, Allah sent two crows and they taught Kabeel how to bury Habeel.

Prophet Adam lived more than 900 years, and had thousands of children. At the time of his death, he declared Sheth (Seth) as his successor and the caliph of the land at Allah's command. Sheth lived 912 years, and nominated one of his sons as the representative, vicegerent by the order of Allah at the time of his death. This process continued till Prophet Idrees became caliph of Allah on earth.

PROPHET IDREES (ENOCH)

Prophet Idrees continued the teachings of Allah on earth. When people did not listen to him, Allah stopped rain, which caused a famine for seven years. People repented, and it rained again. Idrees lived some 365 years.

Prophet Idrees was the one who taught the world the arts of writing with a pen, sewing and stitching, astronomy, etc. One of his sons was appointed his deputy by the order of Allah. This continued till Prophet Noah was assigned the caliphate of the world.

PROPHET NOAH

Prohet Noah was a descendent of Prophet Idrees. His father was Lamak also known as Lamik. He preached the oneness of Allah to his *Ummah* for a long time. His *Ummah* laughed at him, tortured him, almost killing him, for their hearts were hardened. In spite of all this, Noah continued to preach patiently. When he was fed up with his Ummah and was sure that his Ummah would not listen to him, he prayed to Allah for their punishment. Noah was advised by Allah to make a large arch. Noah took a long time in making it. After its completion, he was advised to take on board his family and other believers along with one pair of each species of animals. As soon as Noah boarded the arch, water started pouring from the sky and oozing out of the ground. Initially, it started from Kufa (Iraq). The water rose higher and higher until it engulfed all the earth, even the mountains. One of Noah's sons who did not board the arch was drowned along with the other non-believers. The flood destroyed everyone except those on board. The flood continued for six months. It eventually receded, and the arch came to rest at the mountain called Ararat. The occupants came out of the arch and thanked Allah for their miraculous survival. Prophet Noa lived for more than 950 years. He had three sons and he divided the earth into three regions. His eldest son Yaffis (Japheth) was given north towards Europe and settled there. This is the Japheth race. His middle son Shem remained with his father in the area of the Middle East. The Middle East area is called the Semitic race. His younger son Ham was given the African area and that area is called the Hemitic race.

PROPHET HUD

Prophet Hud belonged to the generation of Ham and was appointed for the people of Aad. These people were rich, strong, tall, and sturdy. They inhabited the region of Hazarmot and Oman. Although Allah had given them very good life, they did not believe in Allah, rather worshipped idols. They never listened to their prophet, and hence, their existence was threatened by a draught for three years. They did not heed the sign of Allah's wrath, so a horrendous storm came. Total darkness took over and debris fell all over. The entire community was destroyed except the Prophet and a few of his followers.

PROPHET SALEH

Prophet Saleh belonged to the generation of Nuh, and was appointed for the people of Thamud. These people inhabited the area between Hejaz and Palestine. They were also very strong people, carved their homes in mountains. They lived long lives and worshipped idols, made of stones.

The people of Thamud refused to listen to Prophet Saleh, although he showed them some miracles to prove his truthfulness. On their persistent demand, Prophet Saleh asked them to gather near a mountain where on his prayer, a camel with a baby came out of the mountain. Most of the people still did not believe the Prophet. The camel and the baby stayed in the area. There was a small lake from which the inhabitants used to get water. It was agreed that the people and the camel would drink the water of the lake on alternate days. The day the camel drank water, it gave milk for the entire town. Some tyrants did not like this idea, and they threatened to kill the camel. Prophet Saleh warned them of the curse of Allah if they did so. They did not listen, and one day the camel was killed by the people. Allah instructed Saleh to leave the territory. No sooner did he leave the territory with his followers a thunderous earthquake shook the land and the entire population was perished.

PROPHET ABRAHAM

Prophet Abraham's father was Tarikh and not Aazir, as is held in popular belief. Aazir was his uncle and was an idol maker and idol worshiper. In Quran, Aazir is written as his guardian father (Ab), and not as 'Walid' (the genitor father), because in most of Arab cultures, sometimes the guardian is called the father. Nimrod was the king in the city where Abraham lived. Nimrod was a powerful tyrant and made people bow to him as god. One night he dreamt that a star was born and it eclipsed the moon and the sun. He asked the sages about the interpretation. They said that someone will be born to wreck your kingdom. Nimrod ordered a ban on all marriages and separated men from women, and killed all new born babies. In his arrogance, he forgot the power of Allah. Abraham's mother got pregnant, and went out of the city to give birth to Abraham in a cave. Abraham remained in the cave until he became adolescent and then came to his town.

One night Abraham selected the brightest of the stars taking it as his God. In the morning when it faded he declared that his God could not be the one who faded away with time. He used the same technique and the same logic with the Sun and the moon to deny these being God. He then invited all the people who worshipped celestial bodies like stars, sun, and moon along with the idols to worship the Almighty who created the world. Some laughed at him, and some scorned him.

Abraham was once invited by the people to an annual festival for their God. Abraham excused himself. When everybody had left, Abraham went into the temple where the idols were kept, broke all the idols, hung the axe around the neck of the biggest idol and came home. The next day, the idolaters were enraged with what had happened to their idols. They immediately came to the conclusion that Abraham must have done it. Abraham was called and enquired. He replied why the people wouldn't ask their biggest idol about it. The people replied embarrassingly that they could not ask him since he did not speak. Abraham then replied that an idol that could not speak or save itself from destruction could hardly be anyone's God. The people got mad and complained to Nimrod.

Abraham was called in Nimrod's court to answer the charges. When Abraham reached the court, he did not bow down before Nimrod. This was an insult to Nimrod, but Abraham said that he would bow down to only the supreme authority and the creator and sustainer of this world. Nimrod asked Abraham to explain who this God was. Abraham said that his God was the one who would give and take away life at will. Nimrod said that he did it too everyday. Abraham then said that his God was the one who brought forth the Sun in the east and made it set in the west everyday. Abraham challenged Nimrod to do it the other way if he were God. Nimrod was dumbfounded and angry. He ordered his guards to throw Abraham in a big fire.

Abraham was thrown in a big fire, whose heat could be felt from miles away. Gabriel came to Abraham to ask him if he wished his help. Abraham replied that he was waiting for the help of the Almighty. The help did come in that Allah ordered the fire to get cold. It was a miracle. Some people started believing in one God, including his uncle's daughter Sara who later married Abraham. Nimrod ordered Abraham, his wife and his relatives to leave the town of Ur. As a result, Abraham migrated to Kinaan and then to Egypt. The king of Egypt was attracted to Sara, and extended his hand to touch her. He got paralyzed. The king repented, and got better by the prayer of Abraham. The king then gave her daughter Hajirah to serve Sara. Since Sara did not have a child, and she was getting old, she pursued Abraham to marry Hajirah. Abraham married Hajirah, and was blessed with Ismail. A few years later, Ishaq was born to Sara. Abraham settled down in the town of Kinaan. After the birth of Ismail, he took him and Hajirah to a deserted place of Mecca and left them there by the order of Allah.

Prophet Abraham dreamt for three nights that he was sacrificing his son Ismail to please Allah. He described his dream to his son Ismail, who happily agreed to be sacrificed. He took Ismail to the place of Mina, laid down Ismail and moved his knife to slaughter his son. At that time, by the order of Allah, Gabriel replaced Ismail by a lamb, which was slaughtered in his place. Prophet Abraham was a bit upset, but Allah consoled him by telling him that his sacrifice was accepted. This act of

Abraham is celebrated every year by all the Muslims as Eid-ul-Azha.

Prophet Abraham and Prophet Ismail built the Ka'bah by the order of Allah at the present site. A stone was sent from heaven and was placed at one corner, called the Black Stone. At the advice of Allah, he called the people for Hajj, which continues till today. Prophet Abraham continued to live in Kenaan. He is the patriarch of the three religions, Judaism, Christianity, and Islam. He is respected by all of them.

Prophet Abraham was a man of great stature. He never ate at night alone without a guest. He was kind, wise, god-fearing, and a friendly person. Many prophets were of his progeny. His son Ismail was a great prophet himself. Prophet Muhammad came from his generation. His other son Ishaq was the prophet of Banu-Israel.

PROPHET LUT

Psorphet Lut was the nephew of Prophet Abraham and left Ur with him. Allah made Lut a Prophet and sent him to the north region of the valley of river Jordan. Two famous cities in the region were Sodom and Gomorrah. The inhabitants of these cities were morally corrupt and practiced homosexuality. They boldly defied the teaching of Prophet Lut, they ridiculed and tortured him.

When the people did not listen, Allah sent a curse on them. Prophet Lut was ordered to leave the city with his family and not to look back. As soon as they left the city, a terrible earthquake struck the town. The two cities were totally destroyed. The wife of the Prophet turned back to look against the warning of the Prophet and was turned into stone.

PROPHET ISMAIL

After the birth of Ismail, Prophet Abraham was ordered to bring Ismail and his mother to Hijaz and get them settled there.

Hijaz was a desolate and uninhabitable place. They had little food and water with them. In desperate search of water, Hajra ran seven times between the two hills of Safa and Marva. Ismail was lying on the ground rubbing his feet. Hajra could not find water, but suddenly she noticed that water was gushing out from the point where Ismail was rubbing his feet. Her happiness knew no bounds. She noticed that the water kept rushing out, and would not stop. She cried Zam Zam (stop stop). The water eventually stopped, but a big well formed there. It has become an unlimited source of water and is used as holy water for the pilgrims for thousands of years. The run between Safa and Marva by Hajirah has become an essential part of Hajj. Later, birds crowded over the well, and the wandering tribe Banu Jarham came by and settled there with their permission. Prophet Ibrahim was ordered to make a house of Allah for worship. Both Prophet Abraham and Prophet Ismail completed the project of building Ka'bah. Prophet Abraham called for Hajj. He prayed to Allah to make that place habitable.

Hajirah died when Ismail was only 15 and was buried near the Ka'bah. Ismail married a girl from Banu Jarham, and had a big progeny. He died at the age of 137. He was a distinguished prophet as Prophet Muhammad is from his progeny. He established Mecca, constructed Ka'abha, started Hajj, and Zam Zam is his miracle.

PROPHET ISHAQ/YAQOOB

Prophet Ishaq was the son of Prophet Abraham from Sara, and was nine years younger than Prophet Ismail. He lived mostly in the area of Syria. Prophet Ishaq named his son Yaqoob. Banu Israel was the name of the children of Prophet Yaqoob and he was called Israel, meaning the slave of God. Prophet Ishaq lived for 180 years. After his death, Yaqoob became the prophet. He had 12 sons. The most pious of them was Yousaf. Out of jealousy, his brothers threw him in a well, but he was saved. This happened when Yousaf was 18 and Prophet Yaqoob was 90 years old. For 21 years, Yousaf and Yaqoob remained separated. After that, Yaqoob went to Egypt to meet Prophet Yousaf. He died at the age of 147 years.

PROPHET YOUSAF

He was the youngest of Prophet Yaqoob's sons. His mother's name was Raseel. He had a brother Benyan (Benjamin) and a sister. He was exceptionally handsome and pious. Making long story short, his brothers got jealous of him, and threw him in a well. He was taken from the well by a passing caravan. The people in the caravan sold him to a minister in the Pharaoh government. The wife of the minister wrongly accused him for a grave crime, and he was sentenced to jail. Eventually his innocence was proved, and he was freed. In the end, he became the king of Egypt. He called his parents, and in spite of the ill behavior shown by his brothers, he showered great mercy on them. He lived for 110 years and was buried in Egypt. Later, Prophet Moses took his coffin and buried him in Kenaan next to his ancestors.

PROPHET AYUB

Prophet Ayub was from the progeny of Prophet Ishaq and lived in Damascus. His wife Rahma was a very rich woman. Allah gave him great wealth, prosperity and a large family as well. He was a man of great patience and perseverance. He was very steadfast in his faith.

Allah tested Ayub by taking everything he had. First, he lost his livestock, which was destroyed by lightening. Then all his crops were destroyed, and all his children died because of the collapse of the roof of the house. He himself got sick. During all this time, he remained thankful to Allah and eventually Allah was pleased with him. All his belongings were gradually returned to him.

PROPHET ZULKIFL

Prophet Zulkifl was named Bashar and his title was Zulkifl. He was the son of Prophet Ayub. He lived and preached in Syria, and died at the age of 75.

PROPHET SHOAIB

Prophet Shoaib was a descendent of Prophet Ibrahim's third wife. He was appointed to the people of Midyan and Aykah, who lived east of Mount Sinai. These people cheated in weight and measurement. Prophet Shoaib tried to correct them and warned them against the crime, but they did not listen. They were destroyed by a violent earthquake and a roaring thunder by Allah, except for a few faithful. Prophet Shoaib married his daughter Safora to Prophet Moses.

PROPHET MOSES

The birth of Prophet Moses resembled very closely to the birth of Prophet Abraham. The children of Israel were prospering in Egypt. Pharaoh was afraid of their authority. Around that time, the fore-tellers of the court informed the King of the birth of a child from Banu-Israel who would destroy his kingdom. He ordered all male babies to be killed and separated all males from females. In his rush of judgment, he forgot the power of Allah. Not only was Moses born, but also nourished in his own palace. As Moses was growing, he got into trouble for helping one of the Banu Isreal, so he left Egypt for Midyan, where he met Prophet Shoaib. He married his daughter and stayed there for 10 years.

On his way back to Egypt, he camped near Mount Sinai. He went looking for fire and reached Mount Sinai. He noted a brilliant light emerging from the mountain. He heard sacred voice and the Almighty bestowed upon him prophet hood. He was given two miracles. Allah on his request assigned his brother as his vicegerent. He was ordered to go back to the Pharaoh and teach him a lesson. Prophet Moses asked the Pharaoh to let Banu Israel go out of Egypt. Many miracles and punishments came for the Egyptians and eventually the King let them go. When Moses along with Banu Israel reached near the Red Sea, the Pharaoh changed his mind and rushed to stop them. Prophet Moses at that time hit his stick on the water of the sea, and a path appeared due to the partition of the sea. Prophet Moses and his followers crossed the river with safety, but when Pharoah and his army tried to cross the river, the two sides of the river came together, drowning all of them. Moses returned back to Mount Sinai, and was given his famous 10 commandments and the book of Torah.

He went away from Banu Israel for 40 days. On the grounds that Banu Israel could not wait for him any longer, they started worshipping a statue of a cow made from gold by someone known as Samri. Although Haroon was amongst them, they did not listen to him. Banu Israel were strong headed and defiant people. On the face of difficulty, they would obey Allah's orders, but would turn away from Him in time of calm and prosperity. They were promised a fertile land. As a punishment, they were left roaming in the deserts for 40 years. Prophet Moses died at the age of 120. His brother Haroon had already died. Yusha bin Non became his vicegerent who took Banu Israel to the promised land.

PROPHET HAROON

Prophet Haroon was the elder brother of Prophet Moses, both of whom were sons of Imran. He carried the duties of Prophet Moses in his absence. Yusha bin Non (Joshua) took the place of Moses after Haroon's death. After Joshua, Hizqeel was designated as the leader of Banu Israel. Sixty thousand people died of plague during that time.

PROPHET ILYAS

By the time Prophet Ilyas was made Prophet, Banu Israel had reverted to material world and idol worship. A tyrant king was brought upon them, who would kill innocent people to get their land. They tortured Ilyas and killed many Prophets who tried to bring them to the right path. As a punishment, they had to suffer a drought for several years. Prophet Ilyas prayed to Allah for his protection, designated Ilyasa to take his place and disappeared. According to the book, he is still alive. Prophet Ilyasa became the prophet after Prophet Ilyas. He showed many miracles like walking on water, and curing blindness. He preached for 8 years, but Banu Israel paid no attention to his gospel. In the end, an outsider attacked and conquered Banu Israel.

PROPHET SHAMVEEL (SAMUEL)

Prophet Shamveel has not been mentioned explicitly in the Qur'an. He was a prophet of Banu Israel after Ilyasa. Banu Israel wanted a kingdom of their own. Prophet Shamveel designated Taloot (Saul) their king by the order of Allah.

PROPHET DAUD

Prophet Daud was the descendent of Judha (one of the sons of Prophet Yaqoob). King Taloot sent an army against the infidel king Jaloot (Goliath). Prophet Daud killed Jaloot and then was given the kingdom.

The divine book of Psalm was given to him. He used to read the Psalm in such a melodious voice that even animals used to gather around him. Allah had given him the miracle where iron would melt in his hands. He started building Baitul Muqaddas. He died at the age of 70.

PROPHET SULEMAN

Prophet Suleman was the Son of prophet Daud. Prophet Suleman asked Allah for a great kingdom, and was given the greatest kingdom. He used to rule on everything, even animals, fish, birds, and air. He completed the construction of Baitul Muqaddas, and died at the age of 59.

PROPHET EZRA

He was from the generation of Haroon. Once he was passing by a town totally devastated with thousands of dead bodies lying all around. He thought how Allah would revive them. He was suddenly dead and remained there for 100 years. Allah revived him and his donkey which had turned to ashes by that time, but on revival, even his food was fresh. Allah asked him if he knew how long he had slept. He replied that a day or less. Allah then told him that he had been asleep for 100 years. By that time, the cities had been revived and were bustling. Jews called him the son of Allah.

PROPHET DANYAL (DANIAL)

Prophet Danyal was a descendent of Prophet Yaqoob, and was a genius. There are many beautiful stories about him in the books.

PROPHET YUNUS

Prophet Yunus was the prophet for part of Iraq and Ninevah. His people were headstrong and obstinate and won't listen to him. He got totally disgusted and prayed to Allah for His curse, but without waiting, he took a boat and went out of town. On crossing the river, a storm engulfed the boat. Prophet Yunus was swallowed by a fish, which then placed him on the bank of a river. He was sick while his parts of his skin peeled off. Allah grew a bush next to him. His wounds gradually healed. The people of the town realized the mistake and came back to follow him.

Prophet Yunus died at the age of 47, and is buried next to the river, which is near Kufa.

PROPHET ZAKARIA (ZACHARIA)

Prophet Zakaria is known for the ritual at Baitul Muqaddas. Virgin Marium was the niece of his wife, and he used to take care of her. He got old but did not have a child. He prayed to Allah and was given a child named Yahya who became a Prophet in his childhood. Prophet Zakaria was martyred while hidden in the trunk of a tree at the age of 100.

Prophet Yahya was the cousin of Prophet Jesus. Prophet Jesus was six months elder to him. He became prophet at the age of 6. He was very compassionate, kind hearted, and called unto people to obey Allah. He lived strictly by the Torah. The Roman ruler disapproved of his religious activities and got him killed by King Harrod.

PROPHET ISA (JESUS)

Prophet Isa was the last prophet of Banu Israel. They defied his teachings and doubted his legitimacy. In collaboration with the Roman and the Palestinian governments, Banu Israel framed him as anti church and anti religion. He was to be crucified, but according to the Quran, another person who closely resembled him was crucified instead. Prophet Isa was raised to Heaven. This person who was killed was instrumental in Isa's implication. Prophet Isa's preaching was later adopted by the Romans and lead to the foundation of Christianity.

Prophet Isa showed great miracles. He began talking at the age of three months to prove the innocence of his mother, Mary (Marium). He was 30 years old when he began receiving divine revelations and started preaching to Banu Israel. He made birds from clay and made them fly. He healed the lepers, gave vision to the blind, brought thousands of people back to life, and fed thousands of people. He declared the coming of Prophet Muhammad. He always reminded people that he was a creation of Allah and not Allah Himself. According to the Quran, he will return to earth after the 12th Imam comes back.

EXERCISES

1. Choose one of the prophets mentioned in the Qur'an. Find all the verses about that prophet in the Qur'an and find all the verses about that prophet from another religious text such as the Bible. If you cannot find information on that prophet in a second source, choose a different prophet. Make a chart to compare the information about the prophet in both sources — what do both sources agree on? What information is in Qur'an but not the Bible and vice versa?

2. *Iblees* was once a much-honored worshipper of Allah. Then pride made him one of the lowest of creation. This is a warning to us that just because we are good one day, we are not safe from the danger of becoming bad the next day. Even the highest person can become low. But also, the lowest person can be the highest — think of *Surah Yusuf* and the story of Prophet Joseph as a possible example. He rose from being a captive to being one of the highest people in the land and became a spiritual leader.

   a. What warning signs do you see in pride or another flaw in character which lower your spiritual rank?

   b. What can you do to turn yourself around if you've made mistakes and want to raise yourself back up?

Chapter Five

THE MESSENGER OF ISLAM

To learn about Islam one has to learn about Prophet Muhammad. He is Islam. He personifies Islamic teachings. His life is a total example for all Muslims. No other person in the history of mankind has left any deeper mark than him.

The Qur'an says: "Say (Muhammad): if you love Allah, then follow me. Allah will love you, and forgive you your faults and Allah is Forgiving and Merciful." (3:31)

He was sent to show the world the signs of the Creator, His greatness, and His mercy. He was sent to perfect human life on earth, and he did his job magnificently. His greatness lies in the fact that he was not only the greatest Prophet, and greatest man, but he also lived as an ordinary person. He was apparently a man like any one of us, but in fact a personified divine message of truth, sanity, and morality. He showed the world how one person, if truthful and devoted to Allah, could change the world.

BIRTH AND CHILDHOOD OF THE PROPHET

Prophet Muhammad was born in a noble tribe called Quraish in Mecca, Arabia in 573 A.D. His great grandfather was Hashim, who was a great tribal leader of his time, and gave his tribe the title of Hashimite. His grandfather Abdul-Muttalib was an important Arab leader. During Abdul-Muttalib's time, Abraha tried to destroy the Ka'abah, but was destroyed himself along with his army by birds as narrated in the Qur'an in Surah 105. The Prophet's father,

Abdullah bin Muttalib, died a few months before his birth. His mother, Amina bint Wahab, also passed away when he was only six years old. A few months after his birth, he was given to the care of Halima Saadiyah, a wet nurse from outside the city of Mecca. After the death of his mother, his grandfather, Abdul-Mutlib, took care of him for two years. After his grandfather's death, his uncle Abu Talib took care of him. Abu Talib himself was a leader of the Quraish, and Arabs, and a businessman. He loved, encouraged, and protected the Prophet from age 8 to 53 till his (Abu Talib's) death at the age of 83.

BUHERA – THE MONK

The Prophet was growing in the affectionate care of his loving uncle Abu Talib after his mother passed away. Abu Talib used to go with his merchandise once a year to Yemen, and once to Syria. This time, when the caravan was going to Syria, the Prophet, who was then 12, accompanied his uncle. When the caravan reached Busra, a town in Syria, the local priest Buhera invited them to dinner. This was unusual as Abu-Talib and his caravan had always passed here but had never been invited to dinner. All of them went to dinner except for the Prophet who was left behind. Buhera insisted that the Prophet be called. When the Prophet arrived, Buhera asked him a few questions to which he replied. He then looked in his book for other signs. And now Buhera was convinced that Muhammad was the last Prophet as written in the Bible. He advised Abu Talib to take special care of Muhammad from his enemies. Abu Talib sincerely heeded his advice all his life.

BATTLE OF HUJAR, AND HILF-UL-FUDUL

The prophet was 14 or 15 years old when he saw some of the more negative aspects of the tribal difficulties of Arabs at the time.

Two Arab tribes, the Bani-Kinaan and the Hawazin, who had been fighting intermittently, fought a battle that lasted for several years. The Prophet was greatly grieved by the death and destruction of an unnecessary war. He stirred the people to take steps to avoid unfortunate events like this in future. At the insistence of his uncle Zubair, a meeting was called. A society called Hilf-Ul-Fudul (covenant of higher morals) was formed to help alleviate the sufferings of the oppressed and needy. The Prophet was among the serious advocates of this society. He took the oath along with others for self-sacrifice, and to eradicate evil from society. The study of the life of the Prophet is a story of sacrifice and eradication of the evils of life, even from his youth. This example also shows how even at a very young age the Prophet, through his behavior and words, was gaining notice as a trustworthy, intelligent person.

YOUTH

Like many prophets in the past including Prophet Moses, and Prophet David, Prophet Muhammad used to tend sheep when he was young. During this time, he had plenty of time to think and contemplate and he often walked the Arabian Desert. Walking the Arabian Desert provided him time and place to think about the Creator and His creation. He also used to work in the business caravan of his uncle, where he demonstrated excellent commercial acumen without being deceitful, greedy or unjust in his dealings. In whatever field he entered he excelled. His quick grasp of facts coupled with his straightforward personality made him extraordinary. His faithfulness and trustworthiness made Meccans honor him by the titles of *Al-Ameen* (the trustworthy) and *Al-Sadiq* (the truthful).

Physical Features

The Prophet was a man of beauty inside and out. A handsome

man of medium built, he was neither short nor tall. He had black hair, a broad forehead, heavy eyebrows, black eyes and long lashes. He had a thin nose, pearl-like white teeth, a thick black beard, long neck, a broad chest, and broad shoulders. His skin was rather fair in complexion. He walked gracefully with firm steps. His appearance made an impression of a dignified hard-working man. In essence he created an aura of authority and nobility around him. But it was not physical features that made him have such an aura — it was his inner character showing through.

Marriage

The Prophet's presence in Mecca was like a fresh breeze. His fame of goodness eventually reached Khadeeja, a wealthy and noble lady of Mecca. She sent for Abu Talib, and asked him to ask the Prophet to take a caravan on her behalf for business to Syria and other places. The Prophet accepted the offer, and set out for Syria with Khadeeja's goods. Another employee of Khadeeja, named Maysarah accompanied him. Because of his skill, honesty, and intelligence; he made a great profit for Khadeeja, much more than what she used to make in the past.

During the journey, his companion Maysarah noted very strange things. He noted that during scorching sunlight of Arabia shade hung over Muhammad's head. He noted that dry shrubs turned green by his presence. On the caravan's return, Khadeeja not only got double profit, but also all these stories from her trusted employee. She was impressed.

Khadeeja herself was a determined, intelligent and noble lady. She sent Abu Talib her proposal to marry the Prophet. The Prophet gladly accepted the proposal and the marriage was conducted in a simple way. Abu Talib read the Khutba of Nikah. At the time of the marriage, the Prophet was 25 and Khadeeja was 28. This was the first marriage for both of them. Obviously, it was a very successful marriage for both of them. They had two sons, Qasim and Abdullah, also known as Tahir and Tyab. Unfortunately both died at infancy. They had one daughter, Fatima, who survived, and the progeny of the Prophet was continued from his daughter.

Khadeeja also took care of three daughters from her sister Haalah. The names of her sisters' three daughters were: Zainab, Ruqaiyyiah, and Umm-e-Kulthum. These nieces of Khadeeja used to live with her before marriage and continued to live with her after marriage. Two of these are the very girls whom Caliph Usman married one after another.

Rebuilding of Ka'abah

The Ka'abah, at one time, was badly damaged either by flood or fire and the tribe of Quraish undertook the task of its repair. The Prophet was 35 years old at that time. The rebuilding progressed amicably until the time came to put the *Hajar-e-Aswad,* the black stone, in its place in the wall of the Ka'abah. Meccans regarded the black stone as very sacred even at that time. It is still a sacred stone for Muslims. During Haj and Umra, the *Tawaf* of Ka'abah starts and ends here. Placing the stone in its place was a great honor. Every tribe wanted their leader to do it. There was an almost war-like mood when suddenly someone suggested an alternative. They decided to leave it until the next morning, and then who ever first entered the Ka'abah would decide the matter. The next morning was a pleasant one. It got more pleasant when the first man who entered the mosque was nobody else but the Prophet. The crowd that had gathered inside the Ka'abah shouted with joy. This was Al-Ameen, the trustworthy, and Al-Sadiq, the truthful, so he should be able to come with a good solution. When he came near the Ka'abah, he was asked to decide about the dispute. The Prophet asked for a cloak, which was brought to him. He spread the cloak on the floor and put the stone in the center. He then asked all the leaders of various tribes to pick up the cloak. When it was brought near the wall, he picked up the stone, and placed it in its designated place. Thus a big dispute was solved peacefully because all the leaders got credit to carry the stone. This event showed his decisive and commanding personality.

In Search of Truth

The Prophet was a thinker. From an early age he developed a habit of meditating in solitude. For hours he would sit alone pondering the creation of this world. He detested the miseries of life, war, and disenchantment and wanted to find a remedy for it all. He was a peace-loving man. He found solace at a nearby mountaintop called Mount Hira, also called Mount Noor. This was his regular retreat later during the month of Ramadhan, and sometimes he would stay there for the entire month.

SOCIAL CONDITIONS

Before the advent of the Islam, the Arab world was beset with darkness and covered with a thick cloud of barbarism. There was no concept of government or law. Might was right. Life was regulated by customs and practices, right or wrong, as transmitted from generation to generation. Tribal leaders and astrologers controlled most of the activities. The tribal leaders were the sole rulers and there were hundreds of them. Conflicts and wars were common while tribal peace scarce.

There was not any trade, business, or commercial activities in and around Mecca. Wealth was confined to a few people. The highhanded people loaned to the poor at an interest rate that could never be paid off. This practice is known as usury and still practiced today, in the form of credit cards.

The women had no rights and it was not uncommon for female infants to be buried alive out of a false belief that they were a burden and bad omen. The religion of most people was some form of idol-worshiping. Every tribe had its own idol, and all of them were placed in the Ka'abah. The biggest of these idols were Al-Lat, Al-Uzza, and

Al-Habl. The ignorant people looked at these idols for help. After illiterate people (for their own benefit) carved all these stones, these idols helped none except their creators by earning them a few dollars in sales of the stone idols.

The Prophet was fed up with these absurdities. His heart ached at the injustice, falsehood, and exploitation. He wished to help everyone. The remaining qualities in Meccans were their love of freedom, their adeptness in the use of arms, eagerness to attain excellence, and the respect shown to guests. They were very eloquent in composing poetry, and they loved to fight.

FIRST DIVINE REVELATION

The Prophet tolerated and lived in the degenerated society for 40 years waiting for the command of Allah. Not only did he live with all this nuisance around him, but also kept his own head above water by holding high esteem and keeping his character unblemished. One day, while he was busy in his invocation and meditations at the Mount Hira during the month of Ramadhan he saw Angel Gabriel, who commanded him to read. "What should I read?" asked the Prophet. Gabriel repeated Allah's command, and then said the first revelation of Qur'an aloud: "Read in the name of your Lord who created. He created man from a clot of blood. Read, and your Lord is Most Honorable, He who taught (to write) with pen, Taught man what he knew not." (96:1-5)

The Prophet repeated these words. These were the first words of the Qur'an. The effect of these words on the Prophet was grave, and he became motionless, and full of perspiration. He looked at Gabriel, who was in the form of light. Gabriel spoke to the Prophet, saying, "You are the messenger of Allah, and I am Gabriel."

According to the Qur'an, Prophet Jesus spoke to the world when he was three days old to tell the onlookers that he was the Prophet and that Allah had given him a Book. It is our belief that the last

Prophet like all other prophets was born as prophet but today it is openly declared. After receiving the first revelation, the Prophet was overwhelmed with Allah's greatness, gratitude, fear and happiness. Gabriel also brought some water and the Prophet performed Wazu and offered two rakats of Namaz as explained by Gabriel.

The Prophet headed home engulfed with grace and blessings of Allah. He felt as if every thing was congratulating him on his prophethood and he heard sound of *Lailah illulah Muhammad ur Rasool Allah* from every nook and corner. Reaching home he was warmly greeted by his loving and astute wife. She noticed a special glow of light around him. The Prophet told her that he had received the Divine call and that he had been bestowed with the prophethood. She had already seen his kind, noble and God fearing behavior and believed him and looked at him graciously and congratulated him. It was then and there that she declared her acceptance of Islam, becoming the first person to do so. It was a great moment. Khadija accepted Islam believing in the oneness of Allah and the prophethood of her husband. Who else could know her husband better than her? She had been seeing him for the last 15 years day in and day out and knew that her husband was the most noble and honest creation of Allah. A little later Imam Ali came by and he also declared his Islam. They all together offered Zohar prayers, establishing the first congregational prayer in Islam.

The Prophet was lying down covered with a blanket when he heard the voice of Gabriel again, this time saying: "O' you who are blanketed, stand up, deliver the warning, proclaim the greatness of your Lord, and cleanse thy clothes. Stay away from the sins and do not think that by doing such deeds you have done a great favor to Allah. Exercise patience to please your Lord." (74:1-7).

The Prophet got the message loud and clear. He got up and told his wife, Khadeeja, the time of resting and slumber had gone by. Allah had ordered him to start the job of warning the people to believe in Allah, and worship Him.

A few days later, while praying in Kaa'bah the Prophet met

Warqa bin Nufil, a devout and learned Christian who had good knowledge of the history of religions. Warqa asked him about the Prophet's experience of receiving the first revelation and after listening the details Warqa confirmed that according to his Book, Muhammad had been declared the Prophet and that he would be the last Prophet till the day of Resurrection

Thus, the period of prophethood started when the Prophet was 40 years old after fully establishing himself as the most honest and trusted man in the entire country.

GLIMPSES OF THE PROPHET'S CONDUCT

Prophet Muhammad was the finest example of a perfect man in every sense. He was a paragon of virtues and was the best example for the human race. Allah distinguished him by assembling in his sublime personality such fine qualities as modesty, truthfulness, kindness, patience, loyalty, honesty, courage, bravery, generosity, magnanimity, wisdom, and delight. By studying his lofty character and amazing simple life, which he led with his household, companions, wives, and others, we are apt to learn valuable lessons from his conduct and accordingly try to live our lives by his example. Ours could never be an Islamic society unless we sincerely follow the footsteps of the Prophet. The Qur'an says: "Certainly you have in the Apostle of Allah an excellent exemplar for him who hopes in Allah and the latter day and remembers Allah much." (33:21)

The Prophet always used to contemplate about the greatness, majesty, and the glory of Allah and the welfare of the human race. He closely followed the affairs of his people and spread the light of Islam. He talked only when necessary, and when he did his speech was devoid of any fumbling and unnecessary words. It was precise, to the point and full of clear meaning.

Here we share and study some aspects of his admirable character, contemplation and wisdom.

Punctuality and Daily Schedule

He was punctual, active, energetic, and lived an orderly life. His day was divided into four periods:

1. Time for worship.
2. Time for household, relative, and wives during which he behaved like an ordinary family man giving the finest example of social behavior.
3. Time for rest and contemplation.
4. Time for public affairs and receiving visitors.

Modesty and Simplicity

He was the finest embodiment of modesty and greatly abhorred arrogance and haughtiness. Almost all of his companions in the early days were poor, and/or people serving as the worthy champions of the down trodden. His house was simple and modest, built of clay bricks, palm leaves, and wood. His food was simple like that of the poor consisting of mostly barley bread. There were even occasions when he might have skipped that meager meal.

He socialized with his companions as one of them, talking, listening, smiling, and displaying a sense of humor. He would sometimes join in their laughter to cheer up their spirit. He would visit them when they became sick, and would accept an invitation for sharing a meal irrespective of whatever the status of the person. In the case of a companion's death, he would participate in the funeral procession walking alongside with the funeral bearer. He hated to see the people rising to their feet when he would enter an assembly. His magnetic personality showed respect for all. He used to sit on the ground, even while eating, and slept on the ground on a simple mat serving as his bed. He greeted small children and women. If someone would shake hands with him, he would not release their hand until the other person did it first.

Once a Christian Arab chief named Adi Ibn Hatim-Al Taiy came to see the Prophet. The Prophet happened to be sitting on a cushion. On seeing the visitor, he offered his place to his Christian guest, himself moving to sit on the ground. The admirable display of modesty by the Prophet so deeply affected Adi Ibn Hatim, at that time that the Christian chief immediately accepted Islam.

Kindness and Generosity

The Prophet's social ties with his companions portrayed the most wonderful example of Islamic brotherhood. Anas bin Malik, who frequently attended the Prophet's assembly, said that whenever the Prophet did not see one of his companions for several days he would inquire about that person, would pray for him, and if he happened to be ill, would pay him a visit. One of his companions, Jabir Ibn Abdullah, said the Prophet once entered a house and saw it was full of people, with no vacant spot, so he sat outside. He recited another example from the Prophet's life.

Once a man came to the Prophet, but on seeing him he started trembling with fear. The Prophet smiled and comforted him with utmost tenderness telling him to relax and take it easy saying that he was not a king, but the son of a Quraish woman who used to eat dried meat.

Courage and Valor

The Prophet was second to none in Allah's creation from Adam to eternity. He was an excellent example of noble manners, indomitable courage, and excellent behavior. His valor was beyond words; while he stood gallantly against the heaviest odds, endured pain and injuries, and victoriously fought, he overcame and showed mercy to the stone-hard ignorance of Arabs. Magnanimity is the finest form of valor and the Prophet excelled in this particular field, sparing enemies, and saving multitudes from injustice and oppression, servitude, and ignorance.

He endured pain and suffered for 13 long years in Mecca for inviting people to Islam without being afraid of the sheer force and number of the Arabs in Mecca, and he did all this single-handedly without any group of supporters except his few devoted followers. After migrating to Medina, he organized an army to defend against the idolaters and he led the faithful in many of the battles. He was not an aggressor, but a defender, and did not promote any of the cruel or sadistic behaviors known to the Arabs in their warfare. His faithful and equally brave cousin Imam Ali, who was the standard-bearer in most decisive battles and who, while defending Islam and the Prophet, was unmatched on the battlefield, described the Prophet's behavior and bravery in these words: "You had beheld me on the day of Badr, all of us proceeded with the Prophet, and he was the nearest one to the enemy's rank. He was on that day the bravest of all."

The Perfect Family Man

The Prophet was the perfect example of a family man; he was a loving husband, an affectionate father, and a caring grandfather. As long as the faithful Khadeeja was alive he never married another woman. Even later in his life, when he had married several women, he used to cherish the loving memory of faithful Khadeeja while yet treating each lady with justice and kindness.

The Prophet's marriages were not for pleasure, but for serving many humanitarian purposes and to further the cause of Islam, as evidenced from the women he married. In the case of Sauda, Uma Salma, and Zaineb binte Uzaima, the purpose of the marriages were to take care of the poor and helpless who were well in their middle ages, while the marriage to Juwairiyah was to grant her freedom from captivity. In the cases of Umi Habiba, Sofia, Ayesha, Hafsa, and

74

Memona the objective was to unite some prominent Arab figures, who often were at odds with each other, and also to safeguard the developing political status of the newly founded Islamic state. His marriage to Zainab binte Jaish was for the sake of enacting a new law, because she was a divorcee of his adopted son, Zaid bin Haris. As the Qur'an justified, the Prophet married her in order to put an end to the wrong notion, common at the time that wives and widows of adopted sons could not be married. The philosophy behind these marriages was entirely visionary, which brought positive changes to Arabia.

The Prophet was an affectionate father, and his only surviving child and daughter, Fatima, was dearer to him then his own life. His famous hadith that Fatima was a part of him, and whoever annoyed her, in fact annoyed him, stood as a firm testimony to his utmost affection to his daughter as well as testifying to her own good character.

History is the witness that the Prophet used to stand up to greet his daughter. Many prominent and wealthy Arabs had approached him for Fatima's hand, but he politely refused them. According to the Divine commandment her hand was given to the leader of the faithful, Imam Ali, with her consent. Fatima and Ali were the parents of his two grandsons Hassan, and Husayn for ensuring the continuity of the Prophet's noble progeny. He used to play with them and take them to the mosque. Once, when the two grandsons were seated on his shoulder like a horse ride, a companion remarked, "What an excellent mount," to which the Prophet replied, "What excellent riders too!" The Prophet's behavior towards his Ahlul Bayt has a lesson for us all. It was not only because of an extreme love of an affectionate father, or a grandfather, but for something divinely ordained. This is supported by several verses of the Qur'an.

Therefore, as we learn from the Qur'an and ahadith, it is obligatory for all Muslims to love and respect his family, and adhere to the Islamic path, which is the only way to save the *Ummah* from disasters.

EXERCISES

1. How do you think the world would be different today if the Prophet Muhammad had not existed and fulfilled his mission?

2. Read Surah 105, and if possible, a *tafsir* or exegesis of the Surah. Explain what you are able to learn about the attempted attack on the Ka'abah. Who did it, when, and why? What happened?

3. Is it good for a woman to propose marriage to a man? What evidence do you find in this chapter to support your answer?

4. Conduct research about the Black Stone in the Ka'abah. What are its origins? Why is it special compared to the other stones?

5. Many ahadith emphasize the importance of taking time to ponder one's actions, the world, and the universe in terms of science, philosophy, morals and so on. The Prophet used to go to a particular place to do this. Arrange for yourself a place in your home or other accessible place where you can concentrate and think, do homework, analyze yourself for self-improvement, and ponder. Describe or draw a diagram of this place. Explain why this place is effective in meeting your goals. When and how do you or will you use it?

6. The Meccan tribes worshipped stone idols. That kind of idolatry is easy to recognize. Today, idolatry persists but it may not be as obvious as worshipping stone statues. Even people who call themselves Muslims are in danger of engaging in subtle forms of idolatry, when their hearts and minds are occupied by something other than Allah and Islam, or when they seek help from other than Allah. What kind of idolatries do you find going on in your generation and location today? How can you remain safe from it?

7. What are the chief excellent characteristics of the Prophet? Which of the characteristics do you find to be particularly well-developed in yourself, your mother, your father, or one

of your siblings? Write a short story about an example of how one of these people demonstrates a good characteristic.

8. Do some people have good characteristics while others don't because of circumstances they can't control, like who their families are and where they live and how they are raised? How much do these things influence your character? How much of your character is decided by you making the choice to do something right or to do something wrong?

Chapter Six

THE EMERGENCE OF ISLAM

The Prophet received the first divine revelation on 27th Rajab, which was the seventh lunar month in 710 AD, and from that date he continued to receive revelations until his death. The period of the prophethood that started at the age of 40 can be divided into two phases. The first phase relates to the early development of Islam until the Prophet's migration to Medina, and the second phase recounts the development from the year of the First Hijra until the death of the Prophet.

FIRST STAGE

The first stage lasted for about three years. During this stage, the Prophet preached the message of Allah to the closest relatives and friends who could be trusted at that time. The first of them to embrace Islam was his wife, and the second person and the first male who accepted Islam was his cousin, Ali ibne Abu Talib. Abu Talib was the Prophet's uncle and his protector. The third person who came to the fold of Islam was the Prophet's servant, Zaid ibne Harisa. Abu Bakr was the fourth person who accepted Islam.

Gradually, the divine revelations became more frequent. Allah taught the Prophet through Angel Gabriel how to make ablution (*wuzu*) and how to offer prayer. The book entitled Kasaes by Nisai relates the first congregational prayer in Ka'abah. According to the book, Yehya bin Afeef related that on one of the pre- Islamic days he visited Ka'abah. He saw a young man came and stood facing

Ka'abah. Soon after a boy came and stood on his right and then a lady came and stood next to him. They read while standing, then bent, and then went into prostration. Afeef asked Abbas, uncle of the Prophet, who was incidentally present, about this group. Abbas told him that the gentleman in front was his nephew, son of Abdullah, the lady is Khadijah, his wife, and the boy was the son of Abu Talib, his nephew. He told Afeef that his nephew told him about Allah, the creator of this world, and they were praying to Him.

In the early period, the Prophet started preaching on an individual level and gradually it was expanded to a group level in the Ka'abah. A few names of the early Muslims were: Ali ibne Abu Talib, Zaid bin Harisah, Abu Bakr ibne Abu Qahafa, Saad ibne Abiwaqas, Abdul Rehman bin Auf, Usman ibne Affan, Talha ibne Ubaidullah, Abuzar Ghaffa'ri, Zubair bin Awwam, Abu Ubaidullah bin Jarrah, Arqam bin Abiarqam, Suhaib Roomi, Abdullah bin Masood, Habbab bin Alarrab, Uthman bin Mazuum, Jaafar bin Abi Talib, and Nowaim bin Abdullah. Women marched side by side with men in accepting Islam. Among the great women who accepted Islam were: Khaddija binte Khawalid, Fatima Binte Assad, Fatimah binte Khattab, Fatimah binte Almujallil, Fukiha binte Yasir, Asma binte Omais, Asma binte Salamah, Ramallah binte Abi Auf, and Umamah binte Khalaf.

During the first three years of the Islamic movement, the messenger of Allah was discreet but still spread Islam gradually. It attracted all age groups, but appealed especially to the youth. About thirty-nine people had accepted Islam during the first phase. The new Muslims took the message very seriously, but the non-Muslims took it lightly. The non-Muslims thought it to be a flagrant idea of an unstable young man.

SECOND STAGE

The second stage of spreading Islam started with an open invitation to accept Islam. The time had changed by then and Gabriel had brought new revelations from Allah to the Prophet: "So, proclaim what has been commanded and stay away from idolators." (15:94)

DINNER FOR KINSMEN

The Prophet invited his kinsmen to a dinner and asked Imam Ali to arrange the dinner. About forty kinsmen of the progeny of Abdul Muttalib were invited. After dinner, the Prophet wanted to address the gathering, but Abu Lahab, one of the Prophet's uncles, interrupted and the guests dispersed without listening to the Prophet. The next day, the dinner was arranged again. After dinner before anyone could disrupt the gathering, Abu Talib stood up and ordered everyone to listen to the Prophet. The Prophet spoke eloquently and said: "I know of no Arab, who had ever come to his people with a nobler message than mine. I have brought to you the best of this world and the hereafter. Believe me that Allah has sent me as His messenger, and entrusted me the task of guiding the entire world. He has commanded me to call my near relatives towards the true creed of Islam, and warn them of the fire of hell. I, thus call upon you, to come forward and testify to my Prophethood. Whoever takes precedence in accepting the faith, shall be my brother, my vicegerent, and my successor in office."

The audience kept quiet and did not speak at all. Imam Ali, who was about 13 or 14 years old, stood up and broke the silence. Imam Ali said: "I am the youngest and may be weak in my legs, but I will help you and assist you in all your work." The Prophet wanted to give others the chance, but no one stood up. The Prophet then held Imam Ali and announced: "Look, Ali is my brother, my vicegerent, and my successor among you. You should listen to him and obey him." Hearing this, they laughed loudly, and said to Abu Talib: "Now see, you have to obey your son." They all departed not realizing that one day this very Ali, under the guidance of the Prophet, would turn the table by spreading Islam throughout Arabia. Through his unflinching support of the Prophet, indomitable courage while facing enemies, and matchless service to the great religion of Islam, Ali would become the best after the Prophet.

PUBLIC DECLARATION OF ISLAM

Having introduced the faith to his kinsmen, the Prophet decided to launch the second phase of spreading Islam. In those days, it was common practice to speak on a matter of common interest to the entire community from the Mount Safa. The Prophet made the call for the people of Mecca to gather. The Prophet, addressing them in a loud voice, said: "If I tell you that an enemy is hiding behind this hill, ready to attack you, would you believe me?" All of them replied with one voice: "Yes certainly, since we have never found you telling a lie." The Prophet then said: "If it is so, then believe me that a divine retribution is soon to overtake you and our community because of evil deeds. You cannot escape it, unless you testify to Allah's religion, and rectify your actions." The Prophet's uncle, Abu Lahab, one of his bitter enemies, shouted: "You wasted the time of all of us only to say this." The crowd dispersed, but from that movement they picked up sharp animosity against the Prophet for his denouncing their gods and calling them to believe in one God.

HOSTILITIES UNLEASHED

The people of Mecca had not taken the Prophet seriously. After the open declaration they became very hostile. They now realized the dangers to their idol worshiping and other antisocial and sometimes antihuman activities. They started teasing him in all possible ways. They would spread thorns in his path. They would incite children to hurl stones at him. They would even throw rubbish at him to try to humiliate him.

Petitioning Abu Talib

The unbelievers realized that the Prophet would not give up his call. They decided to meet Abu Talib, who was the leader of the people of Mecca and the protector of the Prophet. The delegation consisted of Abu Sufian, Rabia, Abu Jehal, Sheeba, Waleed bin Mugheera, and others. They complained to Abu Talib that Prophet Muhammad was preaching to obey one God and denouncing their gods. They were being called ignorant and misguided. This group met Abu Talib at least two times; one time they offered the Prophet all types of bribes if he would stop his mission. Abu Talib, patiently heard their complaints, and after his meeting for the second time he went to the Prophet and told him all about it. The Prophet replied with a determination: "By Allah, if these people placed the sun in my one hand, and the moon on the other, I would not give up what I have been commanded by Allah to carry out as my great mission until Allah makes me accomplish it." Abu Talib extended protection to his nephew, a Prophet of Allah. He said to the Prophet what a servant of Allah was supposed to say: "You do proceed in your great work, no one can cause you any harm so long as I am alive, nor will I ever leave you alone and unprotected."

The Umayyad's Opposition

For a long time the Umayyads had been the staunch enemies of the Hashimites. Added to the already established differences was the new message of equality and justice preached by Islam. Islam was challenging their social status. The Umayyads were indulgent in loaning to the poor and charging exorbitant interest on these loans, a practice denounced by Islam. They were also charging fees for people wishing to place an idol in the Ka'abah. The source of their livelihood was at risk. At this juncture, they took full advantage of their feuds by hatching a plan. Abu Sufian became the leader of this plan, as his sister, Um-I-Jameel, was married to Abu Lahab, an uncle of the Prophet. Others like Utba bin Rabiah and Abu Jehal also supported Abu Sufian.

Temptation Offered

One day Utba came to the Prophet and said to him: "Why are you wasting your life and putting us in trouble. If you want money we can provide it for you, and procure it for you. If you want to marry a beautiful girl we can provide one for you. Even if you want to become the king of the Arabia, we can arrange for it. Just let us know what you want." In reply to Utba's proposal, the Prophet recited the following six verses from the Qur'an:

"In the name of Allah the Beneficent, the Merciful.

"Haa, Meem!

"A revelation from the Beneficent, the Merciful God:

"A Book of which the verses are made plain, an Arabic Qur'an for a people who know:

"A herald of good news and a warner, but most of them turn aside so they hear not. And they say: our hearts are under coverings from that to which you call us, and there is a heaviness in our ears, and a veil hangs between us and you, so work; we too are working.

"Say (O' our Apostle Muhammad!): I am only a mortal like you; it is revealed to me that your God is one God, therefore follow the right way to Him and ask His forgiveness; and vow to the polytheists." (41:1-6)

After hearing these words Utba was completely bewildered. He came back to his group and said to them, "Today, I have heard the Prophet reciting something, which is neither a sorcery nor soothsaying. By Allah, Muhammad will win, will have his way one day, and will win supreme over all of us. I will advise you to leave him alone and watch the developments." These words fell on deaf ears.

EFFECTS OF OPPOSITION

The intensified opposition made the Prophet and Muslims more determined in their faith. As long as Abu Talib was the leader of the tribe nobody could touch the Prophet himself. Likewise, the Muslims belonging to strong tribes of Mecca were left alone. Other Muslims who were poor, destitute, and unrelated to the people of Mecca got the brunt of the punishment. They bore all types of torture. They were made to lie on the hot sand under the scorching sun, with a heavy stone on their chest. They were denied food and drink. Despite the abuse, the Muslims remained firm in their belief. The people of Mecca did all this to stop the spread of Islam and to stop the Prophet from preaching. The infidels did not succeed in their objective and the message of Islam continued to flourish among the people of Mecca.

One day while the Prophet was praying, he was almost strangled by someone throwing intestines of a cow on his head to the amusement of onlookers. His daughter, who happened to be nearby, rescued the Prophet.

Hamza, a strong man, well respected by the Meccans and an uncle of the Prophet, was not in Mecca at that time. On his return, he was told about these incidents. Hamza went straight to Abu Sufian, had an arrangement with him, and went directly to the Prophet and accepted Islam. His acceptance of Islam provided a strong and much-needed boost.

A Desperate Call

The idolaters noted that torture, persecution, and infliction made the Muslims more determined than before. They then presented the Prophet with a proposal saying both parties should mutually accept each other's God to avoid confrontation. Allah commanded the Prophet that there was no compromise on the principles. The Prophet was asked to tell them: "You have your own religion and I have mine." (109:6) The plan of mixing truth and falsehood was nipped.

During this period of agony the only occasion of rejoicing for the Prophet was the birth of his only daughter Fatimah. According to reputable sources, she was born in the fifth year of his Prophethood.

Muslims Immigration to Habshah (Abyssinia)

With the intensification of their persecution, and their equal determination to adhere to their faith, the Prophet permitted a group of Muslims to migrate to Habshah (Abyssinia). About eighty people migrated under the leadership of Jaffar ibne Abu Talib, the cousin of the Prophet and brother of Imam Ali. The King of Habshah, Negus (Najjashi), was a noble King with a cool head. The idolaters of Mecca pursued the Muslims and sent a delegation of their own under Amr bin Aas to bring them back. After bribing the courtiers of the Negus, they presented their case to the King to let this group of Muslims return to Mecca. They alleged that these peoples were apostate as they had forsaken the religion of their forefathers and had started a cult of their own. The King asked the group of Muslims about their beliefs. The leader Jaffar ibne Abi Talib took the lead and said:

"O King, we were ignorant and immoral, worshipped idols made of stone, indulged in all types of indecencies and injustices, and committed crimes. Allah then, with his immense mercy, sent to us a Prophet, one of our own people. His lineage goes back to the Prophet Abraham. His truthfulness, trustworthiness, and honesty were established among the Meccans. He commanded us to worship Allah, the Creator of this world, and denounced idols, which were worshipped by our ancestors. He told us to be truthful and keep our promise, to

be helpful to relatives, to be good to our neighbors, to abstain from bloodshed, and to avoid fornication. He commanded us not to give false witness, misappropriate orphans' property, or falsely accuse anyone. His forbids us to associate anyone with Allah. He advises us to pray, to fast, and to give zakaat. We believed in him as the Prophet of Allah and followed his command. He commanded us to follow good and avoid evil. Thereupon our fellow countrymen attacked us, treated us terribly and persecuted us. They made our lives intolerable. Our Prophet gave us permission to come to you."

The King then asked Jafar ibne Abi Talib to recite some portion of the Qur'an. Jafar recited from *Sura-e-Mariyam*. The King was not only just but was also a worthy scholar. He wept and said, what you had just said, was what was exactly revealed to Moses. He then allowed immigrants to stay and sent the infidels away empty handed.

Umar Accepted Islam

Umar was a harsh man, but he became Muslim in the sixth year of Muhammad's Prophethood. He went out one day to kill the Prophet because of his anger towards Islam. On his way, he met a person by the name of Naeem. On coming to know Umar's intention to kill the Prophet, Naeem told him to take care of his sister Fatimah and her husband Saeed, who had joined Islam. He became enraged and went straight to his sister's home. At his sister's home Habbab bin Alarab was reciting from *Surah Taaha* of the Qur'an to Saeed and Fatimah. Umar entered the house without permission and asked with anger what was being read.

His sister and brother in law refused to tell him, and they hid Habbab in a back room. Umar became furious, and began to hit his brother-in-law, injuring Fatimah who was trying to protect her husband. Seeing the blood from the injuries of his sister, he calmed down and wanted to see the Qur'an. His sister would not let him touch the Qur'an until he cleaned himself, which he did. After reading an Ayah of the Qur'an he calmed down and accepted Islam.

Prophet's Boycott and Confinement

During the seventh year of the declaration of the Prophethood; the Quraish, upset with the spread of Islam, plotted another device to halt the Islamic progress — they joined their forces and all of them signed a total boycott of the Hashimites and the Muttalib family. Afraid for their lives, about forty members of the family, including Khadeejah, were confined to a small place called Shoab-e-Abu Talib, a property belonging to Abu Talib. They had the toughest days of their lives with hardly anything to eat or drink. Sometimes, they had to eat the leaves of trees to survive. Abu Talib and others used to take turns at night to guard the Prophet. The Prophet was forced to sleep at one place, and then later in the night, a different place in order to protect him from any surprise attacks by the enemy. After three long years one day the Prophet told Abu Talib that, as revealed to him by Allah, termites had eaten the papers bearing the signatures of the boycotters. The only words that remained on the papers were the names of Allah. Abu Talib came out and called the leaders of the Quraish to tell them the revelation. Abu Talib believed so much in the truthfulness of the Prophet that he told them that if the Prophet turned out to be wrong in his revelation he would hand him over to them. When the packet of papers was opened, everyone saw the truthfulness of the Prophet's revelation. The social boycott was ended.

THE YEAR OF GRIEF

The end of the first decade of the Prophethood marked the death of two of the strongest supporters and protectors of the Prophet, his uncle Abu Talib and his wife Khadeejah. Abu Talib died in his late

80s. He had worked hard to protect the Prophet since the Prophet was eight. During the last 42 years, he took all types of beatings and difficulties in the way of Allah to protect the message of Islam and the messenger of Allah. The confinement of three years during the social boycott took its toll on Abu Talib, as he could not properly eat or rest. Soon after the death of Abu Talib, the Prophet's most loving and caring wife Khadeejah, also died. It was a terrible blow to the Prophet. But he had to face it, as everyone has to die. There was no escape from his mission. The Prophet had gotten used to shocks and grief all his life from his infancy. He had a mission, and the serious difficulties of this world were to be dealt with. His mission continued.

Glimpses of Abu Talib's Services

Abu Talib was the leader of all Meccans. He was the custodian of Ka'abah. He was called the chief of Batha. He was given a job by his father to protect the Prophet. He discharged it with extreme, perseverance and unflinching courage. He knew the position and status of Muhammad as the Prophet of Allah, whom he believed wholeheartedly. He carried out his job against all odds, with wisdom and secrecy. His steadfastness and love of the Prophet knew no bounds. The Prophet's life was very important to him. He fed the Prophet when he himself was hungry and gave him protection at the risk of his own life. Abu Talib made his own son sleep in place of the Prophet during the night to save the Prophet from a surprise night attack. No wonder that the Prophet cried at his death, led his prayer, and called it the year of grief.

Khadeejah

Khadeejah, the first and most dignified of all the wives of the Prophet, was also a friend to him, and stood like a solid rock to support him, comfort him, and give him courage at a time when no one helped him. She was the first to accept Islam. She was the first to accept him as the Prophet of Allah. She was one of the richest people among the Arabs and gave all her wealth for the cause of Islam. She stood by her husband shoulder to shoulder in all his calamities; even during *jamaat* prayer on the first day not caring about any infliction this could bring her. No wonder the Prophet kept remembering her all his life. She was worthy of his admiration. The Prophet named this year as the 'year of grief'. She was certainly deserving of this gesture of love and remembrance. During the life of Khadeejah, the Prophet did not marry anyone else. After her death he married several ladies, mostly widows. Their names were: Ayesha, Hafsah, Zaineb-binte Alharisa, Zaineb binte Jahash, Umme-Habeeba, Umme-Salma, Jawwareh binte Haris, Memoona binte Alharis, and Safeeah.

Journey to Taif and Back

The departure of his two closest supporters made the Prophet heartbroken and lonely. The harassment in Mecca by his enemies intensified. He decided to leave for Taif, a city about 60 miles from Mecca. He went to Taif accompanied by Zaid bin Harisa. He approached a few important infidel leaders. Not only did they refuse to listen to him, but they also insulted him. They asked their people to drive him out of the city. He could not stay there for more than a few days. Days of Taif were the worst days of the Prophet and Zaid's life, who suffered many injuries. However, the Prophet never insulted the people of Taif with an unkind word.

Returning to Mecca was even worse. He was not welcome there and there was nobody that wanted to listen to him or give him protection. He stayed at mount Hira until Mutim bin Adi gave him protection. He was a notable chief and came with his party to receive the Prophet. Abu Jehal asked Mutim bin Adi if he also had accepted Islam. He said no and told him he had only given protection to the Prophet as a fellow Meccan.

Al-Meraaj: the Ascent

The death of his dearest uncle, his protector, along with passing away of his beloved and supportive wife, was a big shock to the Prophet. His journey of Taif made it worse. He was hurt. At this time, he needed some comfort. Allah, as the Qur'an says, took him to the highest honor which any living being ever had. During this journey, the Prophet saw the glories of Allah, Allah's creation and the workings of the universe.

It was 27th of Rajab, when Gabriel awoke him from sleep. He brought him a horse that was like white light, called *Buraaq*. First, he visited Ka'abah, and then Baitul-Muqaddas. In Baitul-Muqaddas, he led the prayers of all the prophets including Prophet Moses, Prophet Noah, and Jesus. He was then taken to a place in heaven called *Sidra tul-Muntaha* (meaning the end of a limit). Gabriel and the *Buraaq* stopped there. He then was carried by another ride called *Raf Raf* to the highest place of heaven, where nobody had ever reached. He noticed and experienced the glory of Allah, saw heaven and hell, and everything else.

Saying prayers five times a day became *wajib* (obligatory) for Muslims by Allah during this visit. The entire miracle of journey lasted only a short time. It was a physical journey and not just a journey of the soul, like some people think. Allah also gave the Prophet some secrets.

The Qur'an says about the journey: "Glory be to Him Who made His servant go on a night from the Sacred Mosque to the remote mosque of which We have blessed the precincts, so that We may show to him some of Our signs; surely He is the Hearing, the Seeing." (17:1)

"And he is on the highest part of the horizon. Then he drew near, then he bowed, So he was the measure of two bows or closer still." (53:7-9)

The next morning he told the Meccans about his journey. The Muslims believed him, but unbelievers and pagans did not. The journey was meant to show the Prophet the vast limits of his Prophethood as he was a prophet for the entire universe.

Meeting with the Yathrib Delegation

Though the ignorant Quraishites, other tribes of Mecca, and Taif had scoffed at the message of Islam and the Messenger, the divine providence was already at work to help facilitate the spreading of Islam through hidden quarters.

In the eleventh year of Prophethood, the Prophet started meeting delegates who were visiting Mecca from other cities for the annual pilgrimage. He came across a group of people from Yathrib led by Asad bin Zurara of the Khazrag tribe and invited them to Islam. They responded and joined the Muslim rank. On returning to Yathrib, the group started preaching Islam among the local people and made some progress.

First Allegience with Aqaba

The following year a delegation of 12 Muslims from Medina came to Mecca and met the Prophet. They met at a place called Aqaba and swore allegiance to him as Muslims. This was called the first covenant of Aqaba. In this covenant they agreed to obey none but Allah, not to steal, not to commit adultery, not to kill their children, not to commit any evil and not to disobey Allah. The Prophet told them that the reward for following these allegiances would be heaven. Mus'ab bin Amir was sent with them to Medina to give them lessons of the Qur'an.

Second Allegiance of Aqaba

During the following pilgrimage a group of seventy-three men and two women met the Prophet at the same place. They swore allegiance to the Prophet promising to defend and spread Islam in all parts of the country. The meeting was attended by Abbas ibne Muttalib, the uncle of the Prophet. He informed the group of possible dangers and they agreed to face it all. The Medinite Muslims were later called *ansaar,* or "helpers" and the Meccan Muslims were called "migrants," or *muhaajir.*

MIGRATION TO MEDINA (HIJRAT)

The allegiance of Aqaba was happy news for Meccan Muslims as they now had an ally to turn to in time of need. For the infidel Meccans it was a not a happy development and they were alarmed at the growing impact of Islam and their helplessness in stopping it. What had encouraged them most was the death of Abu Talib, who was a solid wall of protection for the Prophet. Their arrogance and ignorance did not realize the presence of the omnipotent and omnipresent Allah, who was protecting his Prophet. The Prophet also changed his strategy. He advised Muslims of Mecca to start migrating to Medina. He was already making arrangements himself to migrate, and could leave on a day's notice. He even bought a camel from Abu Bakr for this purpose. On the other hand, the eldest of the Meccan infidels called a meeting to plan their strategy. It was decided at the meeting to gather a team drawing one member from each tribe to surround the house of the Prophet at night and kill him. The night came, and the Prophet's house was surrounded. The Prophet did not know about it at all, but Allah's machinery went into action. Angel Gabriel came to the Prophet when the infidels had already surrounded his house. He gave him Allah's command to migrate to Medina that night. The Prophet asked Imam Ali to sleep in his bed. Imam Ali asked the Prophet whether his (the Prophet's) life would be saved by doing so. The Prophet answered yes, and that it was the order of Allah. Imam Ali prostrated to thank Allah and slept in his place. This was the first prostration of thanks.

According to the Qur'an, the Prophet picked a handful of sand

and threw it at the watchful eyes of the enemy and walked passed them without being seen by them. While walking silently in darkness he suddenly saw Abu Bakr. He took him with him because he considered it unwise to leave him. This episode of migration (Hijrat) during the month of Rabiul-Awwal in 622 AD marked a turning point for Islam.

The Prophet was gone, and Imam Ali slept in the Prophet's bed to protect him from the enemy. Imam Ali was sleeping as calm and composed as ever. Scores of infidels besieged the house and peeped through the windows, not knowing the real identity of the sleeper. None of this could disturb Imam Ali.

At dawn, the unholy gang burst into the Prophet's house, full of confidence to kill him. But their all night vigil proved worthless as a barrier for the Prophet's escape. To their utter surprise, the figure that calmly emerged from under the cover and stood facing them was the lion of Allah, Imam Ali, not the one they were seeking. Frustrated in their dreadful efforts, the infidels asked Imam Ali about the Prophet's whereabouts. He crisply replied, "did you entrust him to me?" Allah had protected his Prophet from the evil of idolaters and had guarded him from the enemy.

This event brought into focus the personality of Imam Ali and shows his selfless devotion to the cause of Islam and for the life of the Prophet. He agreed to sleep in the Prophet's bed, risking his life without fear. He actually would protect the Prophet at the expense of his own life. Allah rewarded Ali by revealing this Ayah of the Qur'an: "There are those among people who give their lives to seek Allah's pleasure. Allah is affectionate to His servants."(2:207)

Allah had shattered the infidels' plot. By the time the Meccan infidels recovered from the shock, the Prophet was safely out of Mecca and on his way to Yachrib. The Prophet had taken refuge in a cave in a mountain called Thore about three miles out of Mecca. The Quraish left to follow the Prophet and a party of unbelievers did in fact reach the cave of Thore. Strangely, hearing the sound of an idolater, Abu Bakr suddenly started to cry. Before the enemy could spot them the Prophet calmed him down. However, the infidels arrived at the cave's mouth with an expert tracker and looked at the right place, but by Allah's command a spider had spun a cobweb over the entrance of the cave and a Pigeon had laid an egg on it, presenting a semblance of an undisturbed spot as if no soul had been there for a while. Satisfied that no one was in the cave, the unbelievers turned back, giving up hope of finding the Prophet.

The Prophet safely proceeded to Medina, and this migration to Medina marked the start of the Muslims lunar calendar, Hijra, which according to historians took place in Rabi-ul-Awwal.

EXERCISES

1. Give details of the first migration of Muslims to Abyssinia. Also mention few Ayah (translation) of *Sureha Mariam.*

2. Draw a diagram or picture to illustrate the stages of revelation with as many details as possible.

3. Pick one of the first followers of the Prophet (saw) as mentioned in the first stage. Prepare a report or speech that tells whatever you can find out about this person.

4. What are some reasons people accepted Islam? What are some reasons people were hostile against Islam and the Prophet (saw)?

5. Compare and contrast Abu Talib with Abu Lahab.

6. What happened in the Year of Grief?

7. Why did the migration to Medina take place?

8. Research more about Mer'aj and write a poem that gives details of what happened. Or, make a poster or other art form that gives details about Mer'aj. Ask your instructor for guidelines for grading purposes.

Chapter Seven

THE ADVANCEMENT OF ISLAM

Yathrib was the old name of the city of Medina, which later was renamed Medina-tun-Nabi (the city of prophet). It was an old oasis town with plenty of springs and wells. The birches surrounded abundant vineyards and orchards of palm, pomegranates and other food. It is located about 300 miles from Mecca and was inhabited by the idol worshipping Arab tribes of Ous and Khazraj. Certain Jewish tribes, namely Bani Qurdha, Bani Mugheer, and Bani Quinga also lived in Medina. They had migrated to the town centuries before to await the last messenger of Allah whom they found foretold in their scriptures. The two Arab tribes had always been fighting with each other. There was also no love lost between the Arabs and Jews. The Jews were waiting the prediction mentioned in their sacred book about the pagans. They used to say that soon a Prophet would emerge in Arabia and would come to Yathrib to put an end to their wicked ways. By strange circumstances, when the Prophet immigrated to Medina, the two tribes of Ous and Khazraj renounced idolatry and accepted Islam, but the Jews whose forefathers had come to Arabia for this very purpose rejected the Prophet.

FIRST HIJRI YEAR IN MEDINA

The Prophet entered Quba, a suburb of Medina on Monday, 12th Rabiul-Awwal. He stayed there for four days, until Imam Ali arrived with his mother, the prophet's daughter Fatima, and other relatives. At Quba the Prophet built a mosque.

The Prophet entered Medina on Friday, 16th Rabiul-Awwal. When he reached a place called Bani Salim it was time for the Zohr (afternoon) prayer. The Prophet stopped here and offered the first Juma (Friday) prayer. The Juma prayer was thus established. This was the place where the Prophets Mosque was built later.

After entering Medina, the first thing the Prophet established was a place of worship of Allah. Abu Ayyub Ansari bought the land and a simple mosque was built. The Prophet helped in building the mosque along with other companions. Small living quarters were also built along side the mosque. Adhan and Iqamat were also established along with the declaration of the number of Rakaat for each prayer. The foremost task the Prophet had to confront in Medina was to assimilate the *Ansar* and *Mohajjareen*. The *Mohajjareen*, or the immigrants from Mecca who came to Medina before the Prophet, were living as guests with Ansar or the helpers of the Medinites. After the arrival of the Prophet, the conditions changed.

Formation of Brotherhood

He created a brotherly relationship amongst the local population and the immigrants. All Muslims were made brotherly to each whether from Mecca, Medina, or different tribes. For example, Abu Bakr was made brother to Harisa Bin Zaid, Umar Bin Khattab made brother to Utba Bin Malik, Abu Ubaida bin Jarrah, and Saad Bin Muaz, who were friends earlier, were made brothers, and likewise Usman Bin Affan, and Anas Bin Sabit were made brothers. The prophet declared Ali as his brother in this world and hereafter. The *Ansar* practically shared the property with *Mohajjareen* on the basis of shared faith. Besides property they also shared many other things. It was an unheard and unseen event in the history of human beings.

Central Authority

A central authority, with the Prophet at the top, was set up for Medina. Medina thus became the capital of the first Islamic state. There wasn't a huge distinction between the ruler and subjects. Everyone was safe and equal in the community. The only distinction was based on one's personal piety (Taqwa), as stated by the Prophet in his Farewell Speech: "The noblest among you is the one who is the most virtuous." It is also stated in the Qur'an: "Verily the most honored of you in the sight of Allah is (he who is) the most righteous of you." (49:13)

The next step the Prophet took was establishing internal security in Medina between Muslims and non-Muslims including the Jews. A written convent was drawn up and signed by all parties, including non-Muslims. Unfortunately, the Jews did not always live up to their pledges.[1]

Establishment of Prayers

As stated earlier, the five daily prayers, or *salat*, became *wajib* during the Prophet's Miraj. After coming to Medina, the *Adhan* was established, the number of rakat for prayers became fixed, and regular congregational prayers were started. Bilal Habshi became the first *Muezzin* (Caller of the *Adhan*). He did the call to prayer five times a day, and people gathered to pray behind the Prophet. The name of Allah the Great, which was forbidden in Mecca, was now announced five times daily, loud and clear in unison, declaring the greatness of Allah, the Creator of the universe. *Adhan* is the invitation, or call to prayer, which Muslims hear in beautiful and melodious voices all over the world, five times a day.

---

[1] *The Sea of Tranquility (Monogram Series), A Message of Peace Publications, Muslim Foundation Incorporated: New Jersey, U.S.A.*

SECOND HIJRI YEAR

During the second Hijri year, Medina began to thrive as the capital of the first Islamic state under the dynamic leadership of the Prophet. This small city-state changed the history of the world. Gradually, more new orders came. Observing Saum in Ramadhan became obligatory. Zakat was also introduced. Charging of interest (*Ribah*) became *Haram*. The laws governing the offense, inheritance, marriage, and rights of women were implemented by the command of Allah. Later on, in the same year, the direction for prayers (*Qibla*) was changed from Bait ul Muqddas in Jerusalem to Al Kaa'bah in Mecca.

Prophet Guiding the State

The Prophet was not only the religious leader, but also the temporal leader of the new state. The state was established under the exemplary guidance of the Prophet of Allah. He was defending Islam and Muslims on various fronts. In a nutshell, the Prophet was undertaking the following responsibilities:

1. Maintaining a discipline and coherence among Muslims.
2. Guarding Islam against hypocrites.
3. Guarding Islam against the conspiracies of non-Muslims.
4. Guarding Islam against the impending reprisals of the Quraish of Mecca.

Of course, the Prophet did his job perfectly, taking his budding society to its zenith. In the same year, prayers for the two Eids, Eid-Ul-Azha, and Eid-Ul-Fitr, became obligatory along with the sacrifice of animals. During this year, the Prophet's only daughter, Fatima, was married to Imam Ali.

The Battle of Badr

The most important incident of the year was the Battle of Badr. This battle took place when the Quraish with all its big chieftains attacked the Muslims. There were a thousand of them against the 313 companions of the Prophet. This was a vitally important battle. Many leaders of the Quraish were killed including Abu Jehal. Hamza, the uncle of the Prophet and others showed great heroic deeds. Imam Ali was the hero of this battle as he killed half of the seventy infidels killed in the battle. Encouragement and discreet help came from Allah. The Muslims won and the infidels ran away crying.

THIRD HIJRI YEAR

The Battle of Ohad

The most remarkable event of the third Hijri year was the Battle of Ohad imposed by the Quraish as a reprisal to their defeat in the battle of Badr. This time the Quraish attacked Medina with a much greater force and ferocity. Abu Sufuian was the chief of the Quraish army. Two tragedies that happened during the battle were:

1. Hamza (the Prophet's Uncle) was killed and his body mutilated.
2. Some companions of the Prophet, fearing their lives, fled away from the battlefield, leaving Imam Ali and only a few other devoted Muslims to defend the Prophet and Islam.

Eventually, the Quraish were defeated again but the Muslims suffered a great loss too. This loss was only because some companions did not listen to the Prophets strict commands. The same year, Imam Hassan was born on 15th Ramadhan.

FOURTH HIJRI YEAR

During the Fourth Hijri the important events were: (1) The Jewish tribe of Bani Nazir, signatory to the convent of peace, tried to kill the Prophet; (2) Use of alcohol was prohibited; (3) Prayers in times of fear and Qasr, the permission to shorten prayers during travel, were introduced; (4) Fatima binte Asad, wife of Hazrat Abi Talib and mother of Imam Ali passed away; and (5) Imam Husayn, the second grandson of the Prophet was born on 3rd Shaban.

Battle of Khandaq (ditch)

Another important event of this year was the Battle of Ditch (Khandaq), also called the battle of Ahzab. The Prophet had a busy life in Medina. He migrated to Medina so the new state and religion could grow in safety, but no day passed without an incident. Skirmishes, violence and tragedy became a daily occurrence and the violations of pledges were common.

The Quraish had already tried in Badr and Ohad to destroy Islam. Bani Nazir, the Jews of Medina, were forced to leave Medina because they attempted to kill the Prophet, and in doing so, violated a treaty. Ousted from Medina they settled in Khyber along with the other Jews. The Jews visited Mecca and instigated the Quraish to join them in launching a massive attack on Medina. Four-thousand Quraish and six-thousand Jews and others joined forces to attack Medina. The Prophet decided not to leave Medina to face the enemy. Instead it was decided to dig a wide ditch around Medina to stop the onslaught of the enemy. The idea came from the eminent companion of the Prophet, Salman-e-Farsi. The army of the enemy was taken by a total surprise to see the ditch when they reached the outskirts of Medina. They camped at a distance from the ditch for some twenty days, and kept trying to attack the Muslims.

One day, Amr ibne Abd-e-Wad crossed the ditch and challenged the Prophet directly. People were afraid to fight him, since he was a very famous warrior. Imam Ali, with the permission of the Prophet, went out to fight him on foot and killed him. This was a great blow to the enemy, as their best man was killed. The enemy was disheartened, but persisted in their aggression against the Muslims. Small skirmishes kept happening, and there were also reports of attacks from inside Medina by the Jews. Then came help from Allah. One night a strong wind and rain came followed by a bigger storm. "The tents of the enemy's camps were uprooted" so they ran for their lives and the great battle was finally won. The battle of Khandaq had a great psychological effect on the enemy, both for the infidels of Mecca as well as for the Jews. The unique victory of Imam Ali, in single combat against the best warrior and strongest man, engraved fear in the heart of the enemies. The help of Allah in forcing them out of the area, made them think twice in ganging up against Islam.

SIXTH HIJRI YEAR

Treaty of Hudaibiyya

The most important event of the sixth Hijri was the treaty of Hudaibiyya. In the sixth Hijri, the Prophet decided to perform Hajj, which is an obligatory commandment of Allah on all adult males or females who can afford it. The immigrants from Mecca to Medina, the *Muhajjireen* and residents of Medina, the *Ansar* also decided in large numbers to accompany the Prophet. It was a great honor to go on Hajj with the Prophet. The pilgrims took their animals with them to sacrifice, but they did not take their arms, except for their swords.

The Meccans were informed of the Prophet's intention to advance. The Quraish decided to intercept and did not want the Prophet to enter Mecca. The Prophet's caravan continued, and stopped at a place called Hudaibiyya. The Quraish gave signs of war. The Prophet then called all his companions and took an oath of allegiance from all of them to fight to death, if needed. This is known as *Bait-e-Rizwan* in history. During the next few days of talks and exchanges of emissaries with the Quraish, the clouds of war were removed and a treaty was signed known in history as the Treaty of Hudaibiyya. Imam Ali was called to write the treaty. The following were the highlights of the treaty:

1   The Muslims would not perform Hajj that year. They might come back for Hajj the following year.
2   When the Muslims went on Hajj the next year, they would not carry any weapons except their swords.
3   The Muslims would only be allowed to stay in Mecca for three days next year.
4   This treaty would last for ten years, during which each party would guarantee the safety and property of the others.
5   The treaty would also extend to the allied friends of both parties.
6   If someone were to go from Quraish to the Muslims, he would be returned.
7   If a Muslim would come to Quraish, he would not be returned.

Some of the Muslims who did not realize the wisdom of the Prophet were disappointed; even some developed hard feeling towards the Prophet.

The caravan, however, sacrificed their animals, according to the Prophet's orders, and returned to Medina without performing Hajj and Umra. The terms were apparently against the Muslims, but eventually paved the way for conquering Mecca.

The Qu'ran says about the treaty: "Surely, we have given a clear victory." (48:1)

The treaty gave a chance for non-Muslims to understand Islam and the Muslims. It also proved that Muslims loved peace, not war. The Muslims could now recite the Qur'an freely in Mecca and perform their rituals openly.

SEVENTH HIJRI YEAR

Having achieved peace with the people of Mecca through the treaty, the Prophet, during the seventh Hijra, sent letters to many governments and communities including four big rulers of that time to accept Islam.

The Prophet sent a letter to the King Khusro of Iran. He was furious with the letter and torn it up. He ordered the governor of Yemen to arrest the Prophet and send him to Iran. The governor sent two people to Medina. When they met the Prophet, the Prophet told them that the King of Iran was dead. They returned to Yemen, and found out that the Prophet was telling the truth. They became Muslim along with many others.

The Prophet wrote a letter to the ruler of Byzantine, who received the message with honor and sent him some gifts with his reply. He, however, did not accept Islam.

The third letter was sent to the King of Abyssinia (Habsha) to accept Islam. The king kissed the letter and accepted Islam. He asked Jaffar Ibne Abi Talib to return to Medina. The Prophet was so happy with his coming, that he said that he was not sure he was happier at winning the Battle of Khyber, or the return of Jaffar Ibne Abi Talib.

The Battle of Khyber

The battle of Khyber was fought during the seventh Hijri. Here again, Imam Ali was the champion for capturing the fort which could not be captured by the Islam army for the last 39 days. The Jews of Khyber made a peace treaty with the Prophet.

Khyber was a city near Medina. The residents of this city were making things hard for the Muslims of Medina. The Prophet sent his army to dislodge them from the Khyber Fort. The Muslims had been going there for 39 days but could not win them over.

On the 40th day the Prophet called Imam Ali, who was sick at the time. The Prophet treated him, gave him the banner, and praised him saying that he (Imam Ali) loved Allah, and Allah loved him. Imam Ali went running towards the Khyber Fort. The great warrior, Marhab came out to face Imam Ali. Marhab first attacked Imam Ali injuring his forehead. Imam Ali attacked him back and tore him apart. He then opened the Fort door with a single hand. The door was so heavy that many people were usually needed to open it. Later, in reply to a question, Imam Ali said that he tore the door of the Fort by the power given to him by the Allah.

Abu Hurera also accepted Islam in this year. Abu Hurera is the one who is reputed for narrating thousands of ahadith by the Prophet. Some historians have doubted the truthfulness of these ahadith since he lived with the Prophet for only three years, and that he was meeting the Prophet only a few times a day at most, and that he was not a prominent person. Abu Hurera was in fact living near the Prophet's Mosque built for homeless people.

The State of Fadak

Another important event of the seventh Hijri was the giving away of the state of Fadak to the daughter of the Prophet. Having come to know the fall of the fort of Khyber, the people of Fadak, a small village in the vicinity of Khyber, were plotting with the Jews to launch an attack on Medina. The Prophet appointed Imam Ali along with a hundred horsemen to deal with them. The people of Fadak did not offer any resistance and asked for peace on their own accord. Imam Ali accepted it. In exchange they offered him part of the state of Fadak. At the same time, the following verse of the Qur'an was revealed to the Prophet: "Give to near of Kin his due." (17:26)

On receipt of this command from Allah, the Prophet gave the state of Fadak to his only daughter Fatima, and gave a written document transferring the state in her favor. It was this very document on the basis of which Fatima claimed the state of Fadak as her property when the first Caliph, Abu Bakr, confiscated the state soon after the death of the Prophet. The state remained with the government until the Umayad Caliph, Umar Ibne Abdul Aziz, who tried to return it to the family of the Prophet in 99 Hijri.

Mubahila

The other important event of the year was the *mubahila*, or imprecation, with the non-Muslims to whom the Holy Prophet sent a message inviting them to accept Islam. The Prophet wrote a letter to the Bishop of Najaran in the Christian town of Yemen. Upon receipt of the letter, the Bishop decided to send a deputation of 14 persons to the Prophet to ascertain further details about Islam. This high-power deputation included three of their most trusted and reverend leaders namely Abdul Masseh, Asiad, and Abul Haris. On reaching Medina, they met the Prophet and held detailed discussions on various aspects of Islam but with no definite outcome, especially about the status of Prophet Jesus. At last, the Prophet received the following verses and he read it to them:

"Surely the likeness of Isa is with Allah as the likeness of Adam; He created him from dust, then said to him, Be, and he was." (3:59)

"(This, the truth) from your Lord, never has any doubt about it." (3:60)

"But whoever disputes with you in this matter after what has come to you of knowledge, then say: Come let us call our sons and your sons and our women and your women and our near people (our souls) and your near people (your souls), then let us be earnest in prayer, and pray for the curse of Allah on the liars."(3:61)

They would not accept the truth. The Prophet then told them that they should agree to hold *mubahila,* or imprecation, as stated in the Qur'anic verse. This was the command of Allah. Accordingly, the 24th of Zil Hajj was fixed as the date for this great imprecation. Suitable preparations were made for the imprecation in the open field by making shade for the Prophet, and for those who were to participate with him. A separate area was marked for the spectators.

Ahlul-Bayt for Mubahila

On the appointed day for the imprecation, 24th Zil Hajj, the Prophet came out in a small procession of five persons. He led the procession holding Husayn in his arms, Hassan walking with him holding his finger, his daughter Fatima following him with her husband Imam Ali. The five noble figures headed for the platform, which had been prepared for the occasion. The Christian leaders were just standing to see the Prophet come out with the dearest to him by virtue of blood relationship as witnesses to his truth, and the persons to face the great event of imprecation. The Christians seemed to have lost their spiritual courage to be a party to this serious test, imprecation.

Their leaders said to each other that the great faces they were seeing before them; the Prophet, Husayn, Hassan, Fatima, and Imam Ali looked like truthful people and if they commanded to move a mountain it would certainly move, and if the imprecation were held with these truthful persons, all the Christians would be annihilated in no time. They, therefore, decided to have a settlement by payment of tax (*Jizya*). This was a great victory for Islam and achieved without a fight. Some historians believe that the *Mubhila* took place in the 9th Hijri.

EIGHTH HIJRI

During the eighth Hijri, two important events were witnessed. First was the Battle of Mauta, which was fought with Syria since its ruler had ordered the killing of the Prophet's ambassador. In this battle, Jaffer Ibne Abi Talib lost his life. The Prophet grieved much over Jaffer's martyrdom. The second important event was the conquest of Mecca.

The treaty of Hudaibiya had joined both parties and their allies to maintain a perfect state of peace for a period of ten years. In Mecca, there were two tribes, Bani Khazza and Bani Bakr. The former tribe was the ally of Muslims, but the latter was allied with the unbelievers. In 8th Hijri, Bani Bakr attacked Bani Khazza and killed some of their men. The unbelievers of Mecca, namely the Quraish, helped their allies, Bani Bakr, with arms and men and also took part in actual fighting, though in disguise. The Bani Khazza were very badly hit in this clash and lost. Since they were the allies of the Muslims, they sought help from the Prophet. The Prophet started to render suitable assistance to the allied tribe as dictated by the Treaty of Hudaibiya. The Quraish thus abrogated the treaty. The Quraish now realized the gravity of the situation and sent their chief Abu Suffian to renew the treaty but to no avail. On the Muslims side, the preparations were started for a big clash but few people knew where the attack would be made.

On 10th Ramadhan, the Prophet gave the signal for a march and proceeded towards Mecca. His uncle, Abbas, met him on the way and joined in the march. The Muslims, including the Prophet, numbered in the tens of thousands for this march. They set up camp about 4 miles before reaching Mecca. The Prophet's uncle, Abbas, who was strolling on his horse and met Abu Suffian along the journey. Abbas told him that the Muslim army from Medina had arrived. Abu Suffian was completely bewildered with this news. Abbas told him to come along with him to the Prophet and Abu Suffian hesitantly went with him. The Muslims were also surprised to see Abu Suffian and wanted to kill him, but the Prophet gave him a night's time to decide whether he wanted to accept Islam or not. Abbas, later on, tried to convince him since there was no way of escape for him other than the acceptance of Islam. The next morning, the Prophet invited him to Islam, but Abu Suffian stood before him in a state of indecision and Abbas bade him to announce the *Kalima; La-ilaha Illa allaho Mohammad-ur Rasul allah.*

Abu Suffian hesitantly recited the Kalima to save his life and joined the force of Islam. Abu Suffian, with the permission of the Prophet, was sent to Mecca to announce on the behalf of the Prophet that whosoever took shelter in the Kaa'bah, took refuge in the house of Abu Suffian, remained quiet in his home behind closed doors, or appeared in the open without any arms, would be allowed full security of life. On hearing this sudden announcement, the people of Mecca were stunned, but there was no time for them to think it over and they were completely overtaken with dismay. Riding his camel, the Prophet entered without any resistance, but since the passages were overcrowded with spectators, his speed was very slow. Zubair had fixed the standard of Islam on the top of Mount Hajjoon. The Prophet set up his tent near it. From the Mount, he noticed Khalid bin Waleed engaged in some fighting, so the Prophet stopped him. The atmosphere then became completely quiet.

After some time, the Prophet came out of the tent and rode on his camel towards the gate of the city remembering the day when he had left Mecca a few years ago, completely helpless. Now, he was entering the same place as sole master and unquestioned ruler. He bent towards the camel hump by way of prostration offering thanks to Allah. From there, he reached the Kaa'bah where all the Meccans had gathered to hear him pronounce his verdict about their final faith. Glancing at the huge crowd of his former deadly enemies, he asked them how he should behave with them. All of them replied with one voice, that you were a great son of a great father. The Prophet pronounced them free and that there was no reckoning for their past faults. This was certainly an extremely liberal decision. But why shouldn't the Prophet behave this way as Allah had told him, "We have not sent you, O' Prophet but a mercy to the world." (21:107)

After granting general amnesty to the people of Mecca, the

Prophet went around the Kaa'bah seven times and then went inside the Holy sanctuary to clean and clear it of all the idols that were there. He broke the idols himself but some of them were too highly placed for him to reach. He then asked Imam Ali to stand on his shoulders and pull the idols down. Imam Ali accordingly, stood upon the shoulders of the Prophet and pulled down the idols clearing the Kaa'bah of all its idolatry. By now, it was time for offering Zohar prayers. The Prophet asked Bilal to recite the first *Adhan* in Kaa'bah, and thereafter all Muslims present offered the first *Salat* (prayer) with the Prophet. He delivered a speech after the *Salat*, which was followed by the common allegiance by people at large. The Prophet was now unopposed and the undisputed ruler. On the other hand, he forbade people from adopting manners and etiquette of the times of *Jahliyya*.

A man happened to come to the Prophet trembling with fear. He told him there was nothing to fear because he had also been born Al-Quraish like the others. During the ceremony of paying allegiance, all the people who had been responsible for the worst atrocities on the Prophet during the pre-migration days, also came to him. He magnanimously pardoned every one of them whose blood was declared lawful. He didn't pardon eleven people, but not even all of them were punished since some of them converted to Islam, some fled away, and some were pardoned.

NINTH HIJRI

The most important event of the ninth Hijri was the Battle of Tabuk. The expanding power and authority of the Muslims was creating apprehension in the minds of neighboring non-Muslims rulers. One such ruler was the Kaiser of Rome who was the king of Byzantine. He started mobilizing his forces for attack on Medina. On his side, the Prophet took steps to meet the impending danger.

In the month of Rajab, the Prophet ordered his army to march against the Byzantine. It was extremely hot, and the enemy was believed to be very strong, and the distance was long. This was the only *Ghazwa* (battle which is joined by the Prophet) in which the Prophet did not take Imam Ali with him. The reason was that he wanted a strong leader to stay in Medina during his long absence to the expedition to the Byzantine. He, therefore, asked Imam Ali to stay behind. The army with the Prophet marched from Medina towards Tabuk. Meanwhile in Medina, the hypocrites started saying to Ali that the Prophet had left him behind because he did not like him (Imam Ali) any more. Imam Ali joined the Prophet and told him about the incident. Prophet at that time told him: "Are you not satisfied that you hold the same position to me as Haroon [Aaron] held to Moses, except that there would be no Prophet after me." Imam Ali came back to Medina, satisfied and happy, and controlled the city. Anyhow there was no war and the Prophet came back safe and sound.

Recitation of Surah Barat

In the same year, the Prophet sent 300 men for Hajj on his behalf. He gave them 20 camels as a sacrificial offering - part of the Hajj rites. Abu Bakr was commissioned as leader for this journey and was to recite to the unbelievers of Mecca, in public, the first 40 verses of *Surah Barat* (also called *Surah Tauba*) from the Qur'an. Abu Bakr was on his way when the Gabriel told the Prophet to either go himself, or send some one very close to him, to read the Qur'anic verses. Therefore, the Prophet sent Imam Ali ordering him to stop Abu Bakr from reciting the Qur'anic verses. The Prophet asked Imam Ali to get the Qur'anic verses from Abu Bakr and to read them himself to the unbelievers. Imam Ali did accordingly. Upon his return to Medina, Abu Bakr asked the Prophet why he wasn't allowed to recite the verses in question to the unbelievers in Mecca, and why he was forced to hand over them over to Imam

Ali. The Prophet answered by saying it was revealed to him from Allah that no one except the Prophet himself, or a person from his own self, should fulfill this obligation. The Prophet also said that Imam Ali was from him and that was why, at the order of Allah, he assigned Imam Ali the task of reading the *Surah*.

TENTH HIJRI

The Prophet decided to perform the first Hajj during the tenth Hijri year and word spread throughout the Muslim areas. Thousands of people came for the honor of performing Hajj with the Prophet. According to some historians, about 120,000 people gathered to perform Hajj on this occasion. The wives of the Prophet, and his beloved daughter, Fatima, also joined him. Imam Ali was in Yemen, but came back in order to go on Hajj with the Prophet. While performing Hajj, the Prophet told the Muslims how to perform the various rites of Hajj. In Arafat, he gave a sermon in which he said:

"All the customs and practices of pre-Islamic age are, thoroughly trampled under his feet, never to revive again. The Arabs have no preference over non-Arabs, nor have non-Arabs any superiority over the Arabs, except by the way of exercising piety and following the commandants of Allah. All are sons of Adam, where Adam was made from earth.

"The Muslims are brothers among themselves, and they should be mindful of the slaves, give them to eat what they eat and to wear what they wear.

"All the bloodshed during the pre-Islamic period of ignorance has been pardoned, and in this connection, first of all he writes off the blood of his own kin named Zaid, the son of Rabia bin Haris. All the interests on the loans of pre-Islamic days of ignorance have been written off and are no more liable to pay. In this case, also first of all, I write off the interest of my own family namely that of Abbas

bin Abdul Muttalib.

"Fear Allah in the case of women, you have right for women, and women too have rights for you. The life and property of every one of you is sacred, till the Day of Judgment, as it is on this day of Hajj, on this month, and in this city.

"Oh, Muslims, I am leaving among you two very important things, the Qur'an, and my progeny, that is the Ahlul-Bayt, the people of my house. If you hold fast to them, you would never go astray after me. For the Muslims, sincerity of behavior, seeking well for your brotherhood and unity among yourself, shall give you strength.

"Those who are present here should consider it their duty to convey what I am speaking before you here to others who are not present here. Happily, those who get the message directly now from me may preserve it in memory better than those who are getting it through others to read out. On the Day of Judgment, you will answer the question how I lived among you, and how I heard you, behaved with you, and how I delivered the message of Allah.

There were various voices rose from the audience: "Oh Prophet of Allah, we stand witness that you have conveyed to us all the Divine commandments, have thoroughly carried out your Divine mission, and have not left anything unaccomplished. Thereupon, the Prophet raised his finger towards the sky three times saying: "Oh may Allah be witness; I have fully discharged my obligation."

DECLARATION OF THE PROPHET'S SUCCESSOR

After performing Hajj, the Prophet bade farewell to his native Mecca and set out for Medina. When the great procession reached a point where the routes of different caravans, coming from various points of Arabia, normally parted; the sign of Divine revelation suddenly appeared. The Prophet stopped at a place called Al-Juhfa, near the spring of Ghadeer-e-Khumm. The archangel Gabriel came with the following verse: "Oh Apostle! Deliver what has been revealed to you from your Lord; and if you do it not then you have not delivered His message, and Allah will protect you from the (evil designs of) people." (5:67)

At once, the Prophet ordered the whole party to be assembled — even calling back those who had gone ahead — for he had an important message to be delivered. A pulpit made from camel saddles was set up. Standing on it to deliver a sermon, the Prophet asked the people to be witnesses that he had faithfully performed the task of prophethood entrusted to him by Allah. The multitude cried in one voice: "We are witness, oh messenger of Allah." He also asked them who, in their opinion, was more worthy of their obedience than their ownselves. They replied, "Allah and his Prophet knew better. " Then he said: "Oh people, Allah is my Mowlah (Master), and I am the Mowlah (Master) of all the believers." "Verily, Oh Prophet of Allah" came a unanimous voice. The Prophet then went down and lifted up Ali ibne Abi Talib in his hands and showed him to the vast crowd and proclaimed the famous words, which set up the continuation of the Divine leadership. The Prophet said: "For whosoever I am Mowlah (Master), this Ali is Mowlah (Master)." Three times he proclaimed these words before descending the pulpit, relieved for having performed the greatest task that would save the *ummah* from going astray.

The great multitude of Muslims surged towards Ali ibne Abi Talib, congratulating him on his Divine appointment. The first one who came to swear allegiance to Imam Ali was Umar ibne Khattab, who later became the second Caliph. Gabriel descended again with another revelation showing that Allah was pleased with His Prophet for having excellently performed the great final mission for the mankind. The *Ayah* Gabriel brought said: "This day have I perfected for you, your religion, and have completed My favor on you, and chosen for you

Islam (to be) your Religion." (5:3). The official poet of the Prophet, Sabit bin Hasaan, recited an extempore poetry in praise of Ali as the successor of the Prophet.

The most important task completed on that day was to ensure the continuity of the Divine guidance. Since the Prophet was Divinely appointed, so the successor or trustee of the Prophet should also be Divinely appointed, especially in the case of Islam, which is the final Divine message to the human race. All Islamic schools of thought testify to this event. This was the most discussed event in Islamic history, although some later disputed the meaning of the word "Mowlah."

DEATH OF THE PROPHET IN ELEVENTH HIJRI

Two months later, after his return to Medina, the Prophet got sick. Medina looked gloomy since the Prophet of Islam was confined to bed. The dawning of 28th day of Safar, 11 Hijri looked dreadful. The Prophet, although weak with fever, went straight to the mosque to lead prayer. Following a brief speech, he returned to the house. After giving necessary instructions to his divinely ordained successor, Imam Ali, he stopped breathing. This day was the end of all prophethood.

Allah, through His last greatest messenger, has revealed the perfect and most comprehensive set of laws for humankind which are capable of meeting the needs of all generations until Judgment Day. The need for further revelation is not needed. The Almighty, in His eternal reason, has said everything in the Qur'an and has guarded it from falsification and alteration. The Qur'an, along with the Prophet's Sunnah, provides guidance to all humankind, and ensures correct meaning and application. Allah guaranteed the leadership of the ummah to the Prophet's infallible household, the Ahlul-Bayt, who are the torchbearers for the guidance of all Muslims, after the Prophet.

The Prophet's body was washed by Imam Ali with the help of

other close family members. The Ahlul-Bayt offered the funeral prayer behind Imam Ali. The companions were not present at that time, as they were in *Saqifah* deciding who would be the successor of the Prophet. Later on, they all came and one by one they offered the *Namaz-e-Janazah*. The Prophet died on Monday, and he was buried in his place of residence on Wednesday. A mosque, The Prophet's Mosque, was later built around his place of residence and burial place.

EXERCISES

1. Did Abu Ayyub Ansari own the mosque he contributed to? If not, who did? Explain your answer.

2. Pick a pair from the Mohajjareen and Ansar to try to learn more about. Can you find out anything about them?

3. Research about Bilal, how did he become Muslim, and how did he come to the task of reciting adhaan?

4. Make a time line of all the years after hijri in this chapter with all the important events classified as shariah, political, etc. This is a good class project.

5. How did the marriage of Fatima and Ali take place? How does this compare to marriages today? What aspects make up a proper Islamic wedding?

6. Hamza is mentioned is a believing uncle of the Prophet. What other uncles did he have that believed? Did he have any that did not believe?

7. Is beheading or body mutilation a practice of the believers in any of the battles of the life of the Prophet?

8. What are the criteria necessary for a Muslim to engage in battle? What are the rules he must follow during battle?

9. What do you think is the most significant point of the treaty of Hudaibiyya and why?

10. Find and read Fatima's speech about Fadak. Can you find

why she was upset about it?

11. What does the event of Mubahila tell you about Ahlul-bayt?

12. Several battles are mentioned in this chapter. Make a chart that includes all of them along with their causes and results.

13. What is the key importance of the events of Ghadeer e Khumm?

14. Write a eulogy for the Prophet as if you were one who had lived with him, or as yourself.

Chapter Eight

IMMEDIATE SUCCESSORS OF THE PROPHET

Allah has sent a perfect religion in Islam. The Prophet completed all the jobs assigned to him including declaration of his successor before his departure from this life. Allah selected Imam Ali as the successor to the Prophet and the Prophet declared him as his successor on several occasions. The first of these occasions was on the day of the feast of *Zul-Ashira*, when the Prophet first invited his clan members to become Muslim. Thereafter, several times, he renewed the declaration and refreshed the memory of the *ummah*. The last time was on 18th Zil-Hajj, 10th Hijri in the plains of Ghadeer-e-Khum. This declaration was made in front of more than 120,000 *sahabah*. All the historians agree on the declaration except there is some dispute in the meaning of a few of the words used by the Prophet.

However, after the death of the Prophet, the religious and political leadership in Islam was separated. Leaving behind the dead body of the Prophet for the immediate family members to wash and bury, some of the *sahabah* gathered in a small townhouse called Saqifah. There they handpicked Abu-Bakr ibne Qahafa as their leader. Later on, others joined in, either happily or otherwise to endorse his selection.

Historically, the first four Caliphs, who are called *Khulfa-i-Rashedoon*, were: Abu-Bakr ibne Abu Qahafa, Umar ibne Khattab, Usman ibne Afaan, and Imam Ali ibne Abi Talib.

FIRST CALIPH: ABU BAKR:

Abu Bakr was out of the town at the time of death of the Prophet.

He was called after the news of the Prophet's death was known. Therefore, the Prophet's body was to be washed by his family members, so Abu Bakr and his friends gathered at Saqifah to decide the Prophet's successor. The tussle erupted whether the successor or the Caliph should be chosen from amongst the *Muhajireen* or from the *Ansar*. The supporters of the *Muhajireen* group argued that as they were from Quraish, and close to the Prophet they had prior claim. In the midst of this heated argument, Umar ibne Khattab asked Abu Bakr to extend his hand, which he did. Umar holding his hand, declared him the Caliph. Following this, the people accepted him.

Umar later said that the oath of faith on the hands of Abu Bakr was taken in a tussle and without any serious thought. But Allah saved us from various unfavorable effects (*Sahehi Bukhari*). Abu Bakr remained Caliph for over two years and four months: from Safar, 11 Hijri to Jamad-ul-Sani, 13 Hijri. He was an old friend of the Prophet and was a respected man. Many neighboring areas were conquered during his caliphate.

Imam Ali did not accept his caliphate although he was forced to do so.

Two unpleasant incidents happened during his caliphate. First was the forceful taking over of the property Fadak, which was given by the Prophet to his daughter Fatima as is stated in the Qur'an. The property was in the possession of Fatima, but it was taken over by the state at the order of Caliph Abu-Bakr. The other incident was the murder of Malik ibne Nawaira, a companion of the Prophet, by Khalid ibne Waleed. Umar was very angry with this but Caliph Abu Bakr refused to punish Khalid ibne Waleed. Caliph Abu Baker decreed Umar ibne Khattab as his successor after his death.

SECOND CALIPH: UMAR IBNE KHATTAB

Caliph Abu Bakr declared Umar as his successor without consent from anyone. Umar remained Caliph from Jamaad-ul-

Saani, 13 Hijri until Zil-Hajj, 23 Hijri, (about ten years and six months). He was a man with a strong head and strong arm. He extended Islam to Iran and Syria by force. He fired Khalid ibne Waleed as soon as he became Caliph. He established Taraweeh, which he called good innovation (*bidah-al-hasnah*). He also added the phrase *As-salato-khairun-Minnan Nuam* in the morning adhan. His slave, Abu Lulu, murdered him.

THIRD CALIPH: USMAN IBNE AFFAAN

Caliph Umar did not declare anyone as Caliph, but made a committee of seven people with some complicated rules for choosing a Caliph. Some members of the committee were related to Usman. The committee chose Usman as the third Caliph. His period of caliphate lasted for about twelve years: from Muharram, 24 Hijri until Zil-Hajj, 35 Hijri. Caliph Usman belonged to the Ummayad tribe and he was able to extend Islam further by force. He was not a good administrator. He was dependent on the Marwaan ibne Haakim for most of his decisions. Usman had married Marwaan's sister.

There was lot of mismanagement during his rule as he gave all the high posts to all his relatives (Bani Ummayads). People complained severely to him but to no avail. Unfortunately, people got fed up and murdered him in his home. At that time, Muslims from many countries, including Iran and Egypt were in Medina. They all unanimously declared Imam Ali as the fourth Caliph.

FOURTH CALIPH: IMAM ALI

Technically speaking, Imam Ali was the one who was elected by popular votes. The Muslims *en masse*, surrounded his home and almost forced him to accept the caliphate. He had no other alternative but to take over as the fourth Caliph in the month of Zil-Hajj, 35 Hijri. His period of Caliphate lasted until the month of Ramadhan, 40 Hijri.

He strived for Islam in a peaceful manner. The period of his caliphate was marked with justice and a superb administration. He was a man of his word, a brother of the Prophet, and the most knowledgeable person after the Prophet. He worked purely for Allah. He was a brave man called 'Lion of Allah'. He spread Islam through India by peaceful means rather than by force.

Unfortunately, like the Prophet he remained engaged in defending Islam. He had to fight four wars in his five years of rule. The first war, which he had to undertake, was the Al-Jamal. Unfortunately, Ayesha, the wife of the Prophet, was dragged into it; she lost the war and was sent to Mecca. She repented her mistake and continued to cry all her life. Mua'wiya, the governor of Syria also fought Imam Ali, which was absolutely wrong. Fighting a war with a sitting legitimate Caliph was forbidden by the Prophet of Islam

Imam Ali was killed by ibne Muljim, while praying on 19th Ramadhan, 40 Hijri.

EXERCISES

1. What is the feast of Zul-Ashira?
2. Write a play about Ghadeer e Khum. This could be an individual, group, or class project. Talk to your instructor about performing the play for other classes.
3. What verses in Qur'an were revealed at Ghadeer e Khum? Can you find any tafsir about them?
4. Who were the Muhajireen and the Ansar?
5. The chapter says Fadak is mentioned in Qur'an. Can you find out where? Can you find any tafsir about that verse or verses?
6. What do you think about Caliph Umar's "good innovation"? Did he have any authority to make it? Why or why not? Did he make any others?
7. Choose one of the four caliphs to write a report, speech, our

presentation about his life.

8. Who was Marwaan – Usman's brother in law?

9. What specific methods did Imam Ali use to spread Islam? How do these compare with the methods of the other caliphs?

10. What can you find out about the four wars that happened during Imam Ali's caliphate? Can you find the cause, events, and results of one of them for the class?

Chapter Nine

STATUS OF AHLUL-BAYT AND SAHABA

It is an undisputed fact of history, acknowledged by all Muslims, that the Prophet at the end of his mission addressed his companions in the following words:

"I am leaving among you two valuble things, the book of Allah and my household. As long as you adhere to them, you will never go astray after me. These two will never part with each other until they return to me at the pool of Kauthar in paradise."

The Prophet's household, to put it properly as the Qur'an describes them, is "Ahlul-Bayt." They were the guiding stars of the sky of Islam; more so they were par excellence; they personified the light of the Qur'an and the teachings of the messenger of Allah in their lives. They imbibed knowledge from the Prophet, grew up in his house and followed in his footsteps, calling people to the book of Allah and urging them to hold fast to the tradition set by the final messenger of mankind. They were, as the tradition says, the companion of the Qur'an and never departed from it because they embodied all the concepts, guidelines and values brought to us by the Qur'an.

Whoever studies the life of Ahlul-Bayt will at once recognize the pivotal role they played in the great task of shaping the destiny of Islam. They actively endured to keep the Shariah (divine laws) pure and strived to preserve the Islamic ideology in its original form. They even sacrificed their lives in order to safeguard these high principles and rendered them practical for the Muslim nation.

The glorious lives of Ahlul-Bayt have always been a source of inspiration to Muslims in every era and every place, interacting with their consciousness in reaching the highest-level of morality and excellence in both the worlds. Today their tombs are frequently visited by Muslims who make the visits even from the farthest of places around the globe to pay homage and to experience spiritual enlightenment. In short, the Ahlul-Bayt can be described as a crucial part of Islam ensuring the unity of Muslim nations and holding it all together.

We appeal to the Muslim community to gather around the beacons of light and emulate the Ahlul-Bayt's heroic example by bravely facing the subversive elements that are trying to disunite the Muslim ummah and causing discord among Muslims.

At this crucial juncture when Muslim nations are passing through a critical period in the struggle against combined forces of enemies, only the correct application of the message of Islam and the sincere belief in this divine justice will help us weather the storm. This is not possible except by acting on the teaching and by following the path charted out by the Ahlul-Bayt. They were the flag bearer of the peace and cooperation among the human beings.

The energies of a Muslim nation should be directed towards the call of Islam, to defend it and to stop those who are engaged in sowing the seeds of discord and spreading the venoms of blasphemy and extremism among Muslims.

QUR'ANIC VERSES ON AHLUL-BAYT

There are several verses (Ayahs) in the Qur'an as well as the traditions (sayings) of the Prophet, explicitly in praise of the Ahlul-Bayt, which we will describe here. We are mentioning only a few here.

Verse on purity: "Allah only desires to keep away uncleanness from you, O people of the House! And to purify you (thorough) purifying." (33:33)

All commentators of the Qur'an and narrators of the Prophet's traditions unanimously agreed that the word Ahlul-Bayt, or household of the Prophet, as used by Allah in the Qur'an refers only to the following persons: the Prophet; daughter Fatima and her husband Imam Ali, and their two children, Hassan and Husayn; and the nine other Imams.

The famous Suyuti in his renowned commentary, *Durrul-Mansoor* cites the Bawani narration from Umme-Salma that the Messenger of Allah once told his beloved daughter Fatima to call her husband Ali and two of their sons Hassan and Husayn. When they came, the Messenger of Allah covered them with a cloak and put his hand on them and said: "O Allah they are the Ale-Muhammad, so shower your blessings and favors on Ale-Muhammad as you showered them on the Ale-Ibrahim. You are the praise worthy and glorious."

Ayah of Mawadah says: "Say (oh Muhammad) I do not ask of you any reward for it, teaching the message, but love for my relatives (Ahlul-Bayt)." (42:23) Fakhrudin Raazi, while explaining this verse says that without doubt no one was so near to the Prophet as Fatima, Ali, Hassan and Husayn.

Verse on Mubahilah (Imprecation): "But whoever disputes with you in this matter after what has come to you of knowledge, then say: Come let us call our sons and your sons and our women and your women and our near people (our souls) and your near people (your souls), then let us be earnest in prayer, and pray for the curse of Allah on the liars."(3:61)

This verse points towards an epic event narrated by all historians and commentators. This is an event, which revealed to the Muslim leaders that the family of the Prophet comprising Ali, Fatima, Hassan, and Husayn, came out in 9th Hijri to challenge the Christians leaders.

According to Zamakhshari, the Prophet carried his son, Husayn in his arms while holding Hassan's hand and was followed by his daughter Fatima behind whom was Ali until they found a place to sit and the Prophet was heard saying to his Ahlul-Bayt: "When I invoke Allah you all say Ameen". Seeing this, the chief leader of the Christians, Abdul Massih, stated that they did not want to hold an imprecation with them saying "Oh Christians I am beholding such faces that if they wish to move mountain from their places God would move. If it were so do not accept their challenge for Mubahilah and if you do you would all perish and there will remain no Christians on the surface of earth till the day of Resurrection." Heeding this advice, the Christians said to the Prophet "Oh Abul Qasim we decided not to hold Mubahilah with you, you keep your religion and we will keep ours."

Verse on Prayer: "Surely, Allah and His angels bless the Prophet; O you who believe! Call for (Divine) blessings on him and salute him with a (becoming) salutation." (33:56)

In *Tafseer-e-Kabeer*, Fakharuddin Raazi commenting on the above verse narrated the following petition from the Prophet, who was asked by some of his companions on whom and how to send his blessings on him.

The Prophet said: "Say O Allah send blessing on Muhammad and on Muhammad's progeny as you sent blessing on Ibrahim and on Ibrahim's progeny and send grace on Muhammad and Muhammad's progeny as you sent grace on prophet Ibrahim and on Ibrahim's progeny. You are the Praise worthy and Glorious."

The Ayah of Tabligh: "Oh Apostle! Deliver what has been revealed to you from your Lord; and if you do it not then you have not delivered His message, and Allah will protect you from the (evil designs of) people." (5:67)

The above Ayah was revealed on 18th Zil-Hajj, 10 Hijri when the Prophet was returning from his last Hajj at the place of Ghadeer-e-

Khum. He halted the caravan and there declared Ali as his successor.

After his declaration Gabriel came again and revealed the following message: "This day have I perfected for you, your religion, and have completed My favor on you, and chosen for you Islam (to be) the Religion." (5:3)

AHADITH ON AHLUL-BAYT

There are many ahadith, or sayings of the Prophet, like the hadith of two valubale things, which is called *Thaqalain*: "I have been summoned by Allah and the moment is near for me to answer him. I leave among you the two weighty (vitally important) things, the book of Allah, the Almighty, and my progeny."

"Allah's book is like a rope extending from heaven to earth, and my progeny are the Ahlul-Bayt. The Merciful informed me that the two will never part until they come to me at the pool of Kauthar in paradise. I warn you against deserting them."

"The example of my Ahlul-Bayt among you is like Noah's Ark, whoever got aboard it will be saved and whoever remained behind will drown."

"The tradition of security", "the stars are security of earth against drowning and my Ahlul-Bayt as security for the people of the earth."

The *hadith of Qisa* relates how the Prophet gathered all his Ahlul-Bayt including Imam Ali, Fatima, Imam Hassan, and Imam Husayn and covered them with a blanket, and then the Qur'anic Ayah came:"Allah only desires to keep away uncleanliness from you, O people of the House! And to purify you a (thorough) purifying." (33:33)

"I and Ali are from the same light."

"Fatima is a part of me, whoever hurts her, hurts me."

"Al Hassan, and Al-Husayn are the two leaders of youth in heaven."

"I am the city of the knowledge, and Ali is the gate."

"Ali, you have the same relation to me, as Haroon has to Moses, except that there is no Prophet after me."

TWELVE IMAMS

Jaber ibne Abdullah Ansari once asked the Prophet who were his Caliphs. The Prophet gave the names of all the following twelve Imams:

1. Imam Ali ibne Abu Talib Al-Murtaza.
2. Imam Hassan ibne Ali Al-Mujtaba.
3. Imam Husayn ibne Ali Ash-Shaheed.
4. Imam Ali ibne Husayn Al-Sajjad.
5. Imam Mohammad ibne Ali Al-Baqir.
6. Imam Jafar ibne Mohammad As-Sadiq
7. Imam Moosa ibne Jafar Al-Kazim.
8. Imam Ali ibne Mossa Ar-Riza.
9. Imam Muhammad ibne Ali An-Naqi.
10. Imam Ali ibne Mohammad At-Taqi.
11. Imam Hassan ibne Ali Al-Askari.
12. Imam Muhammad Ibne Hassan Al-Mahdi.

In short, the Prophet is the leader of this world followed by his twelve successors. His daughter, Fatima, is included in both household and progeny.

While we will discuss in details the Ahlul-Bayt in the next chapter as to their status, their merits, and our obligation to show respect and love to them, we conclude this section by a quote from Imam Shafi, who said: "If love of Ahlul-Bayt makes you Shi'a, then let the world know, that I am the greatest Shi'a as I love them too much." He also said about Ahlul-Bayt: "It is enough for your honor that if blessings or *Salawat*, are not sent on Ahlul-Bayt during the *salat* (prayer), the *salat* is invalid."

SAHABA

Everyone has his companions. Although the exact definition of the *Sahaba*, or companions, of the Prophet is lacking but generally those who had stayed with the Prophet for some time are called *Sahaba*. Companions of the Prophet are of two types: *Muhajireen*, the Meccan friends, who migrated to Medina; and *Ansar*, the Medinites who hosted the Prophet in Medina. Some of the *Sahaba* were very good, some were mediocre, and some were not so good. We know one thing: most of the *Sahaba*, (singular is Sahab) were friends of the Prophet; they lived with him, loved him, and carried out his orders like a loyal servant. They had seen the Prophet, listened to him, and touched him; they were great warriors, great companions, and great men. We should not underestimate them except for those who were clearly hypocrites. We should have nothing but respect for them, should love them, and should respect their way of life. They were great people, were helpers of the Prophet in the spread of Islam, and torchbearers of the message of Allah. Most of them were very pious.

Some of the verses of Surah Al-Tawba that clearly show the status of the companions of the Prophet are given below:

"And (as for) the foremost, the first of the *Muhajir* and the *Ansar*, and those who followed them in goodness, Allah is well pleased with them, and they are well pleased with Him, and He has prepared for them gardens, beneath which river flow, to abide in them forever; that is the mighty achievement." (9:100)

"And from among those who are round about you of the dwellers of the desert there are hypocrites, and from among the people of Medina (also); they are stubborn in hypocrisy; you do not know them; We know them; We will chastise them twice, then they shall be turned back to a grievous chastisement." (9:101)

"And others have confessed their faults, they have mingled a good deed and an evil one; may be Allah will turn unto them (mercifully); surely Allah is Forgiving, Merciful." (9:102)

EXERCISES

1. Have someone help you to find the Prophet's farewell speech and read it to the class. What does it say about Ahlul-Bayt? What does it say about our obligations?

2. Shias visit the tombs of Ahlul-Bayt. Wahabis are against this. Find the basis of each group's stance on this issue. Who has the greater claim to truth and how do you know?

3. The commentary of Fakharuddin Raazi is mentioned in this chapter a few times. See what you can learn about him. Or, see what you can learn about another Qur'an commentator or about the process of making Qur'an commentary.

4. The Pool of Kauthar has been mentioned several times now. Where this place is and what do we know about it?

5. As an art or calligraphy project, as a class prepare a beautiful presentation of each of the ayahs and ahadith in this chapter about Ahlul-Bayt (as).

Chapter Ten

THE HOUSE OF PROPHET MUHAMMAD

Courtesy of H.I. M. Jawad Chirri (marhoom/late)
– From his book, 'Brother of Prophet Muhammad)

All Muslims glorify the members of the House of Prophet Muhammad who are called *Aal-e-Muhammad* or *Ahle-Bayt-e-Muhammad.* This attitude is in accordance with the instructions of the Prophet who commanded the Muslims to pray simultaneously for the members of his House whenever they pray for him. By so commanding them, he actually required the Muslims to reserve a place for them close to him.

The Qur'an made it mandatory to offer prayers on Prophet Muhammad and to greet him. The Qur'an says: "Surely, Allah and His angels bless the Prophet; O you who believe! Call for (Divine) blessings on him and salute him with a (becoming) salutation." (33:56)

Many companions asked the Prophet to teach them how to comply with this command. Many highly respected ahadith-recorders including Al-Bukhari and Muslim reported in their *Sahihs* (authentics) that Kaab Ibne Ujrah stated that the Prophet said: "Say: God bestow honor on Muhammad and the members of his House, as Thou bestowed on the members of the House of Abraham, Thou are praised and Glorious."[1]

When instructing his followers on a religious matter, the Prophet did not speak out of his human desire. The Qur'an testifies that he only said what was revealed to him: "Nor does he (Muham-

---

[1] *Al-Bukhari, Sahih Al-Bukhari (Authentic of Al-Bukhari), Part 6, (in the Book of the interpretation of the Qur'an) p. 101.*
Muslim, Sahih Muslim, Part 4, (in the Prayer on the Prophet after the declaration of the Faith) p. 136.
Muhammad Ibn Majah, Sunan Ibn Majah, Vol 1. Hadith No. 904.
Al-Termathi, No. 483, Part No.1. Other ahadiths are reported by Abu-Sa-eed. Abu Mas-ood, Talhah and Ibn Mas-ood. All accord with the above noted of Kaab Ibn Ujra.

mad) say (aught about religion) of (his own) desire. It is not but a revelation sent to him." (53:3 &4)

REASONS FOR HONORING MEMBERS OF THE HOUSE

It may appear that inclusion of the members of the House of Muhammad in prayers for him is due to their blood relationship. If so, it would not be in accord with the spirit of Islamic teachings. To bestow on them such a unique honor because of their relationship to Prophet Muhammad is to advocate a family supremacy and is in conflict with following principles of Islam:

1. All peoples in the eyes of God are equal, the Qur'an declared: "Surely, the most honorable of you with Allah is the one among you most careful (of his duty); surely Allah is Knowing, Aware." (49:13)

2. God does not penalize or reward a servant of His for the sin or good deeds of his parents or his close or distant relatives. The Qur'an says: "O people! Guard against (the punishment of) your Lord and dread the day when a father will be of no avail to his son, nor shall the child will carry any burden for his father…"(31:33)

3. Allah does not penalize nor reward a human being for what is beyond his ability and without his choice. Being related or unrelated to the Prophet is not a matter of personal choice. None of us chose to be related or unrelated to a particular family, nationality or race.

It would, therefore, be very difficult for Muslims to believe that they should include Muhammad's relatives in their prayers simply because they are his relatives.

MERIT OR INHERITANCE

To dispel this apparent conflict, it is important to know that the words *Aal-e-Muhammad (Ahle-Bayt)*, which are repeatedly mentioned in the daily prayer, do not include all his relatives. Only a very small number of them are included. Had they all been included it would be clannish or a tribal discrimination because many of them did not walk on the path of Prophet Muhammad, and to place them above others is to advocate a clan's supremacy.

Kinship to Prophet Muhammad does not mean acceptance by Allah, nor does it secure for his relatives a place in paradise or insure them against divine punishment. Allah, according to Islamic teachings, has created paradise for whoever obeys Him and the place of punishment for whoever disobeys Him, regardless of family affiliation, nationality or race.

The Qur'an even contains a chapter titled "The Flame" *(Lahab)*, defaming Abu Lahab, who was an uncle of Prophet Muhammad. The chapter says: "Destroyed will be the hands of Abu Lahab, and he himself will perish. Of no avail shall be his wealth, or what he has acquired. He will be roasted in the fire, and his wife, the porteress of firewood will have a strap of coir rope around her neck." (Chapter 111)

The truth is that the words *Aal-e-Muhammad* mean the only chosen relatives of Prophet Muhammad. These chosen individuals are not chosen, not honored because of their relationship to Prophet Muhammad, but because of their virtues. They lived the true Islamic life, followed the instructions of the Qur'an and the Messenger and never parted with them in words or deeds. When Allah informs us in His book that the noblest among His human creatures are the most righteous, and His messenger commands us to honor the members of his House when we honor him, we infer that they are the most righteous after the Prophet. Had they not been so, they would not deserve such a unique honor and the Prophet would not have instructed us to honor them whenever we honor his name.

To do otherwise would not be in accord with the Qur'an. Thus, by commanding us to pray for them whenever we pray for him, the Prophet was actually informing us of their high merit, being the most obedient to Allah and His Messenger.

Merit Attested

All Muslims agree that Ali, the Prophet's cousin, whom the Prophet brothered and his wife Fatima, the lady of light, the dearest child of Muhammad and their two children, Al-Hassan and Al-Husayn are from the chosen members of the House of Muhammad and they are included in our prayer for the Prophet. The high qualifications of the chosen relatives of Muhammad are the main reason for the very unique honor bestowed upon them.

Imam Ali stood above all others after the Prophet. He was the strongest supporter of the Prophet. He never hesitated to give his life for the promotion of Islam. The readers of history can easily know that Imam Ali was the top defender of Islam and the most adherent to its rules.

Imam Ali's attitude towards personal power and prestige was unique. Whenever he had to choose between adherence to his ideals and the pleasures of earthly life, he unhesitatingly chose the former. History testifies that he preferred to lose the leadership of the Muslim world rather than accept a condition in which he did not believe. He was offered leadership contingent on his pledge to follow the book of Allah, the instructions of the Prophet, and the traditions of the first two caliphs in the absence of the Qur'anic and the Prophet's instructions. He replied, "I shall follow the book of Allah and instructions of his Messenger, and in the absence of specific teachings of the two sources, I shall endeavor to act to the best of my knowledge and ability." [2].

----

[2] *Ibn-Atheer, al-kamil (The Complete History), Part 3, p. 35.*

His knowledge was amazing for its depth and extensiveness. His sermons, lectures, and the words contained in *Nahj-ul-Balaghah* (Peak of Eloquence) testify to the authenticity of the reported statements of the Messenger that "I am the city of knowledge and Ali is its gate, so whoever wants to enter the city should come through the gate."[3]

The record of the other three distinguished members of the House of Muhammad, Fatima, and her two children, Al-Hassan and Al-Husayn, shows that they were the most sincere servants of Islam. The authentic ahadith spoke of their distinctions and qualifications as permanent allies of justice and truth. Zeid Ibne Arqam reported that the Messenger of Allah said to Ali, Fatima, Al-Hassan and Al-Husayn,"I am at peace with whom you are at peace, and I am at war with whom you are at war."[4]

Abu Huraira reported that the Prophet said: "Whoever loves Al-Hassan and Al-Husayn, loves me, and whoever hates them hates me."[5]

Hubshi Ibne Janndah, said that he heard the Prophet saying, "Ali is from me and I am from Ali and no one represents me but Ali."

The Prophet did not intend to distinguish Ali simply because he was related to him. Al-Abbas, his uncle, and the rest of the Hashimites including Jaffer, the brother of Ali, all are related to the Prophet. All of them would have been qualified to represent him. But he said, "no one represents me but Ali."[6]

At one time, Mua'wiyah was criticizing Ali in the presence of Saad Ibn-Abu-Vaqass. Saad said to him: "I heard the Messenger of Allah saying to Ali, "You are to me like Aaron to Moses, but there shall be no prophet after me."[7] Thus, the Messenger gave Ali a position next to his own for the position of Aaron was next to that of Moses.

---

[3] *Al-Hakeem, Sahih Al-Mustadrak, Part 3, p. 26.*
[4] *Ibn Majah, Sunan Ibn Majah, Hadith No. 145.*
[5] *Ibid., Hadith No. 143.*
[6] *Ibid., Hadith No. 119.*
[7] *Ibid., Hadith No. 121.*

Al-Bukhari recorded in his *Sahih* that the Prophet said: "Fatima is the leader of women of the paradise."[8] No one enters paradise but through righteousness and whoever enters paradise is noble according to Allah. If Fatima is the leader of the women of paradise, she must be the most righteous and noblest woman in Allah's view.

Al-Hakeem recorded in his *Mustadrak* that Abu-Dharr Al-Ghafari (a famous companion of Prophet Muhammad and whose truthfulness is known to the Muslims) stated that the Prophet said: "The example of members of my house is like that of Noah's ark. Whoever embarked on it was saved and whoever failed to embark was drowned… "[9]

The Messenger of Allah commanded the Muslims to follow his chosen relatives. Therefore the relatives of the Prophet are distinguished because of their merit and work, and they rank among the most righteous servants of Allah.

REASONS FOR SURPASSING IN RIGHTEOUSNESS

Why did the members of the House of Prophet Muhammad surpass others in righteousness? To understand the reason, we have to remember what took place in the House of Prophet was not unprecedented in the history of prophethood. There were many precedents.

Precedents in History

Allah made Aaron a partner to his brother Moses in his heavenly mission. He did not bestow this honor on any other person from the Israelites. He chose Aaron to bestow honor on him because of Aaron's high qualifications and also in response to the prayer of Moses, as mentioned in the Qur'an:"He (Moses) said: O my Lord! Expand my breast for me, And make my affairs easy for me, And loose the knot from my tongue, (That) they may understand my word; And give me

---

[8] *Al- Bukhari, Sahih Al-Bukhari, Part 5, (Chapter on Distinction of Relatives of the Messenger), p. 25.*
[9] *op. cit., Part 3, p. 151.*

138

an helper from my family: Aaron, my brother, Strengthen my back by him, And associate him (with me) in my affairs, So that we should glorify Thee much, And remember Thee oft." (20:25 to 34)

Prophet Abraham prayed to Allah to make some of his offspring Imams of the people. Allah responded to his prayers and promised to make Imams of the good offspring, without allowing any of the wrongdoers to reach the high rank. The Qur'an says: "And We granted him Ishaq (Isaac) and Yaqoub (Jacob) and caused the prophethood and the book remain in his seed, and We gave him his reward in this world, and in the hereafter he will most surely be among the good." (29:27)

Allah also had chosen along with the relatives of Abraham, the relatives of Imran and preferred them to others. The Qur'an says: "Surely Allah chose Adam and Nuh and the descendants of Abraham and the descendants of Imran above the nations."(3:33) Offspring, one of the other; and Allah is Hearing and knowing."(3:34)

Zakaria prayed to Allah to grant him a righteous child. Allah answered his prayers and the angels gave him good tidings. The Qur'an says: "There did Zakaria pray to his Lord; he said: My Lord! Grant me (from Thee) good offspring; surely Thou art the Hearer of prayer." (3:38) "Then the angels called to him as he stood praying in the sanctuary: That Allah gives you the good news of Yahya verifying a Word from Allah, and honorable and chaste and a prophet from among the good ones." (3:39)

According to these verses, the prophethood, which preceded that of Prophet Muhammad, took the same course. From among the offspring and kinsmen of these Messengers were chosen persons, who reached the highest degree of piety and therefore deserved to be commissioned by Allah.

Distinguished Children and Relatives — A Reward

Allah created noble offspring of these Messengers in response to their prayers, or as a reward to them for their endeavors in spreading the Message of Allah. Like other prophets, Prophet Muhammad was given unusual relatives and offspring as a reward for his endeavor in the service of Allah and in response to his prayers.

He commanded us to say: "Allah, honor Muhammad and the members of his family", and he prayed for the purity of these members on various occasions.

Al-Hakim reported that the Prophet covered Ali, Fatima, Al-Hassan and Al-Husayn with a garment and prayed, saying: "Allah these are my family. I ask Thee to honor Muhammad and the family of Muhammad." In response to this prayer the Qur'anic revelation came: "God wants only to keep abomination away from you and make you, members of the family of Muhammad spotless."[10]

Thus, it was not unusual to have kinsmen and offspring of Muhammad to be distinguished men and women of the highest degree of righteousness. On the contrary, if such persons did not exist among the relatives of the Prophet, it would have been very unusual. Allah honored Abraham, Moses, Zakaria, and other Prophets by creating in their progeny and relatives distinguished persons, and preferring them to others. Why should He not honor His final and most important Prophet by creating in some of his offspring and relatives high distinction?

The Prophet's Reward

The Qur'an makes it explicitly clear that the love of relatives of the Prophet is an Islamic duty. Allah commanded Prophet Muhammad to ask the Muslims to reward him for his true achievement of heavenly mission by loving his close kin. The Qur'an says: "That is of which Allah gives the good news to His servants, (to) those who believe and do good deeds. Say: I do not ask of you any reward for it but love for my near relatives; and whoever earns good, We give him

---

[10] *Op. cit., Part 3, p.148.*

more of good therein; surely Allah is Forgiving, Grateful." (42:23)

Allah was telling Prophet Muhammad to inform all Muslims that the only reward he wanted for fulfilling his heavenly mission was that Muslims love his relatives. This was only because his relatives were the most obedient to Allah and His most beloved servants among the Muslims. By commanding His Messenger to do so, He actually commanded the Muslims to glorify the chosen relatives of Prophet Muhammad, place their confidence in them, and walk on their path.

In compliance with this heavenly command the Prophet asked all his followers to love them. He stated that he was at peace with whomever they were at peace, and that he was at war with whoever they were at war. He considered them to be similar to the Ark of Noah. Whoever embarked on it was safe and whoever failed to be on it was drowned.

The House of Muhammad can be a means of unity to the Muslims. This unity can be realized if Muslims take the attitude that Allah and His Messenger wanted them to take towards these people. It would be erroneous for Muslims to separate Prophet Muhammad from the members of his House while he himself wanted to be united with them. This is clearly evidenced by his instructions that his followers couple him with his chosen relatives whenever they pray for him, whether in or outside their daily prayers.

EVIDENCE DOCUMENTED ON HOUSE MEMBERS

Relying on the tacit agreement among the Muslims, it is assumed that the members of the blessed House of Prophet Muhammad include Imam Ali, his wife Fatima, and their two children, Al-Hassan and Al-Husayn. The most reliable evidence in this matter is the reported words of Prophet Muhammad when he spoke of the Ahlul-Bayt or his *Itrah*. The reported words of the Prophet on this subject can be classified into two types:

1   The ahadith that contained descriptions distinguishing the House of Prophet Muhammad from those who would be excluded by the same description.

2   The ahadith that specified these members.

DESCRIPTIVE AHADITH

Jaber Ibn-e-Abdullah, a famous companion, reported that the Messenger of Allah said:"O people, I have left for you that which if you follow, you will never go astray: the book of Allah and the members of my House who are my *Itrah* (close relatives and progeny)."[11]

Zeid Ibn Arqam, a well known companion of Prophet Muhammad reported that the Prophet said: "I have left for you that which if you hold fast you shall not go astray after me, the book of God, a rope extended between heaven and the earth, and the members of my House who are my Itrah. Certainly, both (the book of Allah and the members of my House) shall not part from each other until they join me on the Day of Judgment. Beware how you will treat both of them after me."[12]

Zaid Ibn Thabit, reported that the Prophet said: "I am leaving among you two successors: the book of God, a rope extended between the Heaven and the earth, and the members of my House who are my Itrah. Certainly the book and *Itrah* will not part from each other until the Day Of Judgment."[13]

Zeid Ibn Arqam again reported that the Prophet said on the day of Ghadeer-e-Khum: "I am about to be summoned by Allah and I shall respond. Certainly, I have left for you the two most valuable legacies. One of them is bigger than the other: The Book of Allah and my *Itrah* or members of my House. Beware how you will treat both of them after me. They will not part from each other until the Day of Judgment." Then he said: "Certainly God is my Mowlah

---

[11] *Al-Termazi, Sunan Al-Termazi, Part 5, p.1328 (Hadith No. 3874).*
[12] *Ibid., Part 5, p. 329 (Hadith No. 3876).*
[13] *Imam Ahamed Ibn-e-Humbal reported this in his Musnad by two authentic ways, Part 5, p. 181.*

(Guardian) and I am the Mowlah of every believer." Then he held Ali's hand and said: "Whoever, I am Mowlah, this Ali is his Mowlah. O God love, whoever loves him and cast out of Thy favor whoever, antagonizes him."[14]

Accordingly, the members of the House of the Messengers are the ones who possessed the following qualifications:

1. *Belonging to Prophet Muhammad's Itrah.* One's *Itrah* includes one's close relative by birth. By this definition the wives of the Prophet and his companions from the non-Hashimites clans are excluded.

2. *Possessing righteousness of the highest degree.* The members of the House of the Prophet were described in the above ahadith as true allies of the Qur'an who would never part from it. Thus, impious men and women would be disqualified, whether they were from the Hashimite or non-Hashimite clans.

3. *Possessing the highest degree of knowledge regarding the content of the Qur'an and the teachings of the Messenger.* Those who possessed limited knowledge of religion were excluded even if they were closely related to Prophet Muhammad. Their lack of knowledge would certainly fall intentionally or unintentionally into disagreement with the Qur'an. The members of the blessed House, according to ahadith, were secured against disagreement with the book of Allah. Such a security could not exist without a profound knowledge of the Qur'an and all the Islamic teachings.

4. *Completely agreeing with each other.* No difference of opinion on the teaching of the Qur'an existed among the members of the House. As all of them were in complete agreement with the Qur'an. They were also in full agreement with each other.

---

[14] *Al-Hakeem in his Al-Mustadrak, Part 3, p.109*

5. *Possessing certitude in all religious knowledge.* The knowledge of the members of the House of Prophet Muhammad was a knowledge of certainty and not conjectural and that is why they were in complete agreement with the Qur'an and amongst themselves.

Certitude of Knowledge

The last qualification for certitude calls for an explanation. By this qualification, the Islamic scholars who are called *Mujtahids*, and are capable of conducting religious research and forming their own opinions are excluded - even if they are Hashimite or related to Hashimite clan. To understand this clearly a few points need to be mentioned. When we try to know the Islamic rules of our devotional or non-devotional actions, our main evidence comes from the Qur'an, or from the ahadith of the Prophet.

When we find clear and specific instructions in the Qur'an about a certain matter, our knowledge reaches the degree of certitude whether we are an Islamic scholar or a layman. When we do not have clear Qur'anic instruction, we look to the ahadith of the Prophet. Some of the ahadith are clear in their indication and are reported by numerous companions. Again our knowledge through this type of hadith attains certitude. The difficulty is that there isn't a lot of hadith of this type and the majority of them are reported by one, two or a few companions. Through such ahadith our knowledge concerning the rules never reaches the level of certainty since the companions did not report it to us directly, nor did they record it in a book.

A person would receive a hadith from a companion. He in turn reported it to another and so on. Later the hadith were recorded in a book after they passed through several people. Thus, our knowledge through this type of ahadith would be, at best, conjectural. There are other places where instructions from the Messenger have been reported unclearly or in different ways. Only professional scholars, or *mujtahid,* can draw conclusions in such cases.

After the scholars reach conclusions, and their opinions are formed, the rulings are still mostly conjectural. They do not usually reach any height of certainty, nor do they necessarily agree with the Qur'an. The probability of disagreement with the Qur'an is very high. If we consider two opposite opinions of two scholars for one question, we would be certain that one of them is in disagreement with the Qur'an because the two opinions contradict one another, and the Qur'an doesn't contain contradictory views.

From this it becomes clear that the *mujtahids,* whether Hashimite or non-Hashimite, are not included in the particular membership of the House of Muhammad. This is because the knowledge of *mujtahids,* while being very great in comparison to a lay person and deserving of respect, is not certain, while the knowledge of the members of the House was securely in agreement with the book of Allah.

This is because the aforementioned hadith clearly indicates that the knowledge of the members of the House of Prophet Muhammad was knowledge of certainty, rather than the knowledge of conjecture, otherwise they would have disagreed in many cases regarding the Qur'an. By this, we ought to consider a *mujtahid,* such as Abdullah-Ibn-Abbas, a cousin of the Prophet, out of the circle of the House, in spite of his extensive knowledge of the religion and his close relation to the Prophet. The rest of the companions, who were not closely related to Prophet Muhammad and did not reach the degree of knowledge of Abdullah Ibn-Abbas, are obviously excluded.

How could it be possible for the members of the House of Prophet Muhammad to obtain knowledge of certainty in all Islamic teachings? Possessing a certainty in religious teachings was highly possible during the life of the Messenger. It is very logical to assume that the Prophet taught a disciple of his, such as Imam Ali, all the contents of the Qur'an and informed him of all the Islamic laws. It is fair to assume that such a close disciple taught some of his disciples all that he learned from the Prophet. These assumptions are supported by certain facts.

Imam Ali was with the Prophet from time of his childhood until the death of the Prophet. Imam Ali was his trusted disciple and close associate. He was his keen-minded student who attended his public as well as his private teachings. Al-Hassan and Al-Husayn (the grandsons of Prophet Muhammad and the sons of Ali) lived with their father many years. They were his close associates. They were his most brilliant disciples and purist Muslims, and resembled their teacher, and in turn, his teacher. Thus, we can say certainty of knowledge regarding the Qur'an, and the instructions of the Prophet, was available and it was possible for some of the disciples of Prophet Muhammad to know all of it.

SPECIFIC AHADITH

Several Ahadith of the Prophet stated the names of the members of the House of Prophet Muhammad. Muslim recorded in his Sahih the following: "When the (following) verse came down (at the time of the debate between the Messenger and Christian from Najran): if anyone disputes in this matter with thee now after the full knowledge has come to thee, say: Let us summon our sons and yours sons, our women and your women, our near people (our selves) and your near people (your selves); then let us earnestly pray and invoke the curse of God on those who lie'. The Messenger of Allah called Ali, Fatima, Hassan and Husayn, and said: Allah, these are the members of my family."[15]

Al-Termazi, Ibn Manthoor, Al-Hakim, Ibn Mardawaih and Al-Bayhaqi in his *Sunnan,* all recorded the report of Umm-e-Salemah, wife of the Prophet in which she said: "In my own house, the Qur'anic verse, (in chapter 33) was revealed saying: 'Certainly God wants to keep away all abomination from you, members of

---

[15] *Muslim, Sahih Muslim, Part 15*

146

House (of Muhammad) to make you pure and spotless'. Ali, Fatima, Al Hassan, and Al Husayn were present at my house. The Prophet covered them with a garment and then said: "These are the members of my House. God keep away abomination from them and make them pure and spotless."[16]

Muslim in his *Sahih* recorded that Ayesha said: "The Messenger of God came out wearing a white cloak, made of black hair. Fatima, Hassan, Husayn and Ali came successively then he covered them with his cloak and said: 'Certainly, God wants to keep all abomination away from you, ye members of the House of Muhammad, and make you pure, spotless."[17]

The following two *ahadiths* are recorded in *Al-Durr Al-Manthoor* by Al-Sayooti: "Abu Al-Hamra (one of the companions of the Prophet) reported that the Prophet continued for eight months in Medina, coming to the door of Ali at every morning prayer, putting his two hands on two sides of the door and exclaiming: "Assalat, Assalat (prayer, prayer). Certainly, God only wants to keep away all abomination from you, ye members of the House of the Prophet and to make you pure and spotless."[18]

Ibn Abbas reported: "We have witnessed the Prophet for nine months coming every day to the door of Ali, son of Abi Talib, at the time of each prayer and saying: *Aslamo Aleikum Wa-Rehmatullahe Ahllel Bayet* (peace and mercy of God be upon you, ye members of the House of the Prophet). Certainly, God wants only to keep away all abomination from you, members of the House, and to make you pure and spotless."[19]

These ahadith clearly indicate that each one of the four is a member of the House of the Prophet. They also exclude all other individuals who were living at the time of Prophet Muhammad,

---

16 *Al-Termazi, Sunan Al-Termazi, Part 5, p. 328, (Hadith No. 3875).*

17 *Muslim, Sahih Muslim, Part 15,*

18 *Al-Sayooti, Al-Durr Al-Manthoor, Part 5, p. 198, (Conveyed by Sayed Taqi Al-Hakeem, Al-Ossol Al-Ammah for Al-Fiqh Al-Muqaram) pp. 155-156.*

19 *Ibid.*

the Hashimites as well the Non-Hashimites, from the Arabs and Non-Arabs.

This restrictive statement, however, does not exclude Al-Hashimites who were born after the time of Prophet Muhammad, and possessed the same excellence of purity in words and action.

MEMBERS BORN AFTER THE PROPHET

The first group of ahadith included in this text indicates that the members of the House are to continue after his death and through numerous centuries because the members according to the hadith shall exist as long as the Qur'an exists. By commanding the Muslims to follow the book of Allah and the members of his House, and by declaring that Ali, Fatima, Hassan, and Husayn as the members of his House, the Prophet actually placed Imam Ali and his two sons at the seat of leadership of the nation.

Thus, the two sons did not need to be appointed by their father, and Al-Hassan did not need to appoint his brother Al-Husayn.

SACRIFICES OF AHLUL-BAYT

Someone asked Imam Jafer As-Sadiq why the Ahlul-Bayt were respectable in the eyes of Allah. The Imam replied, "We are not the relation of Allah but we have given sacrifices in the way of Allah."

From the First Imam to the Eleventh Imam the family sacrificed and suffered for the sake of Islam. The First Imam, from the time of Zul-Ashira till his martyrdom, served, fought, and got killed for the sake of Allah. Islam was his life and fairness was his soul. The historians write that he was killed for his fairness.

Imam Hassan and Imam Husayn sacrificed every child of their family for the sake of Islam. There is no sacrifice comparable to the sacrifices of Imam Husayn. All other Imams were also humiliated and tortured and eventually killed except the current living Imam.

148

EXERCISES

1. Why do we send greetings on the Prophet? Can you find a hadith that explains the best way to send the greetings?

2. Compare and contrast the relationship between Musa and Aaron with that of Muhammad and Ali. How are they the same and how are they different?

3. Are the Aal e Muhammad deserving of special status because they are the Prophet's kin? Explain your answer with evidence.

4. Read a *tafsir* of Qur'an 33:33. If you do not have one, ask your teacher to read one in class. What do you learn from it in relation to the topic of this chapter? Can you find tafsir of another verse in Qur'an that supports the ideas presented here? You may want to look back in the chapter for ideas of which Qur'anic ayahs to investigate.5. What is the reward the Prophet asks of us? Is there something in particular about him or his actions that in your opinion should make him particularly deserving of a reward? What actions should you do to give him his reward? In class, work as a group to make a display showing how each of you will reward the Prophet, *insha'allah*.

6. The Aal e Muhammad have five characteristics mentioned in this chapter. Pick one and write a song or poem about it in praise of Ahlul-Bayt. Your instructor may make this a group assignment and may ask for class presentations.

Chapter Eleven

TWELVE IMAMS: SUCCESSORS TO THE PROPHET

Imams are the successors to the Prophet after his death since Allah had promised not to leave the people without a guide.

The Prophet had worked very hard to further the cause of Islam and establish the religion for the people. It was incumbent upon him to protect Islam's future. Through a decree of Allah, the Prophet designated his successors. An authentic and universally accepted hadith reports the Prophet to have said explicitly on several occasions that twelve Imams would follow him.[1]

According to another version, the Prophet is reported to have said clearly that the first of them would be Imam Ali and the last would be Imam Mahdi.[2]

Allah completed his mission by sending Prophet Muhammad as His last messenger, and Prophet Muhammad completed his mission by designating his successors. He did it on 18th Zilhajj, 10 Hijri on the plain of Ghadeer-e-Khum while returning from Hajj in the presence of some 120,000 Sahaba. At this place he conveyed the message sent by Allah, as stated in the Qur'an (5:67), asking the Prophet to convey the wishes of Allah regarding the Prophet's successor.

FUNCTIONS AND QUALIFICATIONS OF AN IMAM

Islam prescribes very high qualifications for a divine leader

---

[1] *Sahih Bukhari, p. 175, 1355 Egypt; and Sahih Tirmizy Vol. 2, p. 45, 1342, Delhi.*
[2] *Sahih Muslim, Vol. 2, p. 191, 1348, Egypt; Sahih Abi Dawood, Vol. 2, p. 227, Egypt; Musnad Ahmad Bin Hambal, Vol. 5, p. 106, 1313, Egypt; Mustadrak Al-Hakim, Vol. 2, p. 618, Hyderabad; and Tareekh Al-Baghdad, Vol. 14, p. 353*

(Imam). He should be the most knowledgeable and noble of all. And he should be immune from every kind of sin, mistake, and error.

The Prophet and the Imams, besides being religious leaders, were responsible for all government functions and therefore possessed the qualifications to shoulder those responsibilities. The Prophet was the founder of Islam and the Imams were the protectors. Allah appointed both of them. The Prophet alone received the revelation, but the Imams were heirs to the prophetic knowledge. The Imams did not receive revelation, but they were the masters of the details regarding the Prophet's religious system. Both the Prophet and the Imams had special constructive roles and did not spare any sacrifice in the interest of the Muslim *Ummah*. On this note, the prophethood ended successfully and with that, the imamate began. The role of prophethood in short was receiving and teaching of the Qur'an, purification of the soul, and transmitting knowledge. With the inception of the imamate, another important task was added to these objectives: to safeguard and protect the Shariah. All of the Imams had done a marvelous job according to the needs of their times. We will deal with each of the twelve Imams briefly.

THE FIRST IMAM:
IMAM ALI BIN ABI TALIB AL-MURTAZA

Imam Ali was the first Imam. He was the Prophet's cousin and born on Friday, 13 Rajab inside the Ka'abah. He was brought up under the guardianship and instruction of the Prophet. As Imam Ali said: "The Holy Prophet brought me up in his own arms and fed me with his own morsel. I followed him wherever he went like a baby camel following its mother. Each day a new aspect of his character would beam out of his noble person and I would accept it and follow it as a command." This is why Imam Ali was the treasure of the prophetic knowledge.

The Prophet had kept him so close and inseparable for ten years as a child (Imam Ali was with the Prophet for thirty-three years) that he was just like him in character, knowledge, self-sacrifice, forbearance, bravery, generosity, oratory, and eloquence. From his very infancy, Imam Ali prostrated before Allah along with the Prophet. As he said: "I was the first one to pray to Allah along with the Holy Prophet."

"Imam Ali preserved the foot steps of Holy Prophet all along his childhood," says the famous historian Allama Masoodi. Allah created him pure and holy and kept him steadfast on the right path. Although Imam Ali was indisputably the first to embrace Islam when the Prophet called upon his listeners to do so, he could be called a born Muslim since he was brought up by the Prophet from infancy and followed him in every action and deed including prostration before Allah.

Imam Ali, at all times, accompanied the Prophet to help and protect him from his enemies. He used to write down the verses of the Qur'an and discuss them with the Prophet as soon as they were revealed to him.

The Prophet had said to Imam Ali "Oh Ali, you are my brother in this world as well as the hereafter." He also said: "I am the city of knowledge and Ali is its gate."

Allama Masoodi has judged the character and caliber of Imam Ali in these words: "If the glorious name of being the first Muslim, a comrade of the Prophet in exile, his faithful companion in the struggle for faith, his intimate associate in life, and his kinsmen; if a true knowledge of the spirit of his teaching and of the book; if self-abnegation and practice of justice; if honesty, purity, and love of truth; if the knowledge of law and science constitute a claim to pre-eminence, then all must regard Ali as the foremost Muslim. We shall search in vain to find, either among his predecessors or among his successors those attributes."

In the last days of his life, the Prophet had gone to Mecca to perform pilgrimage. On his return journey, when he reached Ghadheer-e-Khum this Qur'anic verse was revealed to him, "O

Apostle! Deliver what has been revealed to you from your Lord; and if you do it not, then you have not delivered His message and Allah will protect you from the people; surely Allah will not guide the unbelieving people." (5:67)

The Prophet stopped there and ordered other Muslims to also stop. About 120,000 people assembled around him. He ordered a pulpit to be raised. After the pulpit was ready he ascended it and lifted Imam Ali up in his hands so that the people might see. Then the Prophet said: "Whoever considers me to be his master and patron he should consider Ali also to be his master and patron." "O Allah! Be the friend of him who is friend of Ali and be the enemy of him who is the enemy of Ali."

Gibbon says: "The birth, the alliance and the character of Ali which exalted him above the rest of his countrymen, might justify his claim to the vacant throne of Arabia. The son of Abu Talib was in his own right the chief of Banu Hashim and the hereditary prince or guardian of the city, temple of Mecca."[3]

Imam Ali had the qualifications of a poet, a soldier and a saint; his wisdom still breathes in a collection of moral and religious sayings[4] and every antagonist, in the combats of tongue or of the sword, was subdued by his eloquence and valor. From the first hour of his mission to the last rite of his funeral, the Prophet was never forsaken by a generous friend, whom he delighted to name his brother, his vicegerent, and faithful Aaron of a second Moses.

In the small hours of 19 Ramadhan, 40 Hijri, Imam Ali was struck with the poisonous sword by a Kharejite while offering his prayers in the Mosque of Kufa. He was born in the house of Allah, the Ka'abah and martyred in the house of Allah. He was the most brave-hearted and gentle Muslim that ever lived after the Prophet, beginning his victorious life with devotion to Allah and His Prophet and ending it in the service of Islam. From the first day of the Feast

---

³ *Gibbon*
⁴ *Peak of Eloquence, English Translation of Nahj al Balagha*

of Zul-Ashira until his death, he defended Islam with all his might.

THE SECOND IMAM:
IMAM HASSAN BIN ALI AL-MUJTABA

Imam Hassan, the elder son of Imam Ali was born on 15 Ramadhan, 3 Hijri in Medina. Upon receiving the happy news of his grandson's birth, the Prophet went to the house of his beloved daughter, Fatima, and took the newly born in his arms and named him Hassan.

The first phase of seven years of the second imam's infancy was blessed with the gracious patronage of the Prophet, who gifted him with all his great qualities and provided him with the divine knowledge to such an extent that he became outstanding in his knowledge, tolerance, intelligence, bounty, and valor. He was infallible by birth and decorated with the heavenly knowledge by Allah.

The demise of the Prophet was followed by an eventful era when the Islamic world was going through a surge of expansion and conquest. But even under such revolutionary phase, Imam Hassan kept devoting himself to the sacred mission peacefully propagating Islam and the teachings of the Prophet along with his great father Imam Ali.

After the martyrdom of his father, Imam Hassan was selected Caliph by the Ummah. The majority of the Muslims pledged their allegiance to him. As soon as he took the reins of the leadership, he met the challenge of Mu'awiyah, the governor of Syria, who declared a war against Imam Hassan as he did against his father, Imam Ali. In compliance with the love of Ummah, the will of Allah, and the decision to refrain from causing massacre of Muslims, he entered into a peace treaty with Mu'awiyah on terms that saved Islam and stopped civil war. This peace treaty never meant surrendering in favor of the permanent leadership of Mu'awiyah. It was meant only as an interim transfer of the administration of the Islamic heritage, subject to the condition that the administration would be surrendered back to Imam Hassan after Mu'awiyah's death and then Imam Husayn would in turn administer it. Having relieved himself of the administrative responsibilities, Imam Hassan kept the religious leadership within him and devoted his life to the propagation of Islam and the teachings of the Prophet in Medina. As noted earlier, the Imam's job was to protect Islamic Shariah. Hence, Imam Hassan acted in the best manner at that time in order to save Islam.

Below are some of the conditions of the peace treaty between Imam Hassan and Mu'awiyah:

1. Mu'awiyah will govern the rein of Islam; so far as he obeys the Qur'an and Sunnah of the Prophet.
2. Mu'awiyah will not designate anyone as his successor.
3. Everyone will keep his rights.
4. Shi'as of Imam Ali will live in peace and will not be harassed.
5. Imam Hassan and Imam Husayn and the other family of the Prophet will remain in peace.
6. The caliphate will return to Imam Hassan or Imam Husayn after the death of Mu'awiyah.

In spite of the fact that Mu'awiyah broke many of the provisions of the peace treaty, Imam Hassan continued to abide by the treaty until his death in 50 Hijri. Not only that, his younger brother Imam Husayn respected the treaty for another ten years until the death of Mu'awiyah.

Imam Hassan was a wonderful man. He safeguarded Islam from civil war and evil. He was killed by poison by one of his wives on 28 Safar, 50 Hijri.

THE THIRD IMAM:
IMAM HUSAYN BIN ALI ASH-SHAHEED

Imam Husayn was born on 3 Shaban, 4 Hijri in Medina. Upon his birth, the Prophet took him in his lap, kissed him and named him Husayn. The Prophet loved his grandchildren profusely and he cared about them at every step of his life. Allah, in the Qur'an, called them Prophet' sons and declared them the leaders of the youth of heaven.

Imam Husayn took responsibility of the Imamate after the death of his brother Imam Hassan in 50 Hijri. He scrupulously abided by the peace treaty signed between his elder brother, Imam Hassan, and Mu'awiyah in order to avoid a civil war among the Muslims. Mu'awiyah, however, did not follow most of the provisions of the peace treaty. The worst violation he made was to nominate his son, Yazid, as his successor against all Islamic norms and the will of Sahaba and, of course, against the wishes of the people.

Mu'awiyah was not the best of Muslims in the world. His entire family, his father, grandfather, mother, and even his grandmother were all great enemies of Islam and tried their best to eradicate Islam. They were compelled to become Muslims only by circumstance. Mu'awiyah never made secret of the fact that he was a shrewd politician and wanted to keep the power to him by hook or crook.

In the case of Yazid, it was altogether a different ball game. He never hid his open animosity towards Islam. He did not observe the Islamic laws or Shariah ever during his life. He openly denounced Islam in his poetry and said there wasn't a Prophet or a *wahi* (revelation). According to him, all of this was part of a plot of the Banu-Hashims to gain power. With his personal background, Yazid succeeded against all tenets of Islam to head the Islamic government on 22 Rajab, 60 Hijri after the death of his father. The first order he issued after inheriting the Caliphate was ordering the governor of Medina to obtain oath of allegiance from Imam Husayn. Obviously,

Imam Husayn refused saying, "Persons like me do not pay allegiance to person like Yazid." Allegiance or *Bay'at* in Arabic means total surrender.

Now the defense of Islamic Shariah, and the religion of Allah was up to Imam Husayn. With Yazid there was no chance of a peace treaty although Imam Husayn tried everything to avoid clashing with him. Yazid would not agree to anything less than Imam Husayn's total surrender, meaning total destruction of the Shariah.

Once all peaceful means towards peace were exhausted, Imam Husayn knew what his fate would be if a battle were to occur. He determined his fate and charted his path very carefully to minimize the damage and maximize the gain. He left Medina for Mecca, a Muslim sanctuary, on 28 Rajab, 60 Hijri. In Mecca, he discovered that many people had disguised themselves as pilgrims and had been sent to secretly kill him. Therefore, he decided to leave for Kufa in Iraq, one day before Hajj. He had earlier received numerous invitations from Kufa to come and guide them to the right path. Before he could reach Kufa he was stopped by a platoon of the enemy under the command of Hurr. There were some arguments but they reached an agreement to camp at the place known as Karbala on 2 Muharram, 61 Hijri.

At Karbala, Imam Husayn had tried several times to avoid the tragic battle. Even the commander of Yazid's army, Omar Saad agreed and sent a note to his superiors to that affect, but Zaid, Yazid's local governor, would not listen to any logic. His only concern was to obtain Imam Husayn's oath of allegiance to which the Imam would never agree.

The Imam's companions numbering 72, stood against at least 30,000 of Yazid's army. On 7th Muharram, the supply of water and food was cut off to Imam Husayn's companions. On the morning of 10th Muharram, Hurr, a commander of Yazid's army, listening to the voice of his conscience, crossed over to the ranks of Imam Husayn to fight for the truth. The fight began around noon on 10th Muharram. The companions of Imam Husayn fought bravely. As Yazid's forces outnumbered them, all of Imam's companions fell as martyrs. Imam Husayn brought his six-month-old son to get some

158

water towards the end of the fight, but Yazid and his army had lost all instinct of humanity and one of the tyrants killed the toddler by shooting an arrow at him. The enemies were numb and devoid of any humanity. After killing the baby, they killed Imam Husayn.

Enemies of Islam and humanity had no limits. After killing Imam Husayn, they burned the camps of the Imam where the children and ladies were sheltered. Only one sick son, Zainul Abedin, survived Imam Husayn. Yazid's army captured him and other family members along with other ladies and children and carried the destitute caravan to Yazid in Syria.

Yazid openly ridiculed the family and proudly declared his victory. The sister of Imam Husayn, Zainab, and the captured son of Imam Husayn refuted their capture as a victory, and reminded him that it was respite given to a tyrant and a killer, according to the Qur'an. Yazid kept them in prison for one year and continued to torture them. Then the day came when Yazid realized his blunder. He tried to blame his subordinates for his actions. He released them from the prison and asked them if they wanted to return to Medina.

After release, Zainab took upon herself to make it known to the people the cruelty and high-handedness of Yazid. She carried out the commemoration of the martyrdom of Husayn in Damascus, the very capital of the tyrant, and tore apart the character of Yazid and his despicable actions. Imam Husayn and most of his family were killed, but Islam came out of this tragedy victorious. Today, Islam owes its existence to Imam Husayn. Thanks to Allah, every learned human being, irrespective of his religion, realizes this all across the world.

THE FOURTH IMAM:
IMAM ALI BIN HUSAYN AL SAJJAD

The Fourth Imam was named Ali after his grandfather, a common practice in Arabia. His title was Zainul-Abedin meaning the pride of worshipper. He was born on 15 Jamad-ul-Awwal, 38 Hijri.

Yazid perpetuated his terrorism over the Islamic world for two and a half years and died a remorseful death. His son Mu'awiyah, a relatively nice person, refused to succeed his father as the Caliph saying the caliphate was snatched wrongly from its owner, the Prophet's family. Not surprisingly, he was killed soon after. Another Ummayid, Marwan-bin-Hakam took over as the next Caliph. During his caliphate, assault on Islam continued. Imam Zainul-Abedin lived in Medina after the tragedy of Karbala. He was not directly victimized but was under house arrest for all practical purposes. Spies were all around him watching every action Imam.

He spent most of his time in the mosque praying and supplicating to Allah. His supplications were not limited to self-serving. Through these supplications, he taught the world great lessons. He taught Islamic spirit, *Nahi-anil-munkar, Amr-bil-maroof,* right and wrong, the oneness of Allah, the importance of the Prophet and his successors. They were not mere supplications, but enlightened utterances which answered many questions confronting the world then and today. They dealt with crisis and turmoil any Muslim, and for that matter a follower of any religion may pass through at some time. These supplications were later collected in a book and called *Sahifa-e-Kamila.*

In the beginning of the last century, when this book was presented to the Chancellor of Al-Azhar University of Egypt by late Dr. Mujtaba H. Kamoonpuri, he was totally amazed and said he never knew such a masterpiece of Arabic literature was available in Islamic treasure. Professor William Chitick of New York University has recently translated it into English.

It may not be out of place to mention here the research study made recently about the effect of supplication. It has been proven beyond doubt that supplication not only helps spiritually but also physically. Two groups of patients, each with thirty people, were selected that were already undergoing surgery. After the surgery, one group was given medication only and the other group was asked to pray for their health along with the medicine. The group that prayed recovered better and faster than the group who was only given medication.

In spite of being under house arrest in Medina, the Imam carried out all his duties of teaching the Qur'an, guiding the *Ummah,* taking care of the poor and destitute and running a school. He also helped adversaries of the Ahlul Bayt when they needed help. When Ummiyads started facing hard times, Marwan, one of the people from Banni Ummiyad came to the Imam for help. His family was given sanctuary in the Imam's house. He later became the ruler. Haseen-bin-Nameer, who killed the Imam's brother in Karbala, came running to the Imam for food and was given more than he needed. His contemporaries accepted the Imam as the most outstanding personality in collecting the sayings of the Prophet (ahadiths).

Imam Zainul-Abedin did not waste a moment of his life in reminding people everyday about the tragedy of Karbala. He was killed by poison on 24 Muharram, 95 Hijri.

THE FIFTH IMAM:
IMAM MUHAMMAD BIN ALI AL-BAQIR

The fifth Imam was born in Medina on 1 Rajab, 57 Hijri. He was popularly titled as Al-Baqir.

Imam Al-Baqir was brought up under the holy guidance of his grandfather Imam Husayn for three years. For thirty-four years, he was under the gracious guidance of his father, Imam Zainul-Abedin. A famous scholar belonging to the Sunnites School says: "Imam Muhammad Al-Baqir has disclosed the secrets of knowledge and wisdom and unfolded the principles of spiritual and religious guidance. Nobody can deny his exalted character, his God-given knowledge and his divinely gifted wisdom and his obligation and gratitude for the spreading of knowledge. He was a sacred and highly talented and spiritual leader, and for this reason he was popularly titled as Al-Baqir, which means the expounder of knowledge."

Kind at heart, spotless in character, sacred of soul, and noble by nature, the Imam devoted all his time submitting to Allah and advocating the teachings of the Prophet and his descendants. It is beyond the power of a man to recount the vast amount of knowledge and guidance he provided for the *Ummah*. As stated earlier, part of the Imam's job was to protect Islam. Following is one example of this service:

In the Imam's time the Islamic empire had become larger than the Roman Empire. However, the entire monetary system (including coins in Islamic countries) was based on the Roman system and Muslims were dependent upon it. The Roman Empire, knowing this, sent a message to the Islamic ruler in Syria to double the charges for the use of the Roman monetary system. When the ruler did not agree, the Roman king sent his emissary with the message that unless the ruler agreed to the increase in charges he would bring out new coins with a carving on it against the Prophet and Islam. This made the Islamic ruler extremely scared and nervous. Imam Muhammad Al-Baqir was urgently called to Syria from Medina for consultation and a solution to this major problem. The Imam told them to hold the emissary in Syria. While the emissary stayed, the Imam traveled to Syria and taught the concerned people how to mint a coin. Coins of different sizes and different values were immediately minted. Having this quietly completed, he sent a few samples of these coins to the Roman King through the emissary. The Roman king could not believe his eyes. The Imam saved Islam from a big embarrassment and calamity.

He also opened a large school in Medina for thousands of students. They were taught religion and many other subjects in the school. Details of this school are provided in the next section on the Sixth Imam, Imam Jafar As-Sadiq. As he continued, he was poisoned by an Ummayid caliph, and died on 1st Rajab, 114 H.

THE SIXTH IMAM:
IMAM JAFAR BIN MUHAMMAD AS-SADIQ

The Sixth Imam was born on Friday, 17 Rabi-ul-Alawwal, 83 Hijri in Medina. He was brought up by his grandfather, the Fourth Imam, Imam Zainul-Abedin for twelve years and then remained under the sacred patronage of his father, Imam Al-Baqir for nineteen years.

The period of his imamate coincided with the most revolutionary and eventful era of Islamic history. The downfall of the Ummayid Empire and the rise of the Abbaside caliphate both occurred during his imamate. The internal wars and political upheavals were bringing about speedy changes in the government. Therefore, the Imam witnessed the reign of various kings starting with Abdul Malik then the Ummayid ruler Marwan bin Hakam, Abu-Al-Abbass Al-Saffah, and Mansoor among the Abbasides. Because of the political strife between the groups of Ummayid and Abbasside, the Imam remained undisturbed during this time and was able to carry out his devotional duties. Because he was left in relative peace, he could carry out his mission to further the cause of Islam and spread the teachings of the Prophet.

Imam Jafar As-Sadiq was acclaimed throughout the Islamic world as a versatile scholar, knowing and teaching all types of knowledge. This attracted students from far off places who wanted to learn from the Imam. His followers soon numbered 4,000. The scholars and experts of Divine Law have quoted many ahadith from Imam Jafar Al-Sadiq. His students and followers compiled hundreds of books on various subjects of science and the arts. Besides teaching *fiqh* (religious law), narrating ahadith, and giving *tafsir* (commentary on the Qur'an), the Imam also imparted lessons in mathematics and chemistry to some of his students. Jabir bin Hayyan Tartoosi, a famous scholar of mathematics, was one of the Imam's students who benefited from the Imam's knowledge and guidance and wrote 400 books on various subjects.

It is an undeniable historical truth that most, if not all, of the scholars of Islam were indebted for their learning to the Ahlul Bayt who were the fountain of knowledge and learning. Allama Shibli in his book, *Seerah Al-Noman,* writes: "Abu Hanifa remained for a considerable period in attendance of Imam Jafar As-Sadiq, acquiring from him a great deal of precious knowledge in *Fiqh* and ahadith. Both the sects – Shi'a and Sunni -- believe that the source of Abu Hanifa's knowledge was mostly derived from his association with Imam Jafar As-Sadiq."

The Imam devoted his life to the cause of religious preaching and making known the teachings of the Prophet. Imam Muhammad Baqir saved Islam from impoverishment when he started the movement of renaissance and Imam Jafaar As-Sadiq continued his father's work.As rulers were involved in their own political strife, Imam Jafar As-Sadiq wasn't attacked as other Imams had been, so he was not interrupted for a few years in his religious activities. He was the first one who imparted knowledge about the origins of this world including its movement on the axis and the opacity and transparency of objects.

He provided a composition of the human body and explained hydrogen gas. He divulged the theory of light, time and space. He explained bacteria and how diseases are spread. He discussed the expansion and contraction of the universe and pollution of the environment. He showed the vastness of the world. Of the knowledge possessed by an Imam, he was one of the most knowledgeable human beings, and he shared this knowledge with ready learners. An Abbaside caliph eventually had him poisoned. He died on 15th Shawal, 148 H.

THE SEVENTH IMAM:
IMAM MOOSA BIN JAFFER AL-KAZIM

The Seventh Imam was born in Abwa—a small town near Medina —on 7 Safar, 128 Hijri.

The Fifth and the Sixth Imams had the time to show glimpses of the vastness of the imamate's knowledge. Students from all over the world came to learn from them. The Abbasside rulers did not like this once they established their rule. They were always afraid of the immense power wielded by Imams among the people. The result was obvious. After the martyrdom of the Sixth Imam, no Imam was allowed to live in Medina to further Islam and share Islamic teachings with the *Ummah*.

For the first ten years, the Seventh Imam remained in Medina to perform his religious duties. He was later called to Iraq. Out of his 35 years of imamate, he spent some 17 years in prison in Iraq. The rulers often shifted him from prison to prison with the instruction to the prisoner guard to treat him cruelly. It so happened that each guard, after seeing Imam's behavior, became his devotee and would eventually was fired by the ruler. Even during his imprisonment, the Imam continued his religious duties of teaching, advising, and leading the *Ummah*.

During this time, a lot of good Muslims, including some of his children, migrated to other countries like Iran and Yemen on the advice of the Imam. The Imam wrote a few books, most important of them being *Musnad Imam Moosa al-Kazim*. He carried out all his duties in the best possible way under the given circumstances. He was poisoned by the Abbaside Caliph and died on 25 Rajab, 183 Hijri.

THE EIGHTH IMAM: IMAM ALI BIN MOOSA AR-RIZA

Imam Ali-Riza was born in Medina on 11 Zilqaad, 148 Hijri. He was brought up under the holy guidance of his father for 35 years. His own insight and brilliance in religious matters combined with excellent training and education given by his father made him unique in his spiritual leadership. He was a living example of the piety of the Prophet and chivalry and generosity of Imam Ali.

165

Imam Reza had inherited great qualities from his ancestors. His mind and heart showed the nobility of his ancestors. He was a versatile person and had full command of many languages. Ibne-Athir Jazeri correctly said that Imam Riza was undoubtedly the greatest saint and greatest scholar of the second Islamic century. He luckily got the opportunity to show his stature to the Muslim world.

The tragedy of Karbala and the education given at the school established by the Fifth and the Sixth Imams had opened the eyes of the Muslims. With the change of regime from Ummayid to Abbasside, people had started deciphering between right and wrong. The thinking of the Arab people had changed. They had finally recognized the importance of Imams, their knowledge, their piety, and their nearness to Allah. The imprisonment of the Seventh Imam had also awakened the people. Now there was a demand all around the Muslim world to benefit from the presence of the Imam.

The above factors forced the ruler of the time, Mamoon-Al-Rasheed, to offer the reign of caliphate to Imam Ali-Riza. Mamoon could not help giving him great esteem because of the Imam's piety, wisdom, knowledge, modesty and personality. In 200 Hijri, Mamoon had sent an invitation to Abbassides to come and stay with him as his guest. About 33,000 Abbassides responded to the invitation and came to stay as royal guests. During their stay at the capital, Mamoon very closely observed them noting their capabilities and he arrived at the conclusion that none of them deserved to succeed him. He, therefore, spoke to them all in an assembly in 201 Hijri telling them that he had decided to appoint Imam Riza to be his successor and he demanded the assembly to give their allegiance to the Imam. Imam Riza initially refused the offer but was forced, and he eventually accepted it with the condition that he would not interfere with the day-to-day administration.

When the Imam went with the royal entourage from Medina to Iraq, about 35,000 *ulema* (learned persons) stood waiting for him to have a glimpse of him with pen in hand ready to write pious words spoken from him. When the Imam reached close to the city of Nishapur, he was asked to narrate at least one hadith. He did so. This hadith is now known as the Golden hadith *(Hadith Al-Zahab),* saying: *"La llaha Illallah* is a castle of Allah and whoever enters it is safe, but there are few conditions to this and I am one of the conditions."

Imam Riza was declared as the successor of Mamoon in front of 35,000 people. It was also declared that future royal robes would be green, the color that had the unique distinction of being that of the Imam's dress. The royal decree was published saying that Imam Riza would succeed Mamoon and his title would be Ali-Riza min Ale-Muhammad. The Caliph also issued a coin with Imam's profile engraved on it

Even after the declaration of the succession when there was an opportunity for the Imam to live a splendid royal life, he did not pay any heed to material comfort and devoted himself entirely with spreading true Islamic ideology with the Prophet's teachings and the Qur'an. He had several hundred discussions with non-Muslims, including Christians Jews, and atheists of the time on religious subjects. He would defeat them in their debates. He also made great contributions in the field of medicine. His rising popularity and reverence, however made Mamoon too jealous to resist his plan to get him secretly poisoned so that he may not remain alive to be his successor. He was poisoned to death on 23 Zeqada, 203 Hijri (or 17th Safar, 203 H.)

THE NINTH IMAM:
IMAM ALI BIN MUHAMMAD AT-TAQI

Imam Muhammad Al-Taqi was born in Medina on Friday, 10 Rajab, 195 Hijri. His famous title was At-Taqi. Imam Muhammad At-Taqi was brought up by his father Imam Ali-Riza for four years. As stated in the previous section, Imam Reza had to migrate from

Medina to Khorasan (Iran) leaving his young son behind. Imam Reza was fully aware of the treacherous character of the ruling king and was sure that he would not return to Medina anymore. So before his departure from Medina, he declared his son Muhammad At-Taqi as his successor and passed all his treasures of divine knowledge and spiritual genius on to him. The lifespan of Muhammad At-Taqi was the shortest among all Imams. He became Imam at the age of eight years old and poisoned at the age of 25, yet he commanded great respect and esteem.

The Ninth Imam had many characteristics of Prophet Muhammad's and Imam Ali's personality. His hereditary qualities comprised of gallantry, boldness, charity, learning, forgiveness, and tolerance. The brightest and the most outstanding aspects of his nature and character were to show hospitality and courtesy to all without discrimination, to help the needy, to observe equality under all circumstances, to ive a simple life, to help the orphans, the poor, and homeless, to impart learning to those interested in the acquisition of knowledge, and guiding people to the right path.

It may be interesting to add here the political climate at that time. For the consolidation of his empire, it was realized by the Abbaside Caliph Mamoon that it was necessary to win the sympathy and support of Iranians who had always been friendly to the Ahlul Bayt, the progeny of Prophet Muhammad. Consequently, Mamoon was forced, from a political point of view, to establish contact with the tribe of Bani Fatima to gain the favor of Shi'as. Accordingly, he declared Imam Riza as his heir - even against the Imam's will. Mamoon also had his sister marry Imam Riza. Mamoon expected that Imam Ali Riza would lend him his support in political affairs of the state. But when Mamoon discovered that the Imam had little interest in political matters and that the masses were more and more committed themselves to him due to his spiritual greatness, he had him poisoned. Yet the necessity to establish contact with the Shi'as still remained. Mamoon, therefore, decided to marry his daughter

Ummal Fazl to the Ninth Imam Muhammad At-Taqi, and with this objective, he summoned the Imam from Medina to Iraq.

Obviously, the Bani Abbass were extremely upset when they came to know that Mamoon was planning to marry his daughter to Imam Muhammad At-Taqi. A delegation of leaders met Mamoon in order to deter him from doing this. Meanwhile, Mamoon continued to admire the knowledge and excellence of the Imam. He said that though Imam Muhammad At-Taqi was still young, he was a true successor to his father and that not even the most profound scholar of the Islamic world could compete with him. When the Abbassides heard this, they chose Yahya Bin Aksam, the greatest scholar and the juror of Baghdad, to challenge the Imam.

Mamoon issued an announcement to organize a grand meeting for the contest. A large number of people from all parts of the kingdom came to watch. Apart from the nobles and high officials, there were as many as 900 chairs reserved for scholars and learned persons only. They wondered how a young child could compete with the veteran judge and greatest scholar of Iraq on religious law.

Imam Muhammad A-Taqi was seated next to Mamoon on his throne face to face with Yahya Bin Aksam. Yahya Bin Aksam started by addressing the Imam in this way: "Do you permit me to ask you a question?" "Ask me whatever you wish," said the Imam in the typical tone of his ancestors.

Yahya Bin Aksam then asked the Imam: "What is your verdict about a man who indulges in hunting while he is in the state of Ehram"? (In the code of religious laws, hunting is forbidden when a person is in Ehram). The Imam at once replied: "The question is vague and is misleading. You should have definitely mentioned whether the person hunted within the jurisdiction of Ka'abah or outside, whether he was literate or illiterate, whether he was a slave or a free citizen, whether he was a minor, whether it was the first time or if he had done it previously. Also, whether the object of his hunting was a bird or some other creature, whether he hunted in the day or at night, whether the hunter repented for his action or persisted on it, whether he hunted secretly or openly, whether the Ehram was for Umra or for Hajj. Unless all these points are explained, no specific answer can be given to this question."

Yahya Bin Aksam was haggard in listening to these words of the Imam and the entire gathering was dumbfounded. There was no limit to Mamoon's pleasure. He expressed his sentiments of joy and admiration openly. He said to the Imam: "Bravo, bravo, well done. Oh Abu Jafar your learning and attainments are beyond all praise."

As Mamoon wanted the Imam's opponent to be fully exposed, he said to the Imam, "You may also put some questions to Yahya bin Aksam."

Then Yahya also reluctantly said to the Imam: "Yes you may ask me some questions. If I know the answer, I will tell it. Otherwise I should request you to give its answer." Thereupon the Imam asked the question to which Yahya could not reply. Eventually, the Imam answered the question. The Mamoon at this moment said:"Did I not say that the Imam comes from the family, which has been chosen by Allah as repository of knowledge and learning? Is there any one in the world who can match even the children of the pious family?" All of them shouted: "Undoubtedly, there is no parallel to Imam Muhammad At-Taqi." At the same assembly, Mamoon wedded his daughter Umul Fazl to the Imam and liberally distributed charity and gifts among his subjects as a mark of rejoicing. One year after his marriage, the Imam returned to Medina from Baghdad with his wife and he set about preaching the commandments of Allah. The Imam was poisoned by King Mo'tasim Abbasi, and died on 29th Zilqad, 220 AH.

THE TENTH IMAM:
IMAM ALI BIN MUHAMMAD AN-NAQI

Iman Ali An-Naqi was born in the suburbs of Medina on Friday,

5 Rajab, 214 Hajri. Like his father he was elevated to the rank of Imam in his childhood. He was six years old when his father, Imam Muhammad At-Taqi, died.

In the political arena, three Abbasides caliphs had changed reins. After the death of Mamoon Rashid, Mo'tasim succeeded him and was later followed by the Caliph Wasiq Billah. Imam Ali An-Naqi lived peacefully in the first five years of the reign of Wasiq Billah. After Wasiq Billah, Mutawakkil came to power. Being too occupied with his state affairs, Mutawakkil did not have the time to harass the Imam and his followers for four years. As soon as he was free from the hassle of his state affairs, he started giving trouble to the Imam. The Imam had devoted himself with the sacred mission of preaching in Medina and thus earned the faith of the people, as well as their allegiance and recognition of his great knowledge and attributes. This reputation of the Imam evoked jealousy and malice in caliph Mutawakkil against him.

The Governor of Medina wrote to Mutawakkil that Imam Ali An-Naqi had been maneuvering a coup against the government and a multitude of Muslims had pledged support to him. Although enraged by this report, Mutawakkil preferred the diplomacy of not arresting the Imam under the garb of pretended respect and love towards the Imam. He planned to put him under life imprisonment after inviting him to his palace. After him, his son Mo'laz Billah became caliph who got the Imam poisoned on 3 Rajab, 254 Hijri.

THE ELEVENTH IMAM:
IMAM HASSAN BIN ALI AL-ASKARI

Imam Hassan Al-Askari was born in Medina on Monday, 10 Rabi-uthani, 232 Hijri. He was popularly known as Al-Askari.

Imam Hassan Al-Askari spent 22 years of his life under the patronage of his father, Imam Ali Ali-Naqi, after whose martyrdom, he became the divinely commissioned Imam. During his life, the

Abbassides rulers were entangled in political tussles. They, however, very much dreaded the existence of Imam Hassan Al-Askari, the rightful and divinely ordained Imam of the family of the Prophet. They knew that the son of this Imam would be Mahdi, or guide, to humanity for all times until the Day of Judgment as declared by the Prophet. So the Abbassides rulers inflicted all sorts of calamities on the Imam. Imam Al-Askari spent the greater part of his life in prison. When he was out of prison many restrictions were placed on his movement. In spite of this, he always fulfilled the duties of the imamate with matchless perseverance.

It has been said that the Imam's job is not only propagating and preserving Islamic teachings and teaching the Qur'an, but also the preservation of Islam as a religion. Whenever a time of crisis came to help Islam, they always stepped foreword to help. One such time came during the eleventh Imam's life.

In Iraq, there had been no rain for a few years and the country was facing a severe draught. A Christian priest prayed for rain in the presence of a big gathering and it started raining heavily. He did this more than once. The Muslim's belief in their religion got shaken. The Abbasside ruler was worried about the people regarding their faith and his kingdom. He was advised by his minister to seek the help of a member of the Prophet's family. Imam Al-Askari was called from the jail for help.

Imam Al-Askari asked the priest to pray for the rain. When the priest started to pray the Imam ordered his servant to take away whatever the priest was holding in his hand. The priest was holding a piece of bone, which was taken from him. The Imam asked him to pray again. The priest prayed but it did not rain this time. The Imam told the crowd that it was the piece of the bone of a prophet held in the open sky by the priest that caused the rain. Allah sent rain due to the blessings (*barkat*) of this bone whenever it was exposed bare under the sky. The Imam buried the bone in the ground and then he went in the open field to pray and it rained heavier than before. The

172

shaken belief of the Muslims was strengthened once again by one prayer of the Imam. He too was poisoned by Caliph Mo'tamad on 8 Rabi-ul-awal, 260 Hijri at the young age of twenty-eight.

THE TWELFTH IMAM:
IMAM MUHAMMAD BIN HASSAN AL-MAHDI

Imam Muhammad Al-Mahdi is the Imam of our times. He was born on 15 Shaban, 256 Hijra in the city of Samarra in Iraq.

The Prophet had prophesied his imamate. Innumerable traditions quoted right from the Prophet can be seen in many books about the coming of Imam Mahdi. In a number of books written by Sunni and Shi'a writers, details about this Imam can be read along with the prophecy of Prophet Muhammad. Many Sunni writers accumulated the ahadith in complete volumes, for example in *Al-Bayan fi Al-akhbar-e-Sahib Al-Zaman* by Hafiz Muhammad Bin Yusuf Shafe'e and Sehah Abu Daud and Sunan ibn Maja. All the above books record the ahadith bearing evidence of the coming of this Imam.

The Imam was brought up by his father Imam Hassan Al-Askari, the Eleventh Imam. The Eleventh Imam used all the protective measures in taking care of his child as Abu Talib had done in connection with safeguarding Prophet Muhammad. While Imam Hassan Askari kept the birth of his child and affair of his infancy a well-guarded secret, he made him accessible only to some exclusive devotees and sincere friends in order to familiarize them with their would-be Imam to whom they would make their allegiance.

When the Twelfth Imam was born, his father named him Muhammad. On the third day after his birth, Imam Hassan Al-Askari brought forth the child to show him to some of his followers and declared: "Here is my successor and yours' would-be Imam! He is the very *Qaim* in whose reverence your head will bow down. He will reappear to fill the earth with blessings and justice after it had been abounding in sins and vices."

Mu'awiyah Ibne Hakeem, Muah Muhammad Ibne Ayub and Muhammad Ibne Usman mentioned that they called upon Imam Al-Hassan Al-Askari with the deputation of forty people. The Imam showed them his newly born child and said: "This is your Imam after me! All of you should unanimously submit your allegiance to him and should not allow any controversy over the matter since that would lead to peril. Also remember that he will no longer be visible to you."

Imam Hassan Askari died on 8 Rabi-ul-Awwal, 260 Hijra and the day marked the inception of his son's imamate being the source of spiritual guidance for the whole universe. As according to Allah's will, all the affairs related to this Imam were to remain strictly behind the curtain. The Twelfth Imam commissioned some of his deputies and ambassadors who had been looking after the religious affairs from the time of his father and advised them to act as associates between the people and concealed Imam. They conveyed the problems and religious queries of the people to the Imam and brought back the verdicts and answers of the Imam to the people. It was by the will of Allah that he disappeared and will again reappear by the will of Allah. This will be a prelude to the Day of Judgment.

During the absence of our Twelfth Imam it is our duty to be expecting his appearance. To remain straight and steadfast in our beliefs we have to follow *Amr–Bil-Maroof* and *Nahi-anil-Munkar*. We have to educate ourselves and our children. We should try to excel in both the worlds. To excel in the world hereafter we have to excel in this world. We have to pass on the torch of education, excellence, and truthfulness of our faith to our next generation to prepare them to meet our Imam and stay under his command.

EXERCISES

1. What are some traits that all the Imams have in common?

2. Write a poem in honor of one of the twelve Imams using some of the information in this chapter.

3. What are the purposes of the commemorations of Karbala today? What activities best honor these purposes and best honor Imam and his sacrifice?

4. What are some events or characteristics of each Imam that distinguish him from all the others?

5. Can you find out about the nicknames of the Imams – what are they and what are their meanings? For example, Sadiq means truthful. Could any of them be applied to you? How could you modify your behavior so that you could be called by one of these nicknames?

6. Name one challenge faced by each Imam and how he overcame it.

7. Where is twelfth Imam now? How can we have faith in his existence while he is hidden from us? Why is he hidden from us?

8. When will twelfth Imam return? What are our duties while he is hidden?

9. How long has twelfth Imam been alive? Why do you believe that someone could live so long when we do not see anyone around us living so long? Are there are other things or events you believe that seem unlikely? Please write about a few to share with classmates and explain your belief in them.

10. How can Imam serve his role while he is hidden?

11. Please read Dua Ahad and discuss as a class the meaning and purpose of this dua. Also study some ziyarat of all the Imams. What is their purpose for Imams and for us? Can you memorize any or prepare a powerpoint presentation of any of them with meaning included?

Chapter Twelve

ISLAMIC WAY OF LEADING LIFE

*"O our God give us goodness of this world and the world after
and keep us away from the fire of hell"*

The Qur'an is the main source for the Islamic social system. It directs Muslims on how to organize society by setting rules regarding family orders, social relations, economic systems, judicial policies, politics, and law and order. In fact, it teaches these things to all humanity, but Muslims are ordered to follow these rules. These complete sets of guidelines or rules help in forming the Islamic society as well as worshipping Allah.

The Prophet explained these Islamic systems to us through his actions and traditions. By obeying the Qur'an, Muslims can live a happy and peaceful life in this world and gain reward in the life hereafter. They can also achieve justice and dignity while leading a life of brotherhood and love. The Qur'an says: "And (as far) the believing men and the believing women, they are guardians of each other, they enjoin good and forbid evil and keep up prayer and pay the poor rate, and obey Allah and His Apostle; (as for) these, Allah will show mercy to them; surely Allah is Mighty and Wise." (9:71)

Islam provides various systems to lead an organized life and create social, political, judicial, and spiritual excellence, so that people can live happily without any problems, conflicts or misery. Among the main systems of Islam, which concern organizing the life of human being, we find six systems. In other words, life can be organized in six categories namely; (1) ritual system, (2) political system, (3) economical system, (4) social system, (5) *Jihad* system, and (6) judicial system. The brief explanation of each of these systems will acquaint the readers how to practice Islam, how to live a happy life by following these principles, and how to avoid man-made system and laws.

THE RITUAL SYSTEM

The main objective of religion is to introduce mankind to their Creator and to teach them to worship Him, the One who has no partner. Islam legislated a series of rituals which explained how to worship and obey the Creator such as prayer, supplication (*Dua*), commemoration, dedication, fasting, pilgrimage, one fifth levy as yearly *Khums*, charity for the poor (*Zakat*), enjoining what is good and forbidding what is bad, calling to accept Islam (*Dawah*), undertaking holy struggle or *jihad* in the way of Allah, and reciting the Qur'an and performing other ritual acts to bring the human beings nearer to Allah.

Islam made it clear that these rituals keep human beings from deviating from the worship of Allah and no one has the right to worship anything or anyone other than Allah, the Creator and the Sustainer of this world.

Worship entails certain conditions such as true intention and true sincerity to Allah alone so that an act or deed is far from being sanctimonious and hypocritical which would nullify the deed for getting reward.

Islam also prevents Muslims from devoting themselves solely to worshipping and not working to earn the necessities of life in this world. Allah has said in the Qur'an: "And seek by means of what Allah has given you the future abode, and do not neglect your portion of this world, and (do good) to other as Allah has done good to you, and do not seek to make mischief in the land, surely Allah does not love the mischief-makers." (28:77)

Islam created a balance between the life of this world and the hereafter. Muslims should strive for both, this life and the hereafter. He should grow crops, undertake development of land and business, indulge in manufacturing, seek knowledge, and obtain good and lawful things of this world and perform all obligatory duties as well as work for his life hereafter.

Worship in Islam besides being obedience to Allah has various social, psychological, and sanitary benefits. Worship encourages people to shun arrogance and vanity. When a Muslim prostrates himself before Allah during prayer he or she wants to make him or herself submissive to the Lord. Prayer needs cleanliness that in turn preserves Muslims' health and beauty. Similarly, fasting gives Muslims strength and determination and fills them with sympathy for the sufferings of the poor while also preserving health of the body.

Congregational prayers instruct the Muslims on how to be cooperative and acquaint themselves with each other. Giving charity and financial offering, helps to solve economic and social problems. Naturally, Hajj teaches endurance and provides an opportunity to interact with Muslims from different nationalities so they can cooperate in understanding and solve their common problems ultimately benefiting Islam and Muslims as a whole.

While reciting supplication or *Dua*, a person feels he or she is in need of Allah, the Most High, and he or she liberates and purifies him or herself from the pride and vanity and asks witness for themselves, his or her parents and other believers. He or she purifies themselves from selfishness and love of good, to all people due to his or her calling for goodness for them. In this way, the best morals are created which benefits all. These virtues educate Muslims perfection, socially and ethically, and encourage them to participate in the progress of society and its reformation besides gaining obedience involved in worshipping Allah alone.

POLITICAL SYSTEM

The Prophet founded an Islamic state after his immigration to Medina. The Prophet obliges the Muslim to establish government and rule people on the foundation of justice and equality so that the people can live happily under Divine just rule. An Islamic state is a state which practices the principals from the Qur'an and the Prophet's traditions, and achieves justice and equality for the people. In Islam the political system is based on the following principles.

Master of the universe is Allah: In Islam, Allah has the sovereign power, the source of all power and He and only He is lawgiver. He knows good from bad and His words are final. This principle is supported by the following Qur'anic verses:

1. "He, to Whom belongs the kingdom of the heaven and the earth, and Who did not take to Himself a son and Who has no associate in the kingdom, and Who created everything, then ordained for it a measurement." (25:2)

2. "Blessed is He in Whose hand is the kingdom and He has power over all things." (67:1)

Human beings are Allah's representatives on earth: Allah has made us human beings as His representatives and taught us good from bad. Now it is up to us to act and carry on good deeds according to the orders of Allah. The Qur'an says:

1. "I am going to place in the earth a Khalifa." (2:30).

2. "Then We made you successors in the land after them, so that We may see how you act." (10:14)

The consultation among the servants of Allah: In Islamic political system, consultation takes the form of Shura, which means participation in listening to other points of view. People should form government, and make legislation by proper consultation among them. Islam does not believe in totalitarianism or despotism. This is based on the Quran.

1. "Take counsel with them in affairs." (3:159)

2. "And those who respond to their Lord and keep up payer,

and their rule is to take counsel among themselves, and who spend out of what We have given them."(42:38).

Accountability of Government: Nobody is above law; everyone is responsible and accountable for his actions to Allah. Rulers are doubly accountable towards Allah and also to the people they govern. By taking an office, the ruler has made himself servant of people. Two Qur'anic verses on this subject are:

Law and order: In Islam, law and order in a society is utmost important. The judiciary is above and independent of the executive ranch. The most important point for the government is to legislate based on the Qur'an and *Sunnah* and its prime objective is to maintain law and order among the citizens of the land without any distinction. The Qur'an says:

1. "O' you who believe! Be custodians of justice (and) witnesses for God, even though against yourselves or your parents or your relatives. Whether a man is rich or poor, God is his greater well-wisher than you. So follow not the behests of lust lest you swerve from justice; and if you prevaricate or avoid (giving evidence), God is cognizant of all that you do." (4:135).

2. "Surely Allah commands you to make over trusts to their owners and that when you judge between people you judge with justice; surely Allah admonishes you with what is excellent; surely Allah is Seeing, Hearing." (4:58)

3. "O you who believe! Be upright for Allah, bearers of witness with justice, and let not hatred of a people incite you not to act equitably; act equitably, that is nearer to piety, and be careful of (your duty to) Allah; surely Allah is Aware of what you do." (5:8)

The equality before law: In the eyes of law and Islamic political system everyone is equal and innocent until proven otherwise. There is no discrimination based on color, caste, religion, territory, language or sex. The Qur'an says:

1. "Surely, the most honorable of you with Allah is the one among you most careful (of his duty); surely Allah is Knowing, Aware." (49:13)

Right of criticism and reckoning: Under the Islamic political system, every Muslim has the right to make constructive criticism of the government and to enter into useful argument with the officials or representative of the government. Any qualified Muslim, man or woman, has the right to take part in government or politics and manage the affairs of the state.

Obedience to the ruler: Obedience to the Muslim ruler is obligatory as long as the ruler complies with the Islamic laws and obligations and establishes justice for the people and he does not act against the interest of the state. The ruler in the Islamic political system is like the father at the family level who is responsible for managing affairs of the family. It is the father who should supervise and educate his children. On the other hand, the children and other family members should obey him; listen to his words and his advice. The Islamic society, similarly, needs the government and head of the state, which should be able to manage the affairs of the Muslim nation. Muslims call this head of the state an Imam or leader.

Imamate or leadership: Islam gives much importance to the leadership or imamate. The Prophet was the Imam and head of the state of the Muslims during his blessed life in addition to his being the Prophet and the Messenger of Allah as declared by Allah in the following Qur'anic verse:

1. "Only Allah is your Vali and His Apostle and those who believe,

those who keep up prayers and pay poor-rate (zakat) while they bow in homage (before God)." (5:55)

The commentators of the Qur'an unanimously agreed that the above verse was revealed in relation to Imam Ali and that he was master of the Muslims. At the end of the last Hajj before his death, the Prophet raised the arms of Imam Ali in presence of tens of thousands of Muslims and posed them the questions. "Am I not more appropriate to rule over you than yourself?" "Yes, oh Messenger of Allah the multitude chided." "Am I not more appropriate to rule over the faithful than themselves?" the Prophet asked. Again he got reply from the crowd "Yes, oh Messenger of Allah." "Then this man (raising Imam Ali's arm) is the master of whom I am his master. Oh Allah support those who support him and desert those who desert him."

It is unanimously agreed that the Islamic *Ummah* is in need of a fair Islamic and a just leader who establishes the right and preserves the *Ummah's* interests. All Muslims should strive to establish the Islamic state, abiding by the Islamic law and ruling according to the Prophet's tradition so they can live in security and sovereignty. The Muslim leader should have the following qualifications.

1. He should be a jurisprudent, (a *faqih*) who should be learned in Islamic laws and teachings.
2. He should be a just man committed to Islam.
3. He should be competent and capable of managing the *ummah's* affairs.
4. He should not fear anyone save Allah.

Allah has said in the Qur'an:

1. "And do not incline on those who are unjust, lest the fire touches you, and you have no guardians besides Allah, then

you shall not be helped." (11:113)

2. "And who ever judges not according to what Allah has sent down they are the transgressor." (5:47)

Unfortunately, at present there are Muslim states ranging from thirty to thirty-five in number and none of them can stand to the real test of the Islamic political system. They are Muslim states more so than Islamic states. The leaders are not elected, they are not just, and the Muslims have no right in their own state. Everyone is looking with hope towards the Islamic Republic of Iran and other new and young emerging rulers of the Middle East and Muslim states for a better political system and better life for their people.

ECONOMIC SYSTEM

A good economy is the backbone of any society; obviously it is one of the most important parts of our life, but not the life itself.

Funds are needed for leading a satisfying life, but life is not for solely to collect funds. One can earn money only the right way, giving away portions assigned for the poor and others. The Islamic economic system is based on the following principles.

Halal earning: Earnings and expenses both should be halal (permissible) and jayz, as laid down by the Qur'an and Sunnah. The following types of earnings are not Jayz:

1. Earning from sale, service, and production of alcohol is forbidden in Islam and cannot be allowed in an Islamic society. Similarly, gambling and interest are haram.

2. Hoarding food and other items of basic necessity of life are forbidden.

3. Earning through fraud, deceit, burglary, and any other matter not recommended by Islam, is haram. Unlawful expenses or being extravagant is severely condemned in Islam. Remember,

our life and all our belongings actually belong to Allah. We are only His servants and will have to answer all our feats.

Economic individual liberty: One can own and posses as much money and property as possible provided (1) it has been earned in the recommended way and (2) its taxes have been paid.

Payment of taxes: There are two taxes in Islam. Zakat is paid on earnings, and Khums is paid on savings. The purposes of these taxes are the same as any other taxes in the world, namely: (1) Welfare and other needs of the state should be fulfilled by these taxes. (2) These taxes should narrow the gap between the rich and the poor.

Interest is haram in Islam: There are many Ayahs in the Qur'an, which forbid interest; it is not a matter of discussion. One of the Ayahs says:

"O, all who believe do not take interest doubling and quadrupling and keep up duty to Allah so that you may prosper."(3:130)

These two taxes have to differentiate from commission and business. Remember, as we said earlier, that *Zakat* and *Khums* help the poor. Someone has said very rightly that *Zakat* and *Khums* help the poor while interest helps the rich.

Law of inheritance: Islamic law of inheritance is very explicit in the Qur'an. The law prevents hoarding of money or wealth among individuals. It keeps money circulating from one person to another.

In summary:

1. The economic system in Islam is a system which outlines how to gain wealth, invest it, spend, and distribute it justly, and

also how to achieve financial equality among the people.

2. In Islam, the economic system is established on the foundation of justice and for meeting the needs of the people to save them from poverty and deprivation.

3. The main reasons of poverty and unemployment are poor consumption habits, weak distribution, hoarding commodities, and cheating with price. The Islamic economic system prohibits these factors to come into play.

4.   Islam forbids usury and monopoly and sets the rules of financial obligations so that money and wealth will not be in the hands of few, while the masses live in poverty and misery.

5. Islam forbids extravagance, vulgarity, and spending money on forbidden things like alcohol, dancing, singing, gambling, etc. It deters human wealth from corruption and loss.

6. The Islamic state is responsible for the poor, disabled, and those who are unable to find a source of living, or who annot find anyone to support them and provide them food.

7. Of course, the Islamic economics system, like any other economic system, is responsible for meeting all needs of the community.

SOCIAL SYSTEM

The social system is comprised of the human relationships and bonds that tie members of the society together. Relationships with one's family members, neighbors, relatives, the orphans of the Muslim nation everywhere, the non-Muslims who live within the Islamic society, are all part of the social system. An Islamic society is a society in which members have faith in Islam, apply its law to their daily life, abide by its moral standards of love, brotherhood, equality, mercy, trust, whose members perform religious duties and abstain from doing what is unlawful in Islam.

In a true Islamic society, drinking alcohol, practicing usury, practicing immorality, deceiving each other, giving or taking bribe, doing injustice, trespassing other's right are prohibited.

The following are some of the principles of Islamic social systems:

Love and loyalty among the faithful: Allah clearly says in the Qur'an: "The believers are but brethren, therefore make peace between your brethren and be careful of (your duty to) Allah that mercy may be bestowed on you." (47:10) Another Qur'anic verse says: "And (as for) the believing men and the believing women, they are guardians of each other; ..."(9:71)

Rights of individual: The Islamic social system respects the rights of individuals and of collective groups, both having mutual rights and duties toward each other. Non-Muslims also have their rights, and they need to be protected.

Mutual Kindness: Islamic society is built on right, just, and mutual kindness. Allah says in the Qur'an: "Surely Allah has enjoined justice, and doing of good (to others) and giving of gifts to your relatives, and He forbids indecency and evil and rebellion; He admonishes you so that you may be mindful." (16:90)

The bond of unity and cooperation: Allah says in the Qur'an: "...And help one another in goodness and piety, and do not help one another in sin and aggression." (5:2) In every aspect of life, the members of an Islamic society should cooperate whole heartedly with each other, for example, in building mosques and schools, helping the needy, fighting oppression, establishing economical, social, and cultural institutions, and for all other forms of cooperation in the society.

Maintaining good moral ethics: Other significant principles of the social system in Islam include honesty, sacrifice, mercy, sympathy, love, faithfulness, keeping ties with near kins, respecting neighbors, and being kind and gentle to elders. These are the factors which consolidate society and make its members happy, thus making them sovereign and free from worries and pressure. It is our responsibility to form an Islamic society and keep it safe from subversive and corrupt elements by means of enjoining the good and forbidding the evil.

SYSTEM OF JIHAD

Jihad has been misinterpreted these days. Allah has ordained Jihad as the means by which the Muslims survive with dignity, and defend their homeland. It is also a way to fight oppression and the threat of outside intervention. It is also a process of internal struggle to overcome our own weaknesses and extravagant desires. Allah made Jihad an obligated duty on all Muslims to defend themselves against the enemies of Allah, and protect their homeland, religion and influence from any aggression of the infidels and oppressors. Allah says in the Qur'an "And fight with them until there is no more persecution and religion should be only for Allah." (8:39).

Jihad does not mean Holy War; it is rather a struggle to achieve your goal and objective. It has to be for Allah, by Allah's rule. One has no right to change Allah's rules.

There are two types of Jihad; *Jihad-ul-Akbar* (major) and *Jihad-e-Asghar* (minor). *Jihad-ul-Akbar* or bigger struggle is against one's own self. It is against the bad habits accumulated in us, like illiteracy, laziness, ignorance, being timid, jealousy, deceitfulness, cheating, lying, stealing and other moral problems that all need to be fought within ourselves. It is important, and difficult to fight these bad habits. If one does not fight against these problems, he cannot be considered a good Muslim.

The second type of Jihad, *Jihad-e-Asghar* is to fight the external enemy. According to our philosophy and belief, this Jihad is undertaken only by the order of the Prophet or Imam. They are the only ones who can order us to fight. Since our Imam is in occultation, we

188

cannot attack anybody and start war. This has to be differentiated from defensive war. If somebody attacks us on our homeland, it is the duty of every dweller to fight with all his might.

Rules of Fighting

There are rules of fighting in Islam. There is a list of do's and don'ts given by the Prophet and explained by Imam Ali. For example: (1). during the battle, the Holy Places and Holy People are to be protected from such attack, (2). farms and farmlands, animals, forest, fields, are not supposed to be burned or destroyed by the enemy, and (3). the elderly, children, and women are to be protected in war. There is a whole list of such restrictions. Islamic Jihad is to purify life and make it better, not to make it miserable for the Muslims or their enemies.

Terrorism and Jihad

The recent terrorist attacks against the American facilities have given rise to a wrong connotation of associating Islam with the terrorism. The followers of terrorism have made people believe for their ulterior political motive that they are waging Jihad. The details of Jihad given above do not lend support to their claim of undertaking Jihad.

All religions teach peace, honesty, love and respect for life, love for family, respect for elders, kindness to the youngsters and above all understanding of each others religions' beliefs. None of the religion advocates hatred. There are three God-given religions, namely Judaism, Christianity, and Islam. These religions have a common source of Prophet Abraham. In fact the message of Islam started with Prophet Adam and ended with Prophet Muhammad including Prophet Moses and Jesus. The message of Islam passed through a process of evolution giving people step by step principles of leading a life in this world and hereafter. The message was completed and made comprehensive by the time it reached Prophet Muhammad. Islam therefore speaks of the rights and obligations of all human beings. It deals with all aspects of life. The life in Islam does not end with death. There is another life after this life. Success of life means goodness and achievements in both the worlds. Islam supply food for the body and the soul alike. It has described rules for living and for the dead bodies. How can such a religion have any connection with terrorism?

The followers of terrorism are governed by tyrants. They believe in death and destruction. They do not believe in peace. They believe in demolishing the fabric of life and indiscriminate mass killing. They hate freedom of speech and they think their words are words of God. Islam and Shi'as have suffered from terrorism as early as in 61 Hijri when Yazid, who was appointed as Caliph by his father Caliph Mua'wiya asked Imam Husayn to accept his brand of terrorism or face death. Imam Husain obviously refused to be directed by a tyrant like Yazid and was brutally murdered in Karbala, Iraq with his family and friends on 10 Moharram, 61 Hijri.

JUDICIAL SYSTEM

Naturally, human societies witness problems and differences among their people. Some may assault others, someone may beat another, and someone may steal another's money, commit murder or otherwise endanger the life of a member of the society. A difference may arise between them over the ownership of a piece of land, a debt, or any other source of contention.

Islam aims to establish justice, security, and stability in society. To do this, it sets certain laws and rules in effect to punish the transgressor and deter them from resorting to violence. These laws oblige Muslims to take their cases before the judiciary to be examined and judged. Islam makes acceptance of the verdict passed by an

190

Islamic court, a requirement of the faith as contained in the following Qur'anic verse:

"But no, by your lord! They will not believe until they make you a judge in what they dispute among themselves, then they will find in themselves no uneasiness in acceding to your verdict and shall submit in full submission." (4:65)

By establishing judiciary in the Islamic society, security, stability, and justice can be preserved. Crime and evil are also controlled. For the criminal and transgressor, fear of punishment tends to urge them to refrain from these acts against society. Were it not for the judiciary system and punishment, human society would be plagued by chaos. The rule is written in the Qur'an: "And that when you judge between people you judge with justice." (4:58)

Certain important and salient features of the judiciary systems of Islam are:

1. The judge should be a jurist, *Faqih* and should have sufficient knowledge with respect to Islamic laws, so that he can pass judgment in the light of his knowledge.
2. The judge should be a pious man who judges justly and rightly.
3. No judgment can be given without evidence, testimony of the witness and/or the admission of the accused.
4. Every accused man is innocent until he is proven guilty. If guilty, he is punished and/or ordered to restore the injurious party's right.
5. The judgment handed down by the Islamic court should be in accordance with the laws and rules of Islam alone.
6. Punish the culprit to save the society is the rule of Islamic law because society has more importance than the individual.
7. Punishment is given to warn others to avoid its repetition.
8. Witnesses are important and they should be truthful. Otherwise, they could be punished for false witness.

9. Circumstances of the crime need be investigated. For instance, in Islamic society, it is the obligation of the state to provide everyone with sustenance. If one who does not have anything to eat, it obviously does not give him a license to steal, but his crime will be dealt differently than others.

10. If someone goes to jail, it is the responsibility of the state to take care of his family, if need be.

11. Some punishments are described. These are called *Hadd* "like eye for eye and nose for nose," and others are called *Tazeerat* given by the judge at that time.

12. Mercy is the basis of punishment. If someone is killed and the victim's party takes money, which is called *Dayat*, and pardons the killer, it is better according to Islam.

ISLAMIC MANNERS

Besides the personal and interpersonal laws governing the Muslims' life, there are Islamic manners that the Muslims are morally committed to observe and practice for every day life. Islam lays emphasis on specific acts of kindness and concern for others, much more clearly than in any other religion. Some specific manners are as follows:

1. Love of neighbors.
2. Respect of elders.
3. Kindness to youngsters.
4. Generosity with wisdom.
5. Bravery
6. Truthfulness at all times.
7. Honesty.
8. Loyalty.
9. Cleanliness.
10. Visiting the sick person.
11. Positive response to greetings.

12. Giving believers the benefit of doubt.
13. Refraining from backbiting and hurting others.
14. Volunteering, help to others.
15. Participation in social work.
16. Respect for the religious scholars.
17. Respect for the people of other religion.
18. Modesty in every aspect of life.

EXERCISES

There are no questions to answer with this chapter. Instead, you will be working on a research project.

1. Choose one of the six systems mentioned in this chapter according to your instructor's approval to research. Your task is to choose a nation and research its version of this system and compare and contrast it with the Islamic system. For example, you could choose to compare and contrast the economic system of the United States with the Islamic economic system, or you could compare and contrast the political system of Iran with the Islamic political system. Here is a list of countries you might want to think about: United States, Canada, Mexico, United Kingdom, Germany, France, Italy, Japan, China, Iran, Saudi Arabia, Kenya, India, Pakistan, Nigeria, Sudan, Sweden, Syria, and Yemen. You may choose a country not on this list. Your instructor must approve your choices of both country and system.

2. Once your choices are approved, begin by researching the system as it works in the country you have chosen. Use this chapter as a guideline on different aspects of the system to research. You may use library books, the Internet, and other approved sources. You must provide information to your instructor about the sources you will use for approval.

3. When your sources are approved, conduct your research and then compare and contrast each point with the Islamic system. Submit your notes to your instructor at the given due date.

4. Prepare a presentation of your research including any changes suggested by your instructor. Suggested formats for presentations include papers, posters, PowerPoint presentations, and speeches. Use the format that your instructor tells you to use. Your instructor may provide you with a check sheet to use for this project.

Chapter Thirteen

SHARIAH: THE ISLAMIC JURISPRUDENCE

Shariah means "straight path" or "code of life" under Islamic law. Basic *deen*, or religion, has been the same from Prophet Adam to Prophet Muhammad. It consisted of belief in the oneness of Allah, Prophethood, and Qiyamah. The code of life under Islamic law, or the *Shariah*, has progressed from time to time as the need arose.

Shariah is a system of law for Muslims to follow in order to lead an Islamic life and by doing so, benefits us in this—and the next—life. The two sources of *Shariah* are the Qur'an and the *Sunnah* of the Prophet.

The Qur'an holds complete instructions for life, but it often needs an interpreter. The Qur'an itself says, "Say (O' Muhammad) if you love Allah, then follow me, Allah will love you and forgive your faults, and Allah is Forgiving and Merciful." (3:31) " And follow him (the Prophet) so that you may be guided." (7:158) As an example, the Qur'an commands us to pray or observe *Salat* and perform *Hajj*. But unless the Prophet had taught us how to pray, we would not have known exactly how to perform *salat* or other *ibadah*.

Laws of *Shariah* were made by Allah and delivered by Prophet Muhammad. Whatever was made *haram* by the Prophet is *haram* until Qiyamah and whatever was made *halal* is *halal* until Qiyamah. Any person, whosoever he may be, cannot change it.

These were laws made by Allah, which are far superior to any man-made laws because He:

1. is Mighty, Just, and Fair.
2. knows the needs of everyone.

3. seeks no personal benefit.
4. knows the future.
5. made His laws to be superior and universal and fair.

Shariah has two other sources of law, the *ijma* of *ulema* or the (consensus of the religious scholars); and the use of common sense. There is no place of *Qiyas*, (guessing) in Islam, but common sense usually dictates *Shariah*. *Ulema*, (singular is *Aalim*) are those who are pious people and are well versed in the Quran and ahadith. They derive the laws of Islam based on the above two sources as the need arises. This process is called *Ijtihad* (research). The door is still open for research in Shi'a Islam.

The *Sunnah* of the Prophet means examples from the life of the Prophet. It includes what he said, what he did, what he allowed and also what he approved. We also believe the Imams including Fatima Zehra, daughter of the Prophet, when they provide information regarding the statements of the Prophet and any aspect of life regarding the Prophet, their statements should also be taken as *Sunnah.* They were the true followers of the Prophet and would reflect only what the Prophet did and said.

The students of history know that the First and the Second Caliphs were not very keen about collecting, writing, or describing the ahadith. Imam Ali was the first to collect the ahadith of the Prophet. In the Shi'a sect there are four authentic books of ahadith:

1. *Kafi* by Abu Jaffar Muhammad bin Yaqoob Kulaimi.
2. *Al-Tahzeeb* by Abu Jaffar Muhammad bin Hassan Toosi.
3. *Al-Ibtesar* by Abu Jaffar Muhammad bin Hassan Toosi.
4. *Man La Yahzar Al-Fakih* by Abu Jaffar Muhammad bin Babavaih Al-qummi.

FIQH

Fiqh means knowledge and understanding of the science of Islamic law and jurisprudence. *Fiqh* is also considered the collection and compilation of Islamic laws based on the Qur'an and *Sunnah* of the Prophet. In the Sunni sect, the first person to do this work was Imam Abu Hanifa, who was born in 80 Hijri, about 70 years after the death of the Prophet. Thus there was a gap of about hundred years before Imam Abu Hanifa started doing his great job of providing *Fiqh*. On the other hand, in the Shi'a sect there wasn't a gap. The Prophet was followed by Imam Ali who continued the *Sunnah* of the Prophet, who was in turn followed by his eleven successors or Imams. The last Imam, Imam Mehdi went into occultation in 329 Hijri, and by that time the *fiqh* of Shi'a sect was well established. After the Imams, the work was taken over by the Shi'a's *ulema*, who are very devoted and honest religious scholars of Islam.

Up to the time of Imam Jafar As-Sadiq there was only one *fiqh*. Abu Hanifa was the first to establish a new *fiqh*. It was based on the combined sources of the Qur'an, *Sunnah,* and Imam Abu Hanifa's own guess work. Imam Jafar As-Sadiq clarified the differences between his *fiqh* and that of Imam Abu Hanifa. This is why the *fiqh* of Shi'as is also called *Fiqh-e-Jafariya.*

ISLAMIC ACTIONS

Basically, all our actions should fall in one of the following five categories:

1. *Waajib* (obligatory) deeds. If one misses this type of deed, he will be sinful.
2. *Haram* (forbidden) acts. Undertaking these acts will be sinful.
3. *Mustahab* (Sunnah or recommended). These acts are good but if one does not perform them, it will not be treated as sin.

4. *Makrooh* (disliked) acts. These acts are not liked but they are not sinful.

5. *Mubah* (Halal). All other acts, which do not fall in the above four categories, fall in this category and are permissible.

Somebody asked the Prophet what Islam was. He answered in one sentence. "Fear of the Creator and love for His creation." All Islamic actions in general are divided between *aqeedah* (Faith) and *Aamal* (action). *Aqeedah* means belief in Islamic terms. The more solid the belief, the better the action will be.

Actions are divided in to two parts: (1) *Huqooq-ul-Lah* are actions undertaken to discharge the rights of Allah, or actions for Allah; and (2) *Huqooq-ul-Abad* are actions undertaken to discharge the rights of fellow human beings, or actions for human beings. The rights of Allah, to obey his commands, are very important, but if someone unintentionally forgets or misses it, Allah has the right to forgive the person. On the contrary, if one misses the obligations towards fellow human beings, even Allah cannot forgive it. To give an example, if one forgets his one-time prayer, Allah may forgive him, but if someone owes you a dollar, Allah cannot pardon it unless it has been pardoned by that individual. This concept is very important because although Allah has all powers and can do everything, He allows His justice to bind Him. He cannot do anything unjust.

HALAL AND HARAM FOODS AND DRINKS

The *Shariah* is a unique legal code, which guides the believer towards the righteousness and steers him away from sin and unjust dealing from the time when a Muslim wakes up each morning until he returns to sleep at night. It guides him to proper conduct. With *Shariah's* given regulations and advice about the things one can eat and drink, we want to briefly explore the *halal* and *haram* in the area of food and drink.

198

From the animals of the sea, only fish can be eaten. Only those fish are allowed for eating which have scales. Other seafood such as clams, crabs and lobsters, oysters, scallops etc. are forbidden for eating, as none of these are fish. Shrimp are allowed due to their having scales. Fish need not be slaughtered according to any particular ritual. It is enough that they are removed from water alive.

From the land animals, meat of the grazing animal is allowed for eating. Meat of animals which possess canine teeth, like the lion and bear are not allowed for eating. The meat of domesticated and wild grazing animals such as sheep, cow, goat, deer and camel is allowed. The meat of horse, donkey and mules is *makrooh*, or disliked, meat. The meat of rabbit, squirrel, raccoon and similar animals are not allowed. The meat of reptiles is also not allowed.

From the animals that fly, meat of predatory birds possessing a talon or claw, like the falcon, eagle or hawk is not allowed. The meat of a bird that flies with an extended wingspan allowing them to fly without flapping their wings constantly, like the eagle or vulture, is not allowed. The meat of birds with a crop, gizzard or a craw like pouch in the neck and an extension in the foot resembling a toe are allowed. The meat of birds such as pheasant or quail, dove or pigeon is *halal* in addition to chicken, duck and goose. Crows and some varieties of lark are *makrooh* for eating. Eating of flying insects is *haram* with the exception of locusts, which are allowed if captured alive.

With the exception of fish, all animals must be slaughtered according to the conditions laid down in the *Shariah*. The conditions are: (1) the person slaughtering the animal must be a Muslim, male or female, sane, and adult. (2) the animal should be made to face the *Qiblah* in such a way that its stomach and feet are facing *Qiblah*. If the animal is absolutely uncontrollable, this condition can be dropped. (3) The person slaughtering the animal must use a sharp knife to sever the windpipe, throat, and two jugular vessels (severing the entire head is not allowed). (4) The name of Allah must be mentioned when slaughtering the animal. (5) There must be some movement of the animal after its throat has been cut and that blood must flow out from the animal. The animal can be hung to allow as much blood as possible to drain out. After the great majority of the blood has drained out, that blood which remains inside is considered clean.

Any animal, which is allowed for eating, but has not been slaughtered according to the above rules, is referred to as *Maitah*. The *Maitah* is a source of impurity and no part of it can be eaten. This prohibition of *Maitah*, is mentioned in the Qur'an: "He has only forbidden you what dies of itself, and blood, and flesh of swine, and that over which any other (name) than (that of) Allah has been invoked;" (2:173) "Forbidden to you is that which dies of itself, and blood, and flesh of swine, and that on which any other name than that of Allah has been invoked, and the strangled (animal) and that beaten to death, and that killed by a fall and that killed by being smitten with the horn, and that which wild beasts have eaten, unless what you slaughter while still alive, and that which has been slaughtered at altars is forbidden, and also dividing the meat by casting lot with gambling arrows (a pagan tradition). All this is sinful." (5:3)

Only meat slaughtered according to these rules can be considered *halal*. All other meat is *haram* and *najis* including kosher meat slaughtered according to the Jewish *Shariah*. While the name of God may be mentioned over the animal when slaughtered by the Jewish tradition, the person is not a Muslim and therefore it is not allowed.

HALAL AND HARAM FOODS

1. *Halal* meats: beef, chicken, lamb, goat, venison, camel, and deer.
2. *Halal* seafood: all type of fish with scales like white fish, salmon, and tuna. Shrimp are also allowed.
3. *Halal* poultry: chicken, duck, geese, pheasant and turkey.
4. *Haram* meats: reptiles, rabbit, raccoon and squirrel.

5. *Haram* seafoods: all types of shellfish (scallop, oysters, etc.) are not allowed. In addition, those creatures which are not fish (like lobster, gray fish, octopus, and whale) are also forbidden. Fish that have no scales are also haram such as catfish and shark.

6. *Haram* poultry: all types of predatory birds, which kill their food like the eagle and falcon are haram.

EXERCISES

1. If the Qur'an is really complete, why do we pay attention to the teachings of the Prophet instead of the just the Qur'an?

2. Use a website, ask a scholar or used any other acceptable method to answer the following. Your class may want to divide these up and report back your answers for each other.

   a. Why do Shias accept hadith from Ahlul-Bayt and not just the Prophet's hadith?

   b. Do our authentic hadith books have any hadith that are doubtful?

   c. Do the Sunni authentic hadith books have any hadith that are doubtful?

   d. Can you think of a good reason about why a pious hadith compiler might purposely leave questionable hadith in his collection?

   e. How and why do fabricated hadith end up in the authentic collections, if at all?

   f. Are all weak, questionable, or doubtful hadith necessarily fabricated? Explain.

   g. What are the basic steps scholars take in investigating hadith?

3. As in #2, use any acceptable method to investigate the following questions.

   a. Why do we rely on the ulema for fiqh?

b. How do ulema become qualified to help us?

c. What are the basic duties of the ulema?

d. What is the history of our fiqh system?

e. Has our system changed at all in the past 100 years?

f. Are there any changes being discussed now for the future of our system?

g. Is our system Islamically correct or is it just something we made up? Does it have a basis in Qur'an and hadith?

h. What are some advantages of our system compared to the Sunni system or compared to a democratic system?

4. In general, why do you think some foods are not permissible to eat?

5. Two conditions of halal slaughter are that the person doing it is Muslim and that the name of Allah is pronounced at the time of slaughter with Bismillah. These conditions do not have an obvious physical effect on our food. Explain your thinking about what these two conditions do for us.

6. Some of the halal meat companies slaughter with the help of a machine. Choose an investigation to report on. Make sure your investigations are done in the spirit of learning and do not set out to raise suspicions. Be polite and friendly to those who help you with your investigation.

a. Contact or visit a halal meat company and find out about their slaughter methods. Also find out where they get their animals, how they are transported, and how the meat is prepared and delivered after slaughtering.

b. Contact a local store or restaurant that provides halal meat and find out about where they get their meat, how they order it, and how they prepare it.

c. Talk to an Islamic scholar about meat slaughter with machines. Are there any special rules about it?

d. Talk to an Islamic scholar about eating in restaurants and rules that might be involved.

e. How should you handle eating out with non-Muslims in their homes? What about in a non-Muslim restaurant?

f. McDonald's was sued for having beef tallow in its fries. To date, they have chosen not to change their fries. Can you find any other cases involving fast food companies? How can you find out the full list of ingredients in fast foods?

Chapter Fourteen

STATUS OF WOMEN IN ISLAM

Each individual in Islam is like a brick in a wall. If any of the bricks are not placed properly, the entire wall of the building will be distorted. Therefore, Islam emphasizes the good in individuals. For a society to be good, individuals must be good. Women play a key role in building a good society.

ISLAM'S RESPECT FOR WOMEN

In the Islamic society, woman has an honored position. Besides her legal and civil rights, she enjoys the special respect, love, affection and gentle feelings which she deserves most. She is the compassionate mother, the beloved wife, and the affectionate daughter. The Qur'an, in various Ayahs, provides the best expression of women's rights. Some of these verses are given below:

1. "And we have enjoined man in respect of his parents—his mother bears him with fainting upon fainting and his weaning takes two years—saying: Be grateful to Me and to both your parents; to Me is the eventual coming." (31:14)
2. "And they if they contend with you that you should associate with Me what you have no knowledge of, do not obey them, and keep company with them in the world kindly, and follow the way of him who return to Me, then to Me is your return, then will I inform you of what you did——." (31:15)
3. "…And treat them (women) kindly;" (4:19).

4. "…And they (women) have rights similar to those against (men) them in a just manner…" (2:228)

Once, a man came to the Prophet and asked him, "Oh messenger of Allah whom should I be more dutiful?" The Prophet replied "To your mother." He asked, "And then to whom?" and the Prophet replied "To your mother." The man again asked "Then to whom?" and the Prophet said "To your father." This clearly shows the importance of the mother.

Imam Jafar As-Sadiq was quoted to have said that whoever provided for three well-behaved daughters or three sisters, paradise was surely his. He was asked "what if two?" and he said "even two." He was asked "what if one?" and he said "even one." From Imam Ar-Riza it has been stated that the Prophet said that Allah was more kind to females than males, and that whoever would bring pleasure to a woman of his close relatives, Allah would be pleased with him on the Day of Judgment. Imam Jafar as-Sadiq also said that sons were considered a favor and daughters good deeds, which implied that Allah would ask questions about the favors and would give rewards for the good deeds.

The above are some of the examples from the Islamic texts concerning women. It is clear that Islam calls for women to be honored, treated affectionately, and cared for. This is unprecedented as no other religion states the rights of women so clearly.

The spirit of Islam commands that mankind be honored, that there is protection of all people's rights, and respect for all of mankind. The Qur'an says: "And we have not sent you but as a mercy to the worlds."(21:107) Islam as mentioned above advises respecting all women whether they be mother, wife, daughter, or sister. Women are deserving of affection, respect, and generosity. Islam recommends honoring women before honoring men. Islam regards the love of woman as a sign of faith.

Islamic societies should grant women the same rights as man

except where there are natural differences such as physical, psychological, and sexual differences. Women also have different rights regarding social position. Islam grants women the following rights:

Right to learn: Islam commands both men and women to learn. The religion teaches that seeking knowledge is a duty imposed on all Muslims, male and female.

Right to work: Both men and women have been given the right to work. All religiously lawful work is open to women as it is open to men. A married woman, however, is not allowed to work unless her husband gives permission. The matrimonial right in the family system comes first in Islam. The matrimonial right is that the husband is obligated to protect his family and is responsible for taking care of the household duties specially earning.

Political rights: In Islam, the woman enjoys full political rights except for the nomination for the post of a judge. The post of a judge in Islam is exclusively reserved for men. Women can participate in all political and social activities like electing the head of state, the nation's representative in the parliament, etc. Women may be a member of all kinds of establishments, organizations, and parties. She may even be a minister, a parliament deputy, and may manage other types of political posts.

Women's Allegiance to the Prophet: The Qur'an speaks about women's allegiance to the Messenger of Allah and history shows that women took the oath accepting the sovereignty of the Prophet and his successor. "O Prophet, when believing women come to you giving you a pledge that they will not associate aught with Allah, and will not steal, and will not commit fornication, and will not kill their children, and will not bring a calumny which they have forged of themselves, and will not disobey you in what is good, accept their pledge, ask forgiveness for them from Allah; surely Allah is Forgiving, Merciful." (60:12)

Civil rights: Women like men enjoy full civil rights. She can inherit, buy and sell products, and conclude a deal or contract. In Islam, women have a legal and independent personality and her obligations are independent from those of her father, husband, or brother.

WOMEN AND FAMILY

Previously we discussed the position of women in Islamic society and her social status. Now we talk about women and family. In Islam, women are the base and cornerstone for building a family and the woman is the beloved whose heart overflows with the sentiment of love, mercy, and calmness. The Qur'an says: "And one of His signs is that He created mates for you from yourselves and that you may find rest in them, and He put between you, love and compassion; most surely there are signs for people who reflect." (30:21)

Women are the source of tranquility, security, and psychological stability for the husbands. Woman is the center of harmony of the family, which protects the children and keeps them from going astray. She is the fountainhead of affection, love, and mercy for the husband and the children. This is why a woman must have social and legal rights. She is the basic unit of the family, therefore, the basic unit of constructing society, and humanity as a whole.

Building of Family in Islam

By studying the Islamic religion and analyzing its ideas, laws, and values concerning the building and organization of the family, two aspects have been emphasized by the Qur'an:

Call to build the family: The Qur'an says, "And one of his signs is that He created mates for you from yourselves that ye may find rest in them, and He put between you love and compassion; most surely there are signs in this for a people who reflect". (30:21)

Another Qur'anic command says, "He it is Who created you from a single being, and of the same (kind) did He make his mate, that He might incline to her..." (7:189)

Another Quranic Ayah says, "...Marry such women as seem good to you..." (4:3)

Organizing the family relations: Marriage is the basic core of the Islamic family. Imam Jafar As-Sadiq quoted the Prophet as saying: "Marry yourself and marry your sons and daughters. Fortunate is the Muslim who can afford to pay for unmarried women. Nothing is more loved in Islam by Allah, the Exalted in Islam, than a home setup by marriage, and nothing is more hated by Allah, the Exalted in Islam, than a home pulled down by divorce." The Imam further explained this by saying "Allah, the Exalted, did emphasize his word about divorce because He strongly dislikes separation."

POLYGAMY AND ISLAM

People, without knowing what Islam says about polygamy criticize it. Islam did not start polygamy but controlled it. No religion has protected women as much as Islam. The Qur'anic verse permitting polygamy does not order a Muslim to be polygamous; in fact, it warns men that if he has more than one wife he must observe total equality among them. Islam permits man to marry up to four wives, but warns that if he cannot maintain justice he should have only one. The Qur'an says: "Then marry those who seem good to you, two, or three, or four, and if ye fear that ye shall not deal justly (with so many) then (marry) only one." (4:3)

The earlier quotation from Annie Besant commends Islam for its treatment of women. And James Michener writes:"Western writers have based their charges of voluptuousness mainly on the question of women. Before Muhammad however, men were encouraged to take innumerable wives; he limited them to four only, and the Koran is explicit that husbands who are unable to maintain strict equality between two or more wives, must confine themselves to one".[1]

EXERCISES

1. Find a hadith or ayah about the high status of women in Islam to share with the class.

2. Choose any culture such as American, Indian, Saudi, etc. Explain a way that culture treats women Islamically and one way that it doesn't. Do all people in the culture behave that way? Explain.

3. There are five rights of women mentioned in this chapter.
   a. How do these rights compare with men's?
   b. Are women equal to men before God?
   c. What is the difference between equal rights and equitable rights? Which is better? Explain.
   d. Compare the rights of women in Islam with the rights of women in any culture of your choice.
   e. Can you think of any women rights in Islam which have not been mentioned in this chapter?

4. Imagine you are getting married. List five of your most important Islamic duties and five of your Islamic rights. Try to avoid expectations that are cultural but not specifically Islamic.

5. What are some things a Shia woman is allowed to put in her marriage contract?

6. What are the different types of divorce and what are rights

---

[1] *James A. Michener, Islam: The Misunderstood Religion, Readers Digest, (American Edition), May 1955, pp. 68-70*

of women involving divorce?

7. What do you think the role of a woman is in the ideal Islamic society? What does she do in the home, in the realm of education, and in the realm of society? This is a good question for a class debate.

8. Many people think women in Islam are oppressed. Why does that opinion exist? What should be done about it? This is a good question for a class debate.

9. Why are divorce rates rising among Muslims? What can be done about it? This is a good question for a class debate.

10. What is the best way in this society for pious Muslims to find good life mates? What should the role of the parents be? This is a good question for a class debate.

Chapter Fifteen

TWO MAJOR SECTS OF ISLAM

SHI'A AND SUNNI

At present, there are two major sects of Islam, namely Sunni and Shi'a. Without going into the historical development of how these and other sects came into being in Islam we will deal here with the common and different beliefs of the two major sects. As a number of historical treatises on the development of Shi'a sect are available in the academic world we will confine ourselves here with highlighting the Shi'a beliefs in order to bring out the Islamic teachings in the correct perspective.

Shi'as are the flag bearer of original Islam as they derive their beliefs directly from the Prophet and the Qur'an. Many beliefs are common in the two sects of Shi'a and Sunni. The common beliefs are:

1. One God, Who is the Creator of this universe.
2. One-hundred-twenty-four-thousand Prophets were sent by Allah, the last being Prophet Muhammad who would be the Prophet until the time of Resurrection.
3. Qiyamah, the Day of Resurrection.
4. Ka'abah is regarded as Qibla and it should always be faced during prayers.
5. The Qur'an is the original book revealed by Allah to the Prophet and it has not been changed at all from the beginning of the first Surah Alhamd to the last Surah Wannas.
6. Salat, Saum, Hajj, Zakat, Khums, Jihad, *Amer bil Maaroof*

and *Nahi-Anil-Munkir.*

7. Social and economic laws of Islam.
8. Laws of inheritance of Islam.
9. Laws of marriage and divorce.
10. Many other ideas/beliefs are common to both.

DIFFERENCES BETWEEN SHI'AS AND SUNNIS BELIEFS

There are a few differences. There are five in number.

First, Shi'as believe in the total submission to Allah. This is carried out in following the Prophet believing in him totally and following his orders without any doubt or without any hesitation. The Qur'an say: "it is not for a believer, man or woman, to have any choice in the matter when God and his Apostle have decided the matter and whoever disobeyed God and his Apostle indeed he has truly gone astray." (33:36)

Second, and the major difference, Shi'as believe in the Divine leadership of 14 infallible (*Masoomeen*) who include 12 Imams for providing guidance after the passing away of the Prophet. Based on the Qur'an and the Prophet's saying and actions (Ahadith and Sunnah), Shi'as believe that the divine leadership, after Prophet Muhammad was continued by designated Imams. In the Qur'an Allah says that He sent the Prophet and He designated his Caliphs, and that Allah does not leave any nation without a guide. (For details on Imamate please refer to Chapter Twelve on Imams.)

The designation of the divine leadership was based on a criterion of the highest education, perfect understanding of Shariah unwavering faith in God and His Messenger, and the qualities of being God fearing and being brave.

The 12 imams of Shi'as fulfill these criteria and were appointed by Allah. The Prophet therefore designated Imam Ali as his Caliph.

This was announced for the first time on the day of Zul-Ashira in the early days of Islam. The last declaration was made on the day in Ghadeer-e-Khum on 18 Zilhaj, 10 Hijri.

Since Sunnis do not believe in the divine leadership, they made Abu Bakr the first Caliph after the death of the Prophet. A few *Sahaba* (companions) chose him. Abu Bakr designated Umar as his successor by his personal liking establishing the principle of designating the successor. Umar formed a consultant committee of seven people to designate the next Caliph after his death. This committee chose Usman. The fourth Caliph Imam Ali was elected by a majority of the *Ummah*. Mua'wiya became Caliph by force.

Third, there is a difference between the two sects concerning the sources of Islamic jurisprudence or the *Shariah.* For Shi'as, the sources of Shariah are the Qur'an, the Prophet's Sunnah, and the Ahlul-Bayt, whereas for Sunnis the sources are from the companions of the Prophet rather than Ahlul-Bayt.

In the Shi'a sect, a direct link is therefore maintained to the Prophet through Ahlul-Bayt. For Shi'as, the basis of law is the Qur'an, the Prophet's Sunnah including that of Ahlul-Bayt, Ijma of *ulema* (consensus of learned scholars) and common sense.

Fourth, there is a difference on the avenue of research for interpreting Islamic teachings to present day situations. In the Shi'a sect, the avenue of research or *Ijtihad* is open. For the Sunni sect, the *Ijtihad* is not allowed.

Fifth, in the Shi'a sect there is a great emphasis on the general rule that whatever common sense dictates is usually the rule of Shariah. It is said that if someone after relinquishing his faith is researching with all his sincerity to find out the best religion and he dies in this process, he will not die as a pagan and will find his place in heaven, according to Shia *fiqah.*

Shi'as believe in justice (Adil) at every level. In terms of tolerance towards others faith, the Shi'a sect takes a liberal attitude. For a non-Muslim there is no compulsion to come to the fold of Islam and forcing someone to become Shi'a is forbidden. All Muslims are free to have friendship with non-Muslims specially people belonging to the religions of Ahle Kitab (Heavenly Books) so far as no offense is made to one's belief. Difference of opinion is fair and is welcomed. Based on this the authenticities of various war undertaken to spread the message of Islam after the death of the Prophet are highly doubtful as Islam does not allow aggression and attacking other nations and countries to force them to become Muslims.

The differences in the beliefs in fact emerged significantly during the caliphate of Mua'wiya when he founded the rule of Ummayid dynasty and declared the year as the year of Sunnah Al-jammat. He had also started the practice of cursing Imam Ali from 70,000 pulpits of mosques every day, particularly during Friday prayers. This was a major step in separating the Shi'as of Ali.

It is interesting to note that the two separate *fiqahs* emerged about 100 years after the Prophet death during the time of Imam Jafar As-Sadiq, the sixth Shi'a Imam. Imam Jafar had established a religious school in Medina where he had his student by the name of Abu Hanifa who later gave his interpretation of the Qur'an and named it *Fiqah Hanifiya* as against the original *fiqah* which could be termed as *Shi'a Fiqah* till that point of time. Later the three other imams Hambali, Maliki, and Shafei declared their respective *fiqahs*. The Shi'a *fiqah* was termed as *Fiqah-e-Jaferia* after the name of Imam Jafer Before the two *fiqahs* came to be separated it was a routine practice that all matters pertaining to the interpretation of the Qur'an and religious issues were referred to the Ahlul-Byat of the Prophet even during the Ummayid dynasty till 126 Hijri. During the caliphate of the first Caliph, Umar was reported to have said that "I do not wish to live if Ali is not around" (to help interpret the Qur'an and answer other religious questions).

216

Some other differences in basic beliefs are:

1. Shi'as believe that Allah can never be seen by eyes. Some Sunnis believe otherwise.
2. The Prophet, according to Shi'as, is always infallible. Not only the Prophet Mohammad but all prophets, for all times, are infallible from the day of their birth until their death. Sunnis believe that the Prophet could make mistakes.
3. The Qur'an says about Imamate that, on the Day of Resurrection everyone will be called by the Imam of his time. Sunnis do not believe in Imamate and do not have an Imam for modern times.
4. Shi'as believe that Allah is all-powerful as well as just. If you owe ten dollars to someone, Allah, despite being all-powerful, cannot pardon it until the one to whom you owe ten dollars pardons you. Allah would not pardon you because He is Almighty. He is also *just*. Justice will be done before His might will pardon someone.
5. Sunnis believe that Allah can send anybody to heaven or hell. Shi'as believe His sending someone to heaven or hell is based on justice.
6. Within the Shias, the rules and principles are clearly laid down first and foremost. After that, the personalities are chosen accordingly. Whereas with the Sunnis, the personalities are first selected, and then the rules are laid down accordingly.

Other differences in practices. are:

1. For offering prayer, or Salat, the Qur'an says wash your hands and face and touch your head and feet. Sunnis wash their feet (the Qur'an uses the words touching not washing).
2. For *Saum* (fasting), the Qur'an says; observe fasting from dawn to night. Sunnis open their fast at sunset and do not

wait for night to fall.

3. The Prophet offered Salat with open hands. Sunnis fold their hands while offering Salat.

4. The prayers for *Zuhr* and *Asr*, and for *Maghrib* and *Isha*, were offered by the Prophet sometimes together and sometimes separately. Sunnis insist on offering each prayer separately.

5. The Prophet used the words *Haiyya ala khayril Amal* in Azan, but Sunnis have left it out. Sunnis say *As Sallatu Khayru-m-minan Naum* for the Morning Prayer, which was not included at the time of the Prophet.

6. The Prophet forbade offering Sunnah prayer in *Jamat*. Sunnis offer *Taraweeh* prayers with *Jamat* which was started by Umar.

7. The first two Caliphs changed some *Halal* and *Haram* of the Prophet, although it was supposed to remain like that, for what the Prophet said stays up to *Qiyamah*. For example, *Hajj-e-Tamatt* and *Muta* are *Halal* for Shi'as and Haram for *Sunnis*, but they were both *halal* during the time of the Prophet

8. For Shi'as, Jihad is permissible only with the permission of the Imam. Defense is different than offensive Jihad, Sunnis can attack anyone in the name of Jihad. All the victories achieved by various Islamic kings fall under this category.

SOME CRITICISMS AGAINST SHI'AS

Shi'as are criticized for kissing or bowing to certain signs established in the name of God. We all believe that prostration is forbidden except for God. But Allah has ordered us to respect His signs. Erery thing in His universe is a sign of Allah particularly those associated with Godly objects and the men of God. The Qur'an say: "Verily Saffah and Marwah are among the signs of God. Who ever therefore makes a pilgrim to the house or performs Umrah therefore it shall be no blame on him to go around these both and whoever of his own accord does anything good in deed, verily God is gracious and all knowing. (2:158)

As for the camels we have made them for you of the signs of God." (22:36)

"That shall be so and whosoever respect the signs of God then that verily is the outcome of the piety of the heart" (22:32)

It is obvious that if the mountains of Saffah and Marwa and animal for sacrifices are worthy to be signs of God these should be revered. If so, the Prophet of Islam and his Ahlul-Byat who while establishing the truth got killed in the way of Allah should be the signs of God. Shi'as who are the followers of the Qur'anic faith and original Islam kiss the grave of the Prophet and other Imams or their replicas only out of respect and nothing else.

The other criticism against Shi'as is that they mourn for the martyrs. The Qur'an declares that heaven and earth also mourn, but they do not mourn for the wicked. It means they mourn for the righteous particularly for those who laid their lives for the Lord in Godly behavior. There is an authentic tradition of the Prophet that he shed tears for the prophesied martyr of Imam Husyan even before the event took place. The Prophet also shed tears for Jafar ibne Abi Talib and for Hamza. There is a Qur'anic reference about Jacob weeping for his son who had disappeared even though as an Apostle he knew that his son was not dead.

Shi'as mourn for Imam Husain as he laid down his life for the judicious freedom of speech and action for the entire humanity. It is his spirit that speaks through the souls of all freedom loving people.

Shi'as belief in Imam Mahdi's coming back as a Messiah is also criticized. All God-given religion in one way or the other believe that someone will come at the end of this world to save the humanity. It is a belief of all religion and in Shi'a belief it has been made crystal clear that a Messiah or savior is alive under Allah's supervision and will appear.

HOW TO UNITE THE UMMAH

DIVIDED UMMAH

There are 1.5 billion Muslims in the world. They all believe in one God, one Qur'an, one Prophet, one Qibla, and many more common beliefs. In spite of all these common beliefs there are so many differences that two Muslims often cannot agree.

Every fourth person who walks on this earth is a Muslim. Every fourth dollar is a Muslim dollar. There are more than 35 Muslim nations in the world. If they just stand hand-to-hand they will encircle the world, and beyond. Still Muslims are unorganized, humiliated, and outcasts. There is no respect for Muslims in their own Muslim countries, or any other countries for that matter. Muslims cannot practice Islam in most of the Muslim countries as they should be allowed.

REASONS FOR DIVISION

Muslims failed to listen to the Prophet. The Qur'an provides the basic principles and the Prophet explained and interpreted these principles through his Sunnah. The Muslims have a basic duty to follow the Prophet's Sunnah if the *Ummah* wants to succeed. The Qur'an says:

1. "…Whatever the Apostle gives you, accept it, and from whatever he forbids you, keep back…" (59:7)
2. "And it behooves not a believing man and believing women that they should have any choice in their matter when Allah and His Apostle have decided a matter; and whoever disobeys

Allah and His Apostle, he surely strays off a manifest straying". (33:36)

3. "Say if you love Allah then follow me and Allah will love you." (3:31)

The Qur'an says to worship Allah. The Prophet explained how to do it. The Qur'an says observe fast, and perform Hajj; the Prophet explained how to do these, and Muslims follow his example almost the same way with some minor differences. On the contrary when the Qur'an says, "… hold fast the rope of Allah and do not get divided," (3:103) no one followed the Prophet. The Qur'an says, "Say Prophet I do not want any payment for my hard work except the love of my near relative," and many do not obey this. The Prophet explained to the people, "O people, I leave behind amongst you two things, which, if you follow, you will never go astray: they are the book of Allah, and my Ahlul-Bayt, my family," the majority of the Muslims do not pay any attention to the Prophet's advice.

The Prophet also said: "The messenger of Allah is about to be called. I shall answer, I am leaving with you two magnificent sources; the first is the book of Allah in which you will find guidance and enlightenment, and the second is the people of my house. I remind you by Allah, of the people of my house, I remind you by Allah of the people of my house." He repeated this four or five times."[1]

The Prophet also said: "Behold my Ahlul-Bayt because they are like the ark of Noah, whoever embarks on it will be saved and whoever turns away from it will be drowned."[2]

The Prophet also said: "O Ali, you hold in relation to me, the same position as Haroon hold in the relation to Moses, except that

---

[1] *Sahih Muslim, Chapter on the virtue of Ali, Vol. 5, p. 122. Sahih Tirmidhi, Vol. 2, p. 328. Mustadrak Al-Hakim, Vol. 3, p. 148. Masnad Imam Hamble, Vol. 3, p. 17.*

[2] *Al-Hakim, Almustadrak, Vol. 3, p. 151. Nayabul Mowwadah, Chapter 30, p. 370. Ibne-Hajaf Al-Swaiqul Moharaqa, pp. 184 and 234.*

there would be no prophet after me."

The Prophet said at Ghadeer-e-Khum: "Ali is the master of all those of whom I am the master. O Allah, love him, who loves Ali and hate him who hates Ali. Help him who helps him, forsake him, who forsakes him and turn justice with him whenever he turns."

At his deathbed, the Prophet asked for a pen and a paper to write a note, so that the *Ummah* would never get astray. People around him did not listen to him; the result is what we see today.

The Prophet also said: "Islam will not be finished until there are twelve Caliphs from the Quraish."[3] The Prophet named these caliphs as: Ali, Hassan, Husyan, Ali ibne Husain, Mohammad ibne Ali, Jafar Ibne Muhammad, Musa ibne Jafar, Ali ibne Musa, Muhammad ibne Ali, Ali Ibne Mohammad, Hasan Ibne Ali, and Al-Hujjat Nayabul Mowadah.[4]

The above quotations have been provided to show what was not listened to by Muslims during the formative period of Islam and even at the present time. The Muslims will remain divided until they start practicing the beliefs based on the Qur'an, Prophet's Sunnah, and guidance provided by the House of Prophet Muhammad.

And last but not the lease, the adherence of principle. Shias are a Community of principles and ideals. If they make a promise, then they adhere to it. Allah commands us in the Quran while common sense attests to it, the leader of the Community should be the best amongst them. Our Prophet and Imams were the best. Shia always added but on the contrary the sec selected them a leader and made the rule.

For example, the first Caliph was selected by a Shura, then 2nd one by a decree while the third by a committee. First, they

---

[3] *Sahih Muslim, Vol. 2, p. 194. Sahih Bukhari, Kitabul Ahkam, Vol. 3, p. 144.*
[4] *Nayabul-Mowwadah, Chapter 76, p.369.*

secluded the individuals, and then they established a rule. Should always follow the rule made by Allah regardless, the leaders best among you.

And last but not the least, the adherence to that principle. Shias are a Community of principles and ideals. If they make a rule, then they adhere to it. Allah commands us in the Quran while common sense attests to it, that the leader of the Community should be the best amongst them. Our Prophet and Imams were the best. Shia always adhered to this principle on the contrary the Sunni sect selected their leader and made the rule.

For example, the first Caliph of the Sunnis was selected by a Shura, then 2nd one by a decree while the third by a committee. First, they secluded the individuals, and then they established a rule. Shias always follow the rule made by Allah regardless of the consequences.

EXERCISES

1. Find the ayahs in Qur'an mentioned in this chapter that say Allah designates leaders, does not leave us without a guide, and does not change the Sunnah after the Prophet. You might try using a Qur'an keyword search engine on the Internet, or a concordance, or ask someone for help.
2. Why is it preferable that our Shariah comes via Ahlul-Bayt instead of the Sahaba? What are some of the problems when Shariah comes through the Companions?
3. Can you find out why it is said that *ijtihad* is closed in Sunni Islam? What sort of problems does this lead to?
4. You may know some Sunnis or Shias who believe and practice differently than mentioned in this chapter. Can you explain why that happens?
5. Design a project as a class or in groups to build unity in a positive way that does not compromise beliefs and practices. Get approval to carry out your project and report on it to

QUOTES FROM THE QUR'AN AND SELECTED AHADITH

EXCERPTS FROM THE QUR'AN

Of all the heavenly books revealed to different prophets, for guidance of mankind, the Qur'an occupies a unique position in the sense that it is the last word of Allah after which no revealed book is to come. The Qur'an is the miracle of Islam. It deals with every aspect of life. Some of the Qur'anic commandments and orders on selected subjects are given here for reference.

QUR'ANIC COMMANDMENTS

1. O' you who believe obey God and obey the Prophet and do not turn your faces away while you are listening to Him. (8:15)
2. O' you who believe! Obey Allah and obey the Apostle and those in authority from among you; then if you quarrel about anything, refer it to Allah and the Apostle, if you believe in Allah and the last day; this is better and very good in the end. (4:59)

AHLUL-BAYET (THE HOUSE OF PROPHET)

1. Say (O' Muhammad and to mankind) I do not ask of you any reward for it, teaching the message, but love for a relative (Ahlul Bayet). (42:23)
2. O' you who believe, fear God and be with those who are true in words and deeds. (9:119).

3. Allah only desires to keep away the uncleanness from you, O people of the House! And to purify you a (thorough) purifying. (33:33)

CHARITY

1. And they feed for the love of God, the poor, the orphans and the captive; we feed you for the sake of God alone. No reward do we desire from you nor thanks. (76:8-9)
2. And for those who spend their property by night and by day, secretly and openly, they shall have their reward from their Lord and they shall have no fear, nor shall they grieve. (2:274)
3. Who gives away his wealth, purifying himself. (92:18)

FASTING

1. O' you who believe! Fasting is prescribed for you, as it was prescribed for those before you that you may guard (against evil). (2:183)

FEAR OF ALLAH (TAQUA)

1. And be careful of (your duty to) Allah, surely Allah is witness of all the things. (33:55)
2. As for those who fear their Lord in secret, they shall surely have forgiveness and great reward. (63-12).
3. Fear Allah, and know that Allah is with the God-fearing people. (2:194)

FOOD

1. O' men! Eat the lawful and good things out of what is in the earth and do not follow the footsteps of the Shaitan; surely

he is your open enemy. (2:168)

GREETING

1. And when you are greeted with a greeting, greet with a better (greeting) than it or return it; surely Allah takes account of all things. (4:86)

GIVING GUIDANCE

1. Surely we have shown him the way; he maybe thankful or unthankful. (76:3)
2. Who created death and life that He may try you—which of you is best in deeds; and He is the Mighty the Forgiving. (67:2)
3. And Allah increases in guidance those who go aright; and ever abiding good works are with your Lord, best in recompense and best in yielding food. (19:76)
4. Those who do not believe in Allah communication, surely Allah will not guide them and they shall have a painful punishment.(18:104)
5. There is no compulsion in religion. (2:256).
6. And surely it (The Quran) is a guidance and (???) for the believers. (27:76)

HOUR OF DEATH, RESURRECTION AND THE HEREAFTER

1. O' people! If you are in doubt about the raising, then surely We created you from dust, then from a small seed, then from a clot, them from a lump of flesh, complete in make and incomplete, that We make clear to you; and what We cause what We please to stay in the wombs till an appointed time, then We bring you forth as babies, then that you may attain your maturity; and of you is he who is caused to die,

and of you is he who is brought back to the worst part of life, so that after having knowledge he does not know anything; and you see the earth sterile land, but when We send down on it the water, it stirs and swell and bring forth of every kind a beautiful herbage. (22:5)

2. This is because Allah is the Truth and because He gives life to the dead and because He has power over all things, (22:6)

HYPOCRITE

1. A party of the followers of the Book desires that they should lead you astray, and they lead not astray but themselves, and they do not perceive. (3:69)
2. O followers of the Book! Why do you disbelieve in the communications of Allah while you witness (them)? (3:70).
3. O followers of the Book! Why do you confound the truth with the falsehood and hide the truth while you know? (3:71)

INTERCESSION FOR MINOR SINS

God is kind and merciful on his servants. He has sent his clear commands for us to follow. But we are human beings. In spite of our love for God we may commit minor sin by mistake or unintentionally. Allah will out of his mercy pardon us if we repent the sin. He has provided another mechanism of intercession by the Prophet and other dignitaries on our behalf. This mechanism is not to commit sin but to give us hope for his pardon. Following are the Qur'anic ayahs in this regard:

1. Who is he, who can intercede on to Him but by His permission. (2:255)
2. None will have power to intercede for them except one who obtains a promise from Ar-Rahman. (19:87)
3. On that day shall avail not intercession of any save that of

whom has permitted God and who's words He is pleased with. (20.109)

4. He knows what was there before them and what came after them; and they did not intercede for any one but whom He willed, and they were filled with awe of Him. (21:28)

5. And will avail not ought any intercession with Him save of him who He has permitted. (34:23)

JESUS

1. And when Isa the son of Mary said, O' children of Israel! Surely I am the Apostle of Allah, verifying that which is before me of the Tawrate and giving the good news of an Apostle who will come after me, his name being Ahmad. (61:6)

JUSTICE

1. O' you who believe! Be maintainers of justice, bearers of witness of Allah's sake, though it may be against your own selves or (your) parents or near relatives; if he be rich or poor, Allah is nearer to them both in compassion; therefore do not follow (your) low desires, lest you deviate; and if you swerve or turn aside, then surely Allah is aware of what you do. (4:135)

2. Whoever does good whether male or female and he is a believer, We will most certainly make him live a happy life, and We will most certainly give them their reward for the best of what they did. (16:97)

MARTYRS

1. And reckon not those who are killed in Allah's way as dead; nay, they are alive (and) are provided sustenance from their Lord; (3:169)

MERCY

1. Say: O my servants! Who have acted extravagantly against
    their own souls, do not despair of the mercy of Allah; surely
    Allah forgives the faults altogether; surely He is the Forgiving,
    the Merciful. (39:53)
2. And return to your Lord time after time and submit to Him
    before there comes to you the punishment, then you shall
    not be helped. (39:54)

MOSQUE

1. Only he shall visit the mosques of Allah who believes in Allah
    and the latter day, and keeps up prayer and pays the poor-rate
    and fears none but Allah; so (as for) these, it may be that
    they are of the followers of the right course. (9:18)

PARENTS

1. And Your Lord has commanded that you shall not serve (any)
    but Him, and goodness to your parents, If either or both of them
    reach old age with you, say not to them (so much as) 'Ugh' nor
    chide them, and speak to them a generous word. (17:23).
2. And make yourself submissively gentle to them with com-
    passion, and say: O my Lord! Have compassion on them, as
    they brought me up (when I was) little. (17:24)

PATIENCE

1. O You who believe! Seek assistance through patience and
    prayer. Surely Allah is with the Patient. (2:153)

ADULTERY

1. Do not even go near to adultery. It is an indecent and evil act. (17:32)

PRAYER

1. Therefore remember Me, I will remember you, and be thankful to Me, and do not be ungrateful to Me. (2:152)
2. If you are grateful I will add more favor to you. But if you showed ingratitude, truly my punishment is indeed terrible. (14:7)
3. Call on me I will answer your prayer but those who are too arrogant to serve me will surely find themselves in hell in humiliation. (40:60)
4. Now surely by Allah's remembrance, the hearts find rest. (13:28)
5. My Lord! Make me keep up prayers and from my offspring (too) O our Lord, and accept my prayers. (14:40)
6. Our Lord! Grant us mercy from thee, and provide for us a right course in our affairs. (18:10)
7. And they who say: O our Lord! Grant us in our wives and our offspring the joy of our eyes and make us guides to those who guard (against evil). (25:74)
8. Say surely my prayers and my scarifies and my life and my death are all for Allah, Lord of the world. (6:162)
9. Or, Who answers the distressed one when he calls upon Him and removes the evil, and He will make you successors in the earth. Is there a god with Allah? Little is it that you say about (Him). 27:62
10. Blessed is He in Whose hand is the kingdom, and He has the power over all things. (67:1)
11. Pour out upon us patience and cause us to die in submission. (7:126)

12. My Lord: grant me wisdom, and join me with the good; (26:83)

13. O my Lord, increase my knowledge. (20:116)

14. There is no god but Thou, glory be to Thee; surely I was indeed wrong. (21:87)

15. Our Lord surely we believe, therefore forgive our faults and save us from the chastisement of the fire. Our Lord forgives us therefore our fault, and cover all our evil deeds and make us die with righteousness. And protect us and grant us protection and have mercy on us. (2:286)

16. Our lord forgive us therefore our fault and cover all our evil deeds and make us die with righteousness.

17. And protect us and grant us protection and has mercy on us. (2:286)

18. O our Lord! Grant me protection and my parents and the believers on the day when the reckoning shall come to pass. (14:41)

19. And say: O my Lord! Forgive and have mercy, and you are at the best of the Merciful one. (23:118)

20. Say: O my servants! Who have acted extravagantly against their own soul, do not despair of the mercy of Allah; surely Allah forgives the false altogether; surely He is the Forgiving, the Merciful. (39:53)

21. And there are some among them who say: O Lord grant us good in this world and good in the hereafter, and save us from the chastisement of the fire. (2:201)

PRIDE

1. Do no walk around puffed up with pride. (31:18)

PROPHET AND IMAM

1. Surely (as for) those who speak evil things of Allah and His

Apostle, Allah has cursed them in this world and the hereafter, and He has prepared for them a chastisement bringing disgrace. (33:57)

2. Surely Allah and His angels bless the Prophet; O you who believe! Call for (Divine) blessings on him and salute him with a (becoming) salutation. (33:56)

3. I am nothing but a warner and giver of good news to a people who believe. (7:188)

4. Remember the day when we will call every people with their Imam. (17:71)

5. And we have not sent you but as a mercy to the World. (21:107)

6. Say: O people! Surely I am the Apostle of Allah to you all. (7:158)

7. Say if you love Allah, then follow me, Allah will love you and forgive you your faults, Allah is Forgiving, Merciful. (3:31)

8. Say truth has come and falsehood has been banished. It was destined to be banished. (17:81)

9. What remains with Allah is better for you if you are a believer, and I am not a keeper over you. (11:86)

QUR'AN

1. And when the Qur'an is recited, then listen to it and remain silent, that mercy may be shown to you. (7:204)

2. And certainly We have repeated (warnings) in this Qur'an that they may mindful, but it does not add save to their aversion. (17:41)

RIGHTEOUSNESS

1. It is not righteousness that you turn your faces towards the East and the West, but righteousness is this that one should believe

in Allah and the last day and the angels and the Book and the prophets, and give away wealth out of love for him to the near of kin and the orphans and the needy and the wayfarer and the beggars and for (the emancipation of) the captives, and keep up prayer and pay the poor-rate; and the performers of their promise when they make a promise, and the patient in distress and affliction and in time of conflicts—these are they who are true (to themselves) and these are they who guard (against evil). (2:177)

2. As for) those who believe and do good, surely they are the best of men. (98:7)

THANKFULNESS

1. Therefore remember Me, I will remember you, and be thankful to me, and do not be ungrateful to Me. (2:152

2. O you who believe! Eat of the good things that We have provided you with, and give thanks to Allah, if Him it is that you serve. (2:172)

WEALTH AND CHILDREN

1. And know that your property and your children are a temptation, and that Allah is He with Whom there is mighty reward. (8:28)

2. O you believer, let not the riches of your children divert you from the remembrance of God if you act thus, your loss is your own. (63:9)

GENERAL

1. And give full measures when you measures out, and weigh with a true balance; this is fair and better in the end. (17:35)

2. O you who believe! Do not enter houses other than your own house until you have asked permission and saluted their inmates; this is better for you, that you may be mindful. (24:27)

3. But if you do not find anyone therein, then do not enter them until permission is given to you; if it is said to you to go back that makes for greater purity for yourself and God knows well all that you do. (24:28)

4. O you who believe! If an evildoer comes with a report, look carefully into it, lest you harm a people in ignorance, then be sorry for what you have done. (49:6)

5. O you who believe! Let not (one) people laugh at (another) people perchance they may be better than they, nor let women (laugh) at (other) women, perchance they may be better than they; and do not find fault with your own people nor call one another by nicknames; evil is a bad name after faith, and whoever does not turn, these it is that are the unjust. (49:11)

6. O you who believe! Avoid most of suspicion, for surely suspicion in some cases is a sin, and do not spy nor let some of you backbite others. Does one of you like to eat the flesh of his dead brother? But you abhor it; and be careful of (your duty to) Allah, surely Allah is Oft-returning (to mercy), Merciful. (49:12)

7. O you who believe, intoxicants and gambling, dedication of stones, and (divination by) arrows, are all an abomination of Satan's handwork: eschew such (abomination) so that you may prosper. Satan's plan is (but) to excite enmity and hatred between you, with intoxicants and gambling, and hinder you from the remembrance of Allah, and from prayer: will you not then abstain? (5:90-91)

8. Surely Allah does not change the condition of a people until they change their own condition. (13:11)

9. And among His signs are the night and the day and the sun

and the moon; do not make obeisance to the sun or to the moon; and make obeisance to Allah Who created them, if Him it is that you serve. (41:37).

10. (As for) those who swallow the property of the orphans unjustly, surely they only swallow fire into their bellies and they shall enter the burning fire. (4:10)

11. Whoever joins himself (to another) in a good cause shall have a share of it, and whoever joins himself (to another) in an evil cause shall have the responsibility of it; and Allah controls all things. (4:85)

12. O you men! Surely We have created you of a male and female, and made you tribes and families that you may know each other; surely the most honorable of you with Allah is the one among you most careful (of his duty); surely Allah is Knowing, Aware. (49:13)

13. Surely the true religion with Allah is Islam (3:19)

SELECTED AHADITH OF THE PROPHET

The following are selected ahadith out of thousands recorded by historians and narrators from Prophet Muhammad:

1. Say there is no God but Allah and Verily you will be saved.
2. Fear God in your ease and difficulty.
3. Love of this world is at the root of every sin.
4. If you fight your passion, you gain control of yourself.
5. Utmost wisdom is the fear of God.
6. The bravest is he who overcomes his passions.
7. Make yourself known to God during ease; God will recognize you in difficulty.
8. Repentance from sin means to the refraining from it for good.
9. I had been sent to complete the excellent mandate.
10. Whoever wakes up without due concerns of Islamic affairs is

not a Muslim.

11. He is not one of us who sleeps while his neighbor is hungry.
12. Two types of persons will not be given due recognition by God on the day judgment: (1) He who boycotts his relatives; and (2) He who has no regards for a neighbor.
13. Paradise is at the feet of your mother.
14. Associating with the poor is a sign of humility.
15. Be merciful to the people on earth, you will be entitled for the mercy of Him who is in heaven.
16. The ink of the scholar is holier then the blood of the martyr.
17. Seek knowledge even if it is in China. The learned ones are the heirs of the Prophet.
18. The acquisition of knowledge is incumbent upon every Muslim, male and female.
19. With Allah the most detestable of all, permissible is divorced.
20. Give the laborer its wage before his perspiration dries.
21. One of you undertakes certain duty then should bring it to perfection.
22. I order you to restrain from anything intoxicant even in small quantities when excessive consumption of the same leads to drunkenness.
23. All Muslims are as one body, if a man complains of a pain in his head his whole body complains and if his eyes complain the whole body complains.
24. Every child is born with a disposition towards the natural religion, submission to God. It is the parent who makes him a Jew, a Christian or a Muslim.
25. Actions will be judged according to the motives.
26. Do not speak ill of the dead.
27. I am leaving among you two heavy things and you will not go astray so long you hold fast to them, one is the book of God and the other is my progeny, the Ahlul Bayet.
28. I am city of knowledge and Ali is its gate.

29. Fatima is my part, whoever hurts her hurts me.

30. Hassan, Husayn are the leaders of the youths of heaven.

SELECTED SAYINGS OF IMAM ALI

1. There is no treasure like knowledge.
2. The man of learning lives even after his death.
3. One without pity for others will never see mercy.
4. The people of the world are like travelers, who are being transported while they are at sleep.
5. Stableness describes good advice.
6. Greed is a lasting slavery.
7. The fear of Allah is the ultimate result of knowledge.
8. Whosoever knows himself well knows his neighbor.
9. People are asleep when they die they will awake.
10. BE not friend to a fool, he will hurt you even while meaning to be helpful.
11. Better be alone than with a bad companion.
12. Consider not who is speaking but what he is speaking.
13. Do for this world as if you are living forever, do for the next world as if you are dying tomorrow.
14. My best-loved brother is he who presents me my faults and shortcomings as gift.

TABLES

WORLD MUSLIM POPULATION
(AS OF 2005)

Country	Population	Total Muslim (%)	Total Muslim	Shia to Total Muslim (%)	Shia Population
Afghanistan	29,900,000	99%	29,601,000	18%	5,328,180
Albania	3,200,000	68%	2,170,000	20%	640,000
Algeria	32,800,000	99%	32,472,000	4%	1,298,880
Argentina	38,600,000	1%	500,000	10%	50,000
Australia	20,400,000	1%	280,000	10%	28,000
Azerbaijan	8,400,000	93%	7,845,600	80%	6,276,480
Bahrain	700,000	100%	700,000	70%	490,000
Bangladesh	147,365,352	88%	129,681,509	5%	6,484,075
Benin	8,400,000	20%	1,680,000	3%	50,400
Bosnia & Herzegovina	3,800,000	62%	2,340,000	1%	23,400
Bulgaria	7,700,000	12%	890,000	10%	89,000
Burkina Faso	13,900,000	50%	6,950,000	3%	208,500
Canada	32,200,000	2%	620,000	10%	62,000
China	1,303,700,000	3%	39,111,000	6%	2,346,660
Comoros	700,000	98%	686,000	1%	6,860
Djibouti	800,000	94%	752,000	1%	7,520
Egypt	74,000,000	94%	69,560,000	1%	695,600
Eritrea	4,700,000	50%	2,350,000	1%	23,500
Ethiopia	77,400,000	50%	38,700,000	1%	387,000
France	60,700,000	10%	5,980,000	6%	358,800
FYR Macedonia	2,000,000	32%	630,000	1%	6,300
Gambia	1,600,000	95%	1,520,000	2%	30,400
Germany	82,500,000	4%	3,060,000	12%	367,200
Ghana	22,000,000	45%	9,900,000	12%	1,188,000
Guinea	9,500,000	85%	8,075,000	3%	242,250
India	1,080,264,388	14%	154,500,000	18%	30,900,000

Indonesia	221,900,000	88%	195,272,000	1%	1,952,720
Iran	69,500,000	99%	68,805,000	90%	61,924,500
Iraq	28,800,000	97%	27,936,000	65%	18,158,400
Ivory Coast	18,200,000	60%	10,920,000	4%	436,800
Jordan	5,800,000	94%	5,452,000	2%	109,040
Kazakhstan	15,346,500	65%	10,000,000	1,9%	88,000
Kenya	33,800,000	24%	8,000,000	7%	560,000
Kuwait	2,600,000	100%	2,600,000	35%	910,000
Kyrgyzstan	5,200,000	75%	3,900,000	3%	117,000
Lebanon	3,800,000	60%	2,270,000	60%	1,362,000
Libya	5,800,000	97%	5,626,000	1%	56,260
Maldives	300,000	100%	300,000	5%	15,000
Mauritania	3,100,000	100%	3,100,000	1%	31,000
Mongolia	2,600,000	6%	160,000	4%	6,400
Morocco	30,700,000	99%	30,393,000	2%	607,860
Niger	14,000,000	97%	13,580,000	3%	407,400
Nigeria	131,500,000	50%	65,750,000	5%	3,287,500
Oman	2,400,000	99%	2,376,000	10%	237,600
Pakistan	165,803,560	98%	162,487,489	20%	33,160,712
Qatar	800,000	95%	760,000	10%	76,000
Russia	143,000,000	15%	21,513,046	3%	2,212,000
Saudi Arabia	24,600,000	100%	24,600,000	10%	2,460,000
Senegal	11,700,000	94%	10,998,000	5%	549,900
Serbia & Montenegro	10,700,000	19%	2,030,000	2%	40,600
Somalia	8,600,000	100%	8,600,000	1%	86,000
South Africa	46,900,000	2%	938,000	10%	93,800
Sudan	40,200,000	73%	29,346,000	2%	586,920
Syria	18,400,000	90%	16,560,000	15%	2,484,000
Tajikistan	6,800,000	90%	6,120,000	5%	306,000
Tanzania	36,500,000	50%	18,250,000	6%	1,095,000
Tunisia	10,000,000	98%	9,800,000	2%	196,000

Turkey	72,900,000	99%	72,750,000	20%	14,550,000
Turkmenistan	5,200,000	89%	4,628,000	4%	185,120
UAE	4,600,000	96%	4,416,000	15%	662,400
Uganda	26,900,000	16%	4,304,000	7%	301,280
United States	296,500,000	2%	6,000,000	15%	900,000
Uzbekistan	26,400,000	88%	23,232,000	6%	1,393,920
Western Sahara	300,000	100%	300,000	3%	9,000
Yemen	20,700,000	99%	20,680,000	42%	8,685,600
TOTAL	4,882,733,300		1,457,568,612	15%	215,959,328

REFERENCES

- The World Almanac & Book of Facts 1998 (K-111 Reference Corp.: Mahwah, NJ), [Source: 1997 Encyc. Britannica Book of the Year]; pg. 654.
- Individual country data from - https://www.cia.gov/cia/publications/factbook/

Please note that the Shia Population includes all of the sects. Also, the list is based on about 92% of the global Muslim population as of 2005. The actual number of the Shias could be marginally higher.

زكـات *Zakāt*

انما الصدقات للفقراء والعاملين علىا و المساكين و المولف قلوب م و فى
الرقاب والغارمين و فى سبيل الل وابن السبيل فريض من الل والل علىم
حكىم

Alms are for the poor and the needy, and those employed to administer the (funds); for those whose hearts have been (recently) reconciled (to Truth); for those in bondage and in debt; in the cause of God; and for the wayfarer: (thus is it) ordained by God, and God is full of knowledge and wisdom.

(At-Tawbah, 60)

There are two types of *Zakāt*:

1. That which is paid off once every year on *'Eid ul-Fitr*, it is called the *zakāt* of body and life, and is only *wajib* on someone who is capable of paying it.
2. *Zakāt* on wealth, which is as follows:
   a. Wheat
   b. Barley
   c. Dates
   d. Raisins

   Zakāt on these things mentioned above becomes obligatory when their quantity reaches the taxable limit which is 300 صاع (sa'a) which is equal to 847 kg.

   e. Gold
   f. Silver

   The taxable limit for gold is 3.456 grams, and for silver is 483.88 grams. If gold and silver reach these limits 1/40 part of each should be paid as *zakāt*.

   g. Camel
   h. Cow
   i. Sheep and goat
   j. Upon the wealth in business as an obligatory precaution

g. Camel has 12 Taxable limits:

No.	Taxable Limit	Amount of *Zakāt*
1	5 camels	1 sheep, there is no *zakāt* on less than 5 camels
2	10 camels	2 sheep
3	15 camels	3 sheep
4	20 camels	4 sheep
5	25 camels	5 sheep
6	26 camels	A two year old camel
7	36 camels	A three year old camel
8	46 camels	A four year old camel
9	61 camels	A five year old camel
10	76 camels	2 three year old camels
11	91 camels	2 four year old camels
12	121 camels or more	For every 40 camels, a three year old camel is paid as *zakāt*

h. The Minimum Taxable limit of cows

No.	Taxable Limit	Amount of *Zakāt*
1	30 cows	1 male calf which has entered the 2nd year of its life
2	40 cows	1 female calf which has entered the 3rd year of its life
3	60 cows	2 male calves of two years of age
4	70 cows	1 male and 1 female calf as described above

- Between 30 and 40 cows there is no *zakāt* , for example if someone has 39 cows there is no tax on them.
- As the number increases one should calculate either with 30 or 40 cows or in some cases both so nothing is left out, and if there is a situation where there must be something left out it shouldn't be more than 9.

i. Taxable Limit of Sheep (including goats)

The minimum taxable limit for sheep is at 40, and 1 sheep should be paid as its *zakāt*. There is no *zakāt* on less than 40 sheep. For more than 40 sheep it's as follows:

No.	Taxable Limit	Amount of *Zakāt*
1	121 sheep	2 sheep
2	201 sheep	3 Sheep
3	301 sheep	As an obligatory precaution 4 sheep
4	400 or more sheep	For every 100 sheep one sheep should be paid as *zakāt*

If the quantity of sheep exceeds the taxable limit but hasn't reached the next taxable limit the amount of *zakāt* doesn't change, for example is someone has 115 sheep there is only 1 sheep as its *zakāt*.

j. *Zakāt* on Business Goods

Goods earned by commutative contracts, and set aside for investment in business or profit earning, is, as a precaution, liable for *zakāt* if certain conditions are fulfilled. The rate of *zakāt* is 1/40 of all the investments or profits earned.

1. The owner of the Goods should be *baligh* and sane.
2. The goods should have reached the taxable limit, which is equal to that of gold and silver.
3. The goods should have remained for one year ever since the owner intended to invest it for profit.
4. The intention of investing it for profit should have remained unchanged throughout the year. If the intention changes, like, when he decides to spend it for maintenance, then he will not pay its *zakāt*.
5. The owner should be actually capable of its disposal throughout the year.
6. Throughout the year, the owner should have a buyer of the goods equal to the capital or more. If , during the year, he gets a buyer for the goods for less then capital outlay, it will not be obligatory upon him to pay its *zakāt*.

Table 1: Members of the House of the Prophet

Name	Father's name	Mother	Children	Birthday	Death Date	Place of Burial	Cause of Death	Age when Died
Holy Prophet Muhammad or Ahmad	Abdullah bin Muttalib	Amina binte Wahab	Fatima Four others died in infancy	17 Rabbi-ul-Awwal (Year of Elephant) Mecca	28 Safar 11 A.H.	Medina	Poisoned	63
Fatima Butool Razia	Prophet Mohammad	Khadija binte Khalid	4 (Mohsin died before death)	20 Jamdius Sani B.H. 45 Year of Elephant Year Mecca	3 Jamadus Sani, 11 A.H.	Medina	Injuries	18 years and 9 months
Ist Imam Ali (Haider, Asad)	Imran (Abu Talib bin Abdul Muttalib)	Fatima binte Assad	11 sons and 16 daughters	13 Rajab 30 Year of Elephant Inside Ka'abha, Mecca	21 Ramadhan 41 A.H.	Najaf Ashraf Iraq	Killled by sword by Ibne Muljim	63
2nd Imam Hassan (Shabbar)	Imam Ali	Janabe Saiyaddah	8 sons and 7 daughters	15 Ramadhan 3 A.H. Medina	28 Safar 50 A.H.	Medina	Poisoned	47

Table 1: Members of the House of the Prophet (Continued)

Name	Father	Mother	Children	Birthday	Death Day	Place of Burial	Cause of Death	Age when died
3rd Imam Hussain (Shabbir)	Imam Ali	Fatima binte Muhammad	6 sons and 4 daughters	3 Shabban 4 B.H, Medina	10 Muharram 61 A.H.	Karbala Iraq	Martyred by sword	57
4th Imam Ali (Zainul Abedean)	Imam Hussain	Shahr Bano binteYazd Jurd	7 sons and 9 daughters	15 Jamadius Sani or 15 Jamadi Awal 38 A.H. Medina	25 Muharram 95 A.H.	Medina	Poisoned by Waleed bin Malik	57
5th Imam Muhammad Baqar	Imam Ali (Zainul Abedin)	Fatima binte Imam Hasan	5 sons and 2 daughters	1 Rajab 57 A.H. Medina	7 Zilhajj 114 A.H.	Medina	Poisoned by Ibrahim bin Waleed	57
6th Imam Jafar Sadiq	Imam Muhammad Baqar	Umme Farwa binte Qasim	7 sons and 3 daughters	17 Rabi-ul-Awal 83 A.H. Medina	15 Shawwal 148 A.H.	Medina	Poisoned	65
7th Imam Musa Kazim	Imam Jafar Sadiq	Hamida Khatoon	19 sons and 18 daughter	7 Safar 128 A.H. Abwa (between Mecca and Medina)	25 Rajab 183 A.H.	Kazmain (Iraq)	Poisoned by Haroon Rashid	55

Table 1: Members of the House of the Prophet (Continued)

Name	Father	Mother	Children	Birthday	Death Date	Place of Burial	Cause of Death	Age when died
8th Imam Ali Raza	Imam Musa Kazim	Najma Khatoon	One or three	11 Zilqad 148 A.H. Medina	17 Safar 203 AH	Mashhad Iran	Poisoned by Mamoon Rashid	55
9th Imam Muhammad Taqi	Imam Ali Raza	Khazran Khatoon (Rehana)	2 sons and 2 or 3 daughters	10 Rajab 195 A.H. Medina	29 Zilqad 220 A.H.	Kazmain (Iraq)	Poisoned by Motasim Abbasi	25
10th Imam Ali Naqi	Imam Muhammad Taqi	Samana Khatoon	5 sons	5 Rajab 214 A.H. Medina	3 Rajab 254 A.H.	Sarman Rai (Samarah) Iraq	Poisoned by Motaz Abbasi	40
11th Imam Hasan Askari	Imam Ali Naqi	Hadisa Khatoon	One son	10 Rabius Sani 232 A.H. Medina	8 Rabi-ul Awal 261 A.H.	Sarman Rai (Samarah) Iraq	Poisoned by Moatamad Abbasi	28
12th Imam Mehdi (Imam Asr)	Imam Hasan Askari	Narjis Khatoon d/o Qaiser Rome	Only Allah Knows	15 Shaban 256 A.H. Sarman Rai Iraq	Still alive in occultation	Still alive in occultation	Still alive	--

PICTURES

Masjidul Al-Aqsa (The Dome of the Rock Mosque)- Jerusalem

Masjidul Al-Haram (The House of God - Kaaba) - Mecca, Arabia

Masjidul Al-Haram (The House of God – Kaaba) – Mecca, Arabia

Masjid An-Nabawi (The Mosque of the Prophet) - Medina, Arabia

Masjid An-Nabawi (The Mosque of the Last Prophet) – Medina, Arabia

Baaghe Fadak (The Garden of Fadak, behind Masjid Fadheek) - Medina, Arabia

Mausoleum of 1st Imam - Najaf, Iraq

Mausoleum of 1st Imam - Najaf, Iraq

Jannat Al-Baqi, Before its Destruction by the Wahabis (Graves of the 2nd, 4th, 5th and 6th Imams among others

Jannat Al-Baqi, Before its Destruction by the Wahabis - Medina, Arabia

Jannat Al-Baqi, After its Destruction by the Wahabis - Medina, Arabia

Jannat Al-Baqi, After its Destruction by the Wahabis - Medina, Arabia

Mausoleum of 3rd Imam - Karbala, Iraq

Mausoleum of Zaynab binte Ali - Damascus, Syria

Mausoleum of Abbas ibne Ali - Karbala, Iraq

Tomb of Sakina binte Husain - Damascus, Syria

Mausoleum of 7th and 9th Imam - Kazmain, Iraq

Mausoleum of 8th Imam - Mashad, Iran

Mausoleum of Fatima binte Musa (Masoome Qum) - Qum, Iran

Mausoleum of 10th and 11th Imam with the Blue Dome - Samarah, Iraq

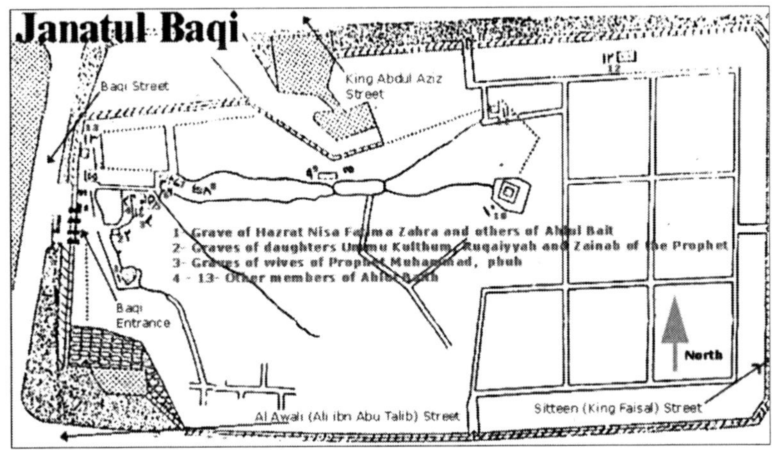
Janatul Baqi
Baqi Street
King Abdul Aziz Street
1- Grave of Hazrat Nisa Fatima Zahra and others of Ahlul Bait
2- Graves of daughters Ummu Kulthum, Ruqaiyyah and Zainab of the Prophet
3- Graves of wives of Prophet Muhammad, pbuh
4 - 13- Other members of Ahlul Bait
Baqi Entrance
North
Al Awali (Ali ibn Abu Talib) Street
Sitteen (King Faisal) Street

ABOUT THE AUTHOR

Dr. Syed Manzoor Rizvi is from a well-respected and highly educated Indian Shia family. He earned his M.D. from King George Medical College, Lucknow (U.P.) India. He completed his medical training as an Internist and Cardiologist from Bronx Lebanon Hospital, Einstein Medical College, Bronx, NY. He is a practicing physician who has specialized in Internal Medicine and Cardiology since 1980 in New Jersey.

Other than working with the sick, Dr. Rizvi's interests also lie in serving his community, enhancing education and moral behavior of youths, as well as developing a mutual understanding and respect between the various religious and ethnic groups in our world.

The Author co-founded the Muslim Foundation, based in New Jersey, in 1980, which is a socioeconomic and religious organization that is not only the voice of the Shias but has also arranged various Interfaith activities among other vital projects.

He has also co-founded Husain Day Organizing Council, which promotes the tolerance, peace and justice aspects of Islam through the personality of Imam Husain, the grandson of the last Prophet of Islam. Dr. Rizvi also founded Message of Peace, which has published around 35 books on various subjects that have been well received. Through this platform, he also co-edited and published the first Shia sub-continental newsmagazine from 1982 to 1992.

Dr. Rizvi has written five books including Imam Ali – Man of All Era and Sea of Tranquility. He has also written numerous articles, including many letters that have been printed in various mainstream newspapers. He also composes poetry in Urdu. His other current pastime is spending time with and pampering his three granddaughters.

Breinigsville, PA USA
13 December 2010
251327BV00001B/28/P